WHAT
THE
EYES
CAN'T
SEE

MARGARET EDDS

WHAT THE EYES CAN'T SEE

Ralph Northam, Black Resolve,
and a Racial Reckoning in Virginia

THE UNIVERSITY OF
SOUTH CAROLINA PRESS

© 2022 University of South Carolina

Published by the University of South Carolina Press
Columbia, South Carolina 29208

www.uscpress.com

Manufactured in the United States of America

31 30 29 28 27 26 25 24 23 22
10 9 8 7 6 5 4 3 2 1

Library of Congress Cataloging-in-Publication Data
can be found at http://catalog.loc.gov/.

ISBN 978-1-64336-352-3 (hardcover)
ISBN 978-1-64336-353-0 (ebook)

For Margaret Simpson

CONTENTS

ILLUSTRATIONS

PROLOGUE

The wait—for Ralph Northam and for the state he nearly lost—lasted fifteen months.

It spanned George Floyd protests. COVID-19 quarantines. An insurrection at the nation's Capitol. Tumultuous social unrest.

When the decision from Virginia's highest court finally arrived, it was everything the governor had dreamed. The unanimous decision, written by the court's senior African American judge, upheld in clear terms Northam's right to remove one of the South's most iconic images from government soil. The statue of Confederate general Robert E. Lee had lorded sixty feet in the air against the Richmond skyline for 131 years.

"The Lee Monument has been, and continues to be, an act of government speech," the opinion affirmed. "Values change and public policy changes." Virginia could not be bound in perpetuity by the actions of a nineteenth-century governor and legislature motivated by belief in the virtue of the Lost Cause, a way of life inseparable from the enslavement of millions of men, women, and children.

Northam was not one to wear his emotions on his sleeve, but the verdict was thrilling. "People of color have been so patient," he said. "There's been a lot of hurt for them over the years. This is another step Virginia has taken to heal the last 400 years."

Thirty-one months after calls for Northam to resign had thundered coast to coast, branding the governor a racist for a blackface photograph on his medical school yearbook page, Robert Edward Lee was about to be dislodged.

And Ralph Shearer Northam was still standing.

One outcome was as astonishing as the other.

This is the story of how many remarkable changes arose early in the third decade of the twenty-first century in the state where much of the nation's history began. One man's quest for personal redemption at first collided and later entwined with Black anger and resolve to create a new chapter in a centuries-old saga—a tale that asks time and again whether the reality of America ever can equal its promise.

PART I

CRISIS IN BLACK AND WHITE

In the sultry, mosquito-infested summer of 1619, two events occurred within a few days and a few miles of each other along the Chesapeake Bay coastline of Virginia that, for better and worse, would define the nation soon to emerge from those shores.

From Friday, July 30, through Wednesday, August 4, with a pause to honor the Sabbath, a small group of White men gathered at the Jamestown church to perform the first formal exercise in representative democracy in the New World. The meeting of that so-called General Assembly, composed of "two sufficient men" from each of various plantations and settlements, as well as Gov. George Yeardley and a few others, would not today be recognized as a true democratic undertaking.

The twenty-two settler-members, called burgesses, were beholden to a long line of superiors, from the Virginia Company of London up through England's King James I himself. But as they considered matters large and small—how to handle a complaint against rogue employees who had stolen corn and a canoe from native Powhatans; how to gain assurance that lands granted to early settlers would not be stripped away; how to treat idleness, drunkenness, and other assorted sins—the participants birthed a tender legacy of self-rule and respect for individual rights. Centuries later, those concepts lie deeply rooted, even as they have yet to reach universal flower. Still, what the Jamestown burgesses did, in the words of historian Brent Tarter, "influenced the whole future of Virginia's history and the history of the United States."[1]

A second event, occurring less than a month later and less than three dozen miles downstream, also has impacted the whole of Virginia and American history, though in a far more malignant way.

"About the latter end of August," wrote John Rolfe, best known to later generations as the English husband of the legendary Pocahontas, a ship containing "20. and odd Negroes" landed at Point Comfort, the tip of a spit of land where the James River empties into the Chesapeake Bay.

That human cargo had left Portuguese Angola earlier in the summer on a slave ship headed for Veracruz. Mid-voyage, two English privateers engaged the ship in a fierce battle, capturing several dozen Black prisoners who had not yet succumbed to the ravages of their tortured weeks at sea. The first twenty of those captives reached Virginia some days later aboard the *White Lion*, entering history as the first shackled Africans to set foot on the English-speaking American mainland. Although they were not termed "slaves" at the time, no one disputes that they arrived against their will and were transferred into the immediate service of White landholders. Rolfe recorded that the Africans were "bought" by Governor Yeardley and an associate in exchange for food "for the best and easiest rates they could."

Over the next two and a half centuries, some four hundred thousand African men, women, and children followed, brought in chains to the North American mainland to help secure the economic underpinnings of a new nation founded on the ideal of liberty and justice for all.[2] The inevitable clash of those contradictions resulted in the bloodiest war in US history, settled in 1865 at Appomattox, yet again on Virginia soil.

In 2019 Americans observed the four hundredth anniversary of the fateful confluence of freedom and oppression at Jamestown and Point Comfort, spotlighting anew the centuries-old, unfinished work of a state and nation birthed and perpetuated in possibility and despair.

CHAPTER 1

A Nightmare Unfolds

For three days, Ralph Northam's future as the seventy-third governor of Virginia dangled by a fraying thread. An amiable, plainspoken doctor, no one's idea of a suave politician, Northam had led a charmed public life. He had won six elections, counting primaries, for the state senate, lieutenant governor, and governor by impressive margins. None stirred up even a hint of scandal. Some national commentators found him a bit of a rube, unsophisticated by Washington, DC, norms. Virginians, by contrast, widely viewed him as trustworthy and sincere.

Then without warning, as if a mischievous Hermes had descended from Mount Olympus to wreak havoc on his life, a nightmare unfolded. A scandalous photo of a man in blackface standing next to a figure draped in a Ku Klux Klan shroud emerged from the spot where it had lurked for decades, undetected by opposition research or even his own campaigns—on Northam's page in his medical school yearbook. Northam did not remember the photo. He did not recognize himself in it. But a quick check confirmed that the image had not been photoshopped onto the page. Undeniably, there it was.

An uproar reverberated coast to coast. Within twenty-four hours, almost every national Democratic politician of note had called on him to resign. His pride in his image as a caring, self-effacing physician and citizen-servant who rose to every task—saving hundreds of brain-injured Iraqi War evacuees in a teeming German hospital, hatching a fragile political alliance to bring health care to four hundred thousand Virginians—lay battered and bruised. And as a fifty-nine-year-old White man who cherished his upbringing in the rural South, he found himself woefully unprepared to understand what had just occurred.

Unlikely as it might seem, on that day, February 1, 2019, Northam had never heard of a minstrel show. He knew from the news that some television personality had gotten into trouble for defending blackface Halloween costumes, although he did not remember Megyn Kelly's name. And he once had gone so far as to ask his young African American aide as they were traveling across Virginia during a campaign trip why blackface was so offensive. As he recalled, the answer had been "it just is," which did not satisfy Northam as an explanation.

A medical school graduate and a college biology major, his expertise was in science and the natural world. He could diagnose and treat complex neurological diseases in children. He was at home in any manner of boat on the tributaries of his beloved Chesapeake Bay. He could happily spend a day pulling a car engine apart and putting it back together. He had a caring and empathic nature, but the liberal arts and the softer sciences took a backseat, or no seat, in his busy, productive life. "I don't want to make excuses, but I didn't know enough about history. I really didn't," Northam later admitted.

A shocking photograph evoking some of the most hurtful and hateful memories of twentieth-century America was about to propel him into a painful crash course, one that would teach him a great deal about both history and himself.

THE FIRST INKLING OF THE CHAOS to come emerged at the end of a grueling week. Two days earlier, Northam had poked a hornet's nest during a routine appearance on a Washington radio call-in show. Asked about a controversial bill before the legislature that would loosen restrictions on third-term abortions, the governor did exactly what his staff had warned him not to do. He answered the question like a doctor, not a politician. Such abortions are a matter between physicians, mothers, and fathers, Northam began, taking on the practiced tone of a medical-school instructor, which he had been just a few years earlier.

He had enjoyed teaching students as a sideline at the Eastern Virginia Medical School (EVMS). Here was an opportunity to educate a wider audience. Late-term abortions occur "in cases where there may be severe deformities, there may be a fetus that's nonviable," he said. Then he trod more dangerously. "So, in this particular example, if a mother is in labor, I can tell you exactly what would happen. The infant would be delivered. The infant would be kept comfortable. The infant would be resuscitated if that's what the mother and the family desired, and then a discussion would ensue between the physicians and the mother."

In Northam's mind, he was describing a rare and tragic event, the withholding of life-prolonging measures when an infant is born with such severe abnormalities—an impossibly impaired or unformed brain, for instance—that no hope of normalcy exists. More than a decade had passed since his first foray into politics, but his naivete at times still astounded aides. To little surprise, national abortion foes responded with outrage. "This is horrific," Republican

National Committee chair Ronna McDaniel exclaimed on Twitter. She charged Northam with "defending born-alive abortions." Senator Marco Rubio, a Florida Republican, saw the comments as an endorsement of "legal infanticide." And President Donald Trump predicted: "This is going to lift up the whole pro-life movement like maybe it's never been lifted up before."[1]

Back in Richmond, exasperated aides assessed the damage. "We friggin' told him not to say that. He did it anyway," sighed Mark Bergman, Northam's closest and most senior political strategist. "That's like the doctor in him coming out. He thought he was being explanatory." Convinced that any further statements would be twisted, the governor followed staff advice. He put his head down and kept his mouth mostly shut. "I have devoted my life to caring for children and any insinuation otherwise is shameful and disgusting," he said at a Thursday press conference. Shaken, he hoped that, with luck, the storm would pass.

Outside forces declined to cooperate. On Friday afternoon, ironically the first day of Black History Month, an obscure right-wing website known to dabble in conspiracy theories posted the blackface photo from the 1984 yearbook of the EVMS. It had come to them, said the owner of Big League Politics, courtesy of a former Northam classmate infuriated by the governor's abortion stance.[2]

The news reached Clark Mercer, Northam's chief of staff, a little after 3 PM. "I was sitting here at this desk. Someone came by and said, 'Have you seen it?' I had no idea what 'it' was," said Mercer. A generation younger than Northam, familiar with both racial dynamics and hard-nosed politics, Mercer saw instantly the peril. Still, he figured the photo was a fake.

"Clark called me into his office," said Northam, who was about to leave for a Gold Star remembrance ceremony honoring a fallen Virginia soldier. "And he said, 'There's a picture in your yearbook of someone in blackface and a KKK garb.'" The two scanned the small image visible on a cellphone. "My initial response was 'somebody's playing games,'" Northam said. He had left Virginia shortly after graduating from medical school for a pediatric residency in San Antonio and had never purchased or seen the yearbook. "I said, 'I don't remember it. I don't have clothes that look like that,'" referring to the distinctive plaid pants worn by the man in blackface. The pair decided that Northam should continue as planned to the ceremony. Mercer would ask Evans Poston, the commissioner of the revenue in Norfolk and a political ally, to run by the medical school and take a look at an actual yearbook.

Northam and his state trooper escorts were already heading down a snowy highway when Mercer summoned them back. The photo was real. The initial trickle of inquiries about it was starting to verge on a flood. Rushing back, the governor arrived to find his office swept up by a tidal wave. Aware suddenly that this was no game, Northam reached as he usually did in a crisis to his eight years of military training as an Army doctor and his four years before that at the rigid Virginia Military Institute. As the office commander, he should be issuing orders. Too late. Quickly he saw that events had passed him by. Someone handed him a list of people to start calling, mostly key Black officials, US Representatives Bobby Scott and Donald McEachin among them. He began dialing. His message? "We're trying to figure out what's going on. Hold tight."

Already a few Republicans were calling for his resignation. "It was kind of surreal, like a dream, like what is happening, right here?" Northam remembered his stunned reaction. He had been trained as a soldier and as a doctor to remain calm in a crisis. When he walked into a hospital room where a patient was coding, or dying, and needed to be resuscitated, he knew the imperative of composure. "If you aren't calm in your leadership, then everybody else is not calm, and it's not as productive. I've always tried to keep my calmness," he said. This time, however, he was less the physician than the patient. And few of those around him were remaining calm. At surface, from long experience, he appeared to be in control. Inside his stomach was starting to churn.

Northam also had been trained to trust experts, and he knew that this sort of political crisis lay outside his expertise. The way he had bungled the abortion question was proof that instinct did not suffice. He began to feel a pressing weight, driven partly by a question he could not answer with certainty. Was he in the photograph? He did not think so. He had no memory of any such costume or party. But was he forgetting a lapse in judgment more than three decades earlier? "That's not something I would have done," he remembered telling himself. Yet, if so, why was the picture on his page? Everyone wanted to know, and he could not say.

Meanwhile, frantic aides migrated between Northam's office and Mercer's, wrangling over a response. Text messages and phone calls crisscrossed in and out of Washington and up and down the East Coast. How should Northam respond? As the moments passed and media pressure for a statement mounted, the cast grew. Almost everyone who had been involved in Northam's inner circle at any time in his political career chimed in, either in person or on the phone. A few people who no longer worked there showed up to help.

The in-office crowd was topped by Mercer, a talkative policy buff who had held Northam's top staff post since his inauguration as lieutenant governor five years earlier. Also on hand, among others: Brian Coy, who had worked briefly as Northam's communication chief before taking a private-sector job; policy team members Jennie O'Holleran, Carter Hutchinson, and Matt Mansell; Suzette Denslow, the deputy chief of staff; Marianne Radcliff, a prominent lobbyist and trusted Northam friend; Counselor Rita Davis; Keyanna Connor, the secretary of administration; and Ofirah Yheskel, the bright, young director of communications. The former press secretary, Yheskel had held the top public messaging job for just four months.

Mark Bergman, who had served as Northam's political strategist in every campaign but his first, had booked a flight to Richmond and headed to LaGuardia Airport from his home in Connecticut almost as soon as he heard the news in mid-afternoon. David Turner, spokesman in the 2017 gubernatorial campaign, set out down I-95 from Washington, DC.

"The next thing I know, there were probably ten-plus people in here that were starting to figure out what was the best thing for me to do, who I needed to talk to, what we needed to do as far as putting out statements. And some of them, I guess they were well intended, but I didn't invite them in here, and I don't know who did," Northam said. Was there panic? "Oh, my Lord," he nodded.

As aides reached out for advice, various crisis management experts informally augmented the group. Some offered an orthodox strategy. Get ahead of the news cycle. Acknowledge a mistake. Take responsibility before public opinion cements. Hope that, with luck, friends will rally around and aggrieved parties will accept the apology. Bergman got a call through to Anita Dunn, a top strategy and communications adviser to Barack Obama and, later, Joe Biden. Her recommendation, as Bergman recalled, was to apologize for the appearance of the photo on the yearbook page but also to say that Northam was still trying to figure out how it got there. That idea disappeared into the whirlpool.

The assembled wordsmiths and strategists arrived at three options for Northam. One, deny any connection to the picture. Two, own it and apologize. Three, say some version of the fact that he had no memory of the picture and was trying to understand how it wound up on his yearbook page. Each option came with drawbacks.

Consistently, from his first viewing, Northam had said he did not remember the picture and did not think he had ever dressed up in such garb. Everyone's assumption was that he had never donned a KKK robe. If he issued an outright denial about donning blackface, however, and then was proved wrong, it would not matter that memory had failed him regarding a decades-old episode. In Northam's mind, his credibility, which he valued above almost anything else, would be forever tarnished. If he accepted ownership of the picture, he would be contradicting his own tentative memory, as well as aligning himself with a repugnant image. And if he offered the most honest response, that he simply did not remember this photo and was trying to research its history, the crisis management experts believed the claim would be ridiculed as preposterous.

Mercer described the collective thinking on the last point: "The comms [communications] people thought that was a completely untenable position to be in. How can you not remember a photo like this?"

The possibility of temporarily saying nothing did not rise to the list, although that was the course advised by Tim Kaine when Northam reached the US senator a little before 6 PM. A former civil rights attorney, Kaine was on the downtown expressway in Richmond, heading home to take his wife, Anne, out for a birthday dinner. No matter the pressure, "do not put out a statement" until it had been vetted by someone with racial sensitivity who cared about the governor and who also was outside his immediate bubble, Kaine advised. "You only have one chance to do this right."

Later, the 2016 vice-presidential nominee wished he had turned his car around and driven back to Northam's office, prioritizing the crisis over the dinner. He did not. A different action by Kaine might have given Northam something he lacked that night, a mature voice detached from the uproar engulfing the office.

For his part, Northam felt conflicted. Pounded by the din, his internal compass failed. In the moment, he saw two of his inviolate creeds—take responsibility and tell the truth—as hopelessly at odds. Taking responsibility meant acknowledging a mistake (even one he was not sure he had made) and apologizing for it. That might start Virginia down the hard road of healing. Telling the indecisive truth was being dismissed by the professionals as a sure-fire loser, one likely to have a worse political outcome than facing up to something he had doubts about having done. And an outright denial struck Northam as the worst of all options, because if he was mistaken, his integrity would be in ruins. Only one reality seemed clear: everyone was pressuring him for a decision.

Later Mercer said that one of his regrets about the evening was failing to press home to others that indecision about the photograph on Northam's part did not equate to guilt. "I've probably known the governor the longest. I probably understand his thinking more than most folks. Folks there that night didn't appreciate how he thinks. They heard a politician saying, 'I'm not sure.' With most other politicians, you would think, 'It's them,' if they said they were not sure."[3]

More doctor than politician, Northam was different, Mercer said. He was trained to assemble facts and weigh evidence. Sometimes he took longer than most to get clarity. In this case, the governor had wanted to be absolutely certain before attaching his word to a blanket denial.

Pam Northam had hurried from the executive mansion to her husband's office after a late-afternoon telephone call warned that something was amiss. When she arrived, "it was like a bomb had gone off on the third floor. People rushing around, and you could tell something very upsetting had happened," she said. "I got to his office at some point, and I just took one look at his face, and I knew he was exhausted and in shock." The former occupational therapist and science teacher saw her husband's mental and physical state as a significant driver of a choice that later, to many, seemed inexplicable. "It's hard to deal with things when you're at your best, let alone when you're not at your best."

Just after 6 PM, with the office as close to unanimity as it was likely to get, Northam signed off on a statement. It included a fateful acknowledgment of wrongdoing. He had rejected outright denial, and the experts had rejected equivocation. Accepting responsibility was the only option left. Besides, there was no denying that the picture was on his yearbook page. Both he and his advisers thought most Virginians were likely to accept an apology.

"I am deeply sorry for the decision I made to appear as I did in this photo and for the hurt that decision caused then and now," his printed statement began.

"This behavior is not in keeping with who I am today and the values I have fought for throughout my career in the military, in medicine, and in public service. But I want to be clear, I understand how this decision shakes Virginians' faith in that commitment.

"I recognize that it will take time and serious effort to heal the damage this conduct has caused. I am ready to do that important work. The first step is to offer my sincerest apology and to state my absolute commitment to living up to the expectations Virginians set for me when they elected me to be their governor."

A bit later the staff distributed a video of Northam reading a similar but slightly less specific statement. A frown creasing the space between his heavy eyebrows, he gazed directly into the camera and proclaimed himself "deeply sorry" for past behavior. "I cannot change the decisions I made nor can I undo the harm my behavior caused then and today. But I accept responsibility for my past actions and I am ready to do the hard work of regaining your trust," he said.

If Northam and his staff expected an apology to bring respite, they were mistaken. Once Northam spoke, the outrage began to gather its full force.

LAMONT BAGBY WAS ON HIS WAY to pick up his son from an after-school program late Friday afternoon when his phone started dinging with a series of texts. "As I parked, I looked at them and saw the picture. I didn't know what it was. I thought, I'll call the administration and they'll say, 'There's nothing to it.' Instead, they said, 'We'll get back to you.'"

A state delegate from suburban Richmond, the chair of the Virginia Legislative Black Caucus, Bagby is a large, forceful man who grew in a city housing project, stayed out of trouble by playing high school basketball, and went on to earn two college degrees. Bagby and Northam came from two different worlds, but they shared a teasing sense of humor and a preference for action over talk. A Northam ally, he looked forward to the good they could do together, building on the recent Medicaid expansion victory.

Dropping his son at home, he drove back downtown to the state capitol and began calling on members who were within range to join him. "I was in disbelief," he recalled. "I didn't believe it was true." Northam "was always with us. I can't remember any racial issue where he was not with us." But what were they to make of such a hideous photograph?

Astonished and appalled, members were asking questions that Bagby could not answer. Some were furious, some in tears. Delegate Marcia "Cia" Price had been just thirty-six years old, in her first term as a state delegate representing Hampton and Newport News, when Northam tapped her as cochair of his gubernatorial campaign. She had poured her heart and soul into that heady responsibility, vouching for Northam with her political network, ushering him into living rooms and churches. As Black legislators streamed back to the capitol for a caucus, she felt the apparent duplicity as keenly as a razor slash. "I felt betrayed. I felt naive. I felt anger. I felt sadness—mostly anger," she recalled.

Others such as Delegate Delores McQuinn, a respected Richmond minister, reminded the lawmakers of the Northam they knew—a decent, caring man. The caucus was split on next steps.

Bagby called Northam's office and asked if the governor would meet with the group. Black lawmakers wanted to hear an explanation with their own ears. They met. Walking through the situation once more, Northam asked the legislators to hold off until he had a clearer understanding of the origins of the photograph. Remember their relationships, he pleaded. Give him that chance. Despite the confession, "at that point, he was continuing to say that he could not recall that picture," Bagby said. "If he was lying, he was a damn good liar." One response struck the group as particularly odd. Asked whether he was the individual in blackface or the person in the KKK robes, Northam said he did not know. How could he be in the picture without recalling that most basic fact?

As caucus members filed out, Northam felt a tinge of hope. He believed he might have persuaded them not to join the resignation chorus. Shortly, buying time, the Black lawmakers issued a statement that stopped short of outright rejection, but just barely: "We are still processing what we have seen about the Governor, but unequivocally say that what has been revealed is disgusting, reprehensible and offensive. We feel complete betrayal."

Some politicians less familiar with Northam felt no such constraint. At 7:07 PM, former housing secretary Julián Castro became the first Democratic presidential contender to call for Northam to resign. California senator Kamala Harris followed at 7:37 PM. Fired by a Black Lives Matter urgency, by fear of appearing hypocritical after attacks on the racial sins of Republicans, and by their own ambition, a parade followed. Before the night was over, Cory Booker, Elizabeth Warren, Kirsten Gillibrand, Sherrod Brown, John Delaney, Amy Klobuchar, and John Hickenlooper joined the call, as did NAACP president Derrick Johnson. "These images arouse centuries of anger, anguish, and racist violence and they've eroded all confidence in Gov. Northam's ability to lead," said Senator Booker of New Jersey, reflecting the sentiment of the group.[4]

The Virginia reaction to Northam's confession was equally grim. Levar Stoney, Richmond's ambitious young African American mayor who had helped recruit Northam for his initial run for the state senate, became the first major state officeholder to say the governor "should do the honorable thing and step down." Northam had considered Stoney a personal friend, so the rebuke stung. For his part, the mayor said his call to tell Northam of his decision evoked heart-thumping unease, but "I always believe, and I preach this to my team, that one person is not bigger than the agenda."

Other prominent Virginians soon followed.

As the evening stretched on, Pam Northam, putting her usual gracious manners on hold, marched into the executive suite and decreed that her husband must come home. "I needed to get him out of there. I needed to get food in him," she said. The First Lady had seen his exhaustion earlier and knew that it could only have intensified as the assaults on his character mounted. She had also been on the phone, reaching out to longtime friends and former classmates to see if anyone could shed light on the photo. Her search had unearthed a filigree of hope.

Howard Conduff, a Floyd County dentist, Northam's roommate at the Virginia Military Institute (VMI), and one of his closest friends, happened to have spent the previous night at the executive mansion. Pam contacted him by phone as he drove back to southwest Virginia. Had he ever seen the photo? Did it look like Ralph? Once home, Conduff studied the image. "It's not him," he concluded. "His posture, the way he stood. I'm a dentist. The person in that picture has pearly white teeth, very square. Ralph's teeth aren't like that." A secondhand report that a former classmate of Ralph's at EVMS, Virginia Beach cardiologist Dawn Manjoney, had studied the yearbook photo and felt certain that neither figure was Ralph also bolstered the First Lady.

Those opinions might be scant cause for optimism, but they were a tiny life raft in a turbulent sea.

"I WALKED BACK TO THE HOUSE feeling like a beat dog," Northam recalled his mood. When Murphy, his black Labrador retriever, greeted him with the usual exuberance, the governor experienced his first touch of normalcy in a long afternoon and night. The reprieve did not last. A call from Terry McAuliffe, Northam's predecessor, was the first to the governor's mansion after he took refuge there. The pair had served together in the state's two top offices, and Northam considered McAuliffe, like Stoney, a friend. Once again, past camaraderie proved irrelevant. "He didn't ask me any questions," the governor recalled the conversation. "Just said, 'You need to resign.'" For Northam, the bluntness was startling, unexpectedly so. It was not how he believed he would have handled the situation in reverse. "If I have a friend and the friend gets themselves in a jam, I would say, 'So and so, I'm going to try to help you through this,' not pull the rug out from under you."

Northam responded curtly. "I just said, 'Terry, I'm trying to figure out what happened. It was 35 years ago.' And I just left it at that." The statement McAuliffe issued later that evening acknowledged their friendship and Northam's public service while describing the photograph as "racist, unacceptable and inexcusable at any age and any time." Given an untenable situation, "it's time for Ralph to step down."[5] Soon he would be on CNN's *State of the Union* reiterating the message: "We have to move on. . . . We've had a horrible history [on race] in Virginia."

What the masses could not see or hear were the scattered messages to Northam from a smaller but fervent group of friends urging him to resist. That cluster would expand over the next few days to include Conduff, his good friend; Kelvin Jones, his pastor; Mark Bergman, the strategist; Tom Northam, his older brother; his wife, Pam; state senator Richard Stuart, a Republican who shared his rural sensibilities; and a couple of political professionals, including Paul Begala, a close ally of former president Bill Clinton and the father of a Northam staffer. The group advised him to slow down and be sure of what had happened before taking an action he might regret. He welcomed their support. "Don't even think about resigning," counseled his brother Tom, an Eastern Shore lawyer and fellow graduate of VMI. "When you're going through hell, keep going."

LANDING AT THE RICHMOND INTERNATIONAL AIRPORT that evening, Mark Bergman was dismayed to learn that Northam had already issued a statement apologizing for appearing in the photograph. Leaving New York, he'd thought that the opposite—a denial—was in the works. Bergman was a politics buff who caught the bug as a Virginia middle schooler and never lost it. A confirmed pragmatist, he had worked for numerous politicians around the county, but he felt closest to Ralph. The governor, in turn, trusted Bergman's political instincts and often seemed steadied by his presence. Bergman's opinion of the photograph? "I just knew it wasn't him, and even if it was him, he didn't commit a crime, he didn't corrupt his office. I also felt very strongly that if he left office in disgrace, it would personally destroy him. He would not be the same person, because he had not earned that."

On his way into the city, Bergman reached the governor by phone. "That was the first time I had talked to him all day. He was being shuttled from meeting to meeting." His urgent message to Northam: "Don't resign. You should not be the first Virginia governor to resign, and for something you didn't do."

The governor's response made Bergman fear that he had arrived too late. "There's a first time for everything," Northam replied.

PASTOR KELVIN JONES, MINISTER of the historic First Baptist Church Capeville, one of the oldest African American congregations on the Eastern Shore, was meeting with a few other ministers when Northam phoned Friday evening. A deputy sheriff when not in the pulpit, Jones exudes solidity and strength. His preaching skills are such that his invocation at Northam's inauguration prompted enthusiastic applause.

"Pastor," Jones recalled the conversation, "I've got something to share with you. They have found a picture, what they say was me in blackface."

"When was that?" Jones asked.

"In medical school."

Jones's response was spontaneous. He laughed. It did not take him long to realize that, for Northam, it was not a laughing matter. "It's going to blow up. It's going to be ugly," the governor said.

Jones still did not see the depth of the harm. "I just knew the picture was old. I'd hate to be judged on something I did three days ago, let alone twenty-five, thirty years ago. I didn't see the hoopla initially. I didn't get what people were so bent out of shape about."

He offered to drive to Richmond that evening. Northam said no, and Jones promised to come the next morning instead. "That is probably my biggest regret," Jones said. "I wish I had gotten in the car right then and gone."

A PIVOTAL DEFECTION STRUCK DEEPEST on that first night. It was the one Northam had most hoped to avoid. A small delegation, including Delegates Bagby and Price, arrived at the mansion in late evening to tell the governor face-to-face. At 10:56 PM, six minutes after the Congressional Black Caucus in Washington called for Northam to step down, the Virginia Legislative Black Caucus tweeted its similar decision: "We just finished meeting with the governor. We fully appreciate all that he has contributed to our Commonwealth. But given what was revealed today, it is clear that he can no longer effectively serve as governor. It is time for him to resign so that Virginia can begin the process of healing."[6]

The degree of hurt Northam felt in that call and others was directly related to how well he knew the caller. Rejection from national figures bothered him far less than that of the people he believed were his friends. His earlier confidence that the caucus might stand with him felt foolish.

The pain was mutual. "We didn't all feel the same way. We'd developed friendships. We knew the family," said Bagby of the Black Caucus. Even so, the group coalesced around the belief that the yearbook photograph—no matter how ancient—could not be tolerated. Northam had admitted his guilt. Delores McQuinn, who opposed such action, had gone home for the night. "It was tough," Bagby said, "but sometimes you have a job to do."

In quick succession, the dominoes tumbled. McAuliffe followed the Black Caucus at 11:02 PM, Virginia Senate Democrats at 11:13 PM, and Virginia House Democrats four minutes later.

WHEN THE FRONT DOOR of the executive mansion latched shut and the phones quieted late that evening, Northam wearily climbed the stairs to the his and Pam's private apartment. He felt mired in confusion. Shell-shocked and battered, he was beyond tired, moving almost as in a dream.

What had just happened to his life?

Sinking onto the bed, he noticed Pam's iPad, opened to a shot of the yearbook page. For the first time in a dizzying evening, he paused and pored over the image, now larger than the version he'd seen earlier. He took in the unfamiliar flashy pants and the solid legs of the man in blackface, different, he believed, from those of his own thin, lanky self in a bygone era. He tried to match the smile, the shape of the head to his, and for the first time, the confusion he had felt throughout the evening cleared.

Turning to his wife, he said simply, "That's not me."

"You know what the truth is," the First Lady replied, "and you have to tell it, whatever that costs."

CHAPTER 2

A Moonwalking Fiasco

On Day 2, matters for Northam got worse.

Despite a nearly sleepless night, he greeted his closest staff members at the mansion the next morning with coffee and an announcement. He was convinced that he was not in the photograph. He would reveal that fact to the world at a scheduled 2 PM press conference. Feeling more in command, he assigned tasks: drafting remarks for the press conference, getting a copy of the yearbook to Richmond, reaching out to former classmates and others who might have direct knowledge of the picture, and monitoring a flood of messages. With a plan of action, he felt more focused, more hopeful, and more in touch with himself. The troops dispersed.

Arriving at the mansion in late morning, Pastor Jones was astonished by the scene. Capitol Square was overrun with reporters and TV trucks. A line of protesters stretched down the sidewalk dividing the mansion from Northam's offices in the Patrick Henry Building. "Hey, hey, ho, ho, Ralph Northam has got to go," they chanted. When the security team took him upstairs to the family's living quarters, he had expected to see a beehive of activity. Instead he saw "a handful of folks, staff, people who were like themselves walking in a fog. It was like a spirit of concession was being pushed on him."

As the press conference neared, Brian Coy returned with a draft of an opening statement for Northam to read. Coy, who had left government to work for a communications and government relations firm in Richmond, had been asked back by Mercer to shore up the young in-house communications team. That morning he had been assigned no easy role, putting into words why Northam had said one thing about the blackface photo the previous day and now was saying another. The result satisfied neither Northam nor Jones. "I sat there and read through what Brian had written. And it was like, 'Hmmm,'" the governor said. Some of the language made him sound less racially sensitive than he believed he was. "I said, 'Hold on here a second.'"

Jones was blunter. "This isn't going to work," he recalled saying. "You all are writing a speech to speak to politicians. You're not writing a speech that allows him to speak to the heart of the people he's offended. African Americans are by nature, by Christ relationship, forgiving people." Urgently Jones started suggesting tweaks. He wanted to capture what he believed Northam was trying to say: "I'm appalled and hurt by this accusation that has not had time to be researched or anything. And I want my friends to know how bad I'm hurt by this."

With television networks interrupting regular programming and a throng of reporters and camera crews crowding into the first floor of the executive mansion, Northam faced the nation, Pam at his side. Tall and runner thin, he had dropped his usual open-collared informality for a navy suit, a light blue dress shirt, a red tie, and a Commonwealth of Virginia lapel pin. His demeanor differed also. He appeared more somber than usual, as he glanced up and down while reading the prepared text. The last-minute flurry over wording had been unsettling, but Northam also felt freed by his deeper conviction about the truth. He had never been a polished communicator. Still, voters seemed to respond to his naturalness. He hoped that the pattern would persist.

Earlier, peering into her closet, the First Lady had indulged in a bit of gallows humor, asking herself, "What does one wear to an execution?" Glancing out at the crowd, a trim figure in a maroon dress and black jacket, hands clasped formally at her waist, her warm brown eyes trained mostly on her husband, Pam drifted to a scene in the Mel Brooks horror-comedy, *Young Frankenstein*, when actor Gene Wilder faces a mob with pitchforks and torches. "You just had that feeling of this very angry mob, waiting for your demise," she said.

She did not have long to wait.

The previous day, he had taken responsibility for material that was "offensive, racist, and despicable," began Northam, launching the press conference. "When I was confronted with the images yesterday, I was appalled that they appeared on my page, but I believed then and now that I am not either of the people in that photo." A television audience gathered to witness a mea culpa and a possible resignation gasped. The governor continued with an eight-minute defense that elaborated on his dismay over the photo but, to many minds, did not answer the most fundamental question: Why, in heaven's name, had he said one thing one day and the opposite the next?

"I recognize that many people will find this difficult to believe," he said, tackling the whipsaw. "Even in my own statement yesterday, I conceded that based on the evidence presented to me at the time, the most likely explanation was that it was indeed me in the photo. In the hours since I made my statement yesterday, I reflected with my family and classmates from the time and affirmed my conclusion that I am not the person in that photo."

Then his defense took its second surprising turn. Part of what convinced him that he was not in the photo, he said, was the clear recollection of a moment in the same time frame when he did dress up for a costume competition as a Black man, the singer Michael Jackson. The event took place in San Antonio, where he moved for a pediatric residency just after his medical school graduation. "It is because my memory of that episode is so vivid that I truly do not believe I am in the picture in my yearbook. You remember these things," he said. *What?* Urging an "honest conversation" around racial injustice, Northam said he would continue in office so long as he could effectively lead. He hoped that his candor in revealing the Jackson episode would underscore his truthfulness.

For many viewers, the question-and-answer period that followed produced the two most memorable—and cringeworthy—moments of the press conference. First, asked about the Michael Jackson episode, he elaborated: "I had the shoes. I had a glove, and I used just a little bit of shoe polish to put on my cheeks. And the reason I used a very little bit is because, I don't know if anybody's ever tried that, but you cannot get shoe polish off." Northam saw the added detail, drawn from four years of spit-shining his shoes as a VMI cadet, as validating his frankness. Skeptical listeners thought he sounded overly familiar with the risks of applying shoe polish to skin.

Second, picking up on Northam's mention that he had perfected Jackson's trademark moonwalk dance step as part of the costume, a reporter asked: Could he still moonwalk? The snippet that followed lasted no more than three seconds, but it left an enduring image. Head nodding slightly, Northam glanced to his right, as if looking to see whether space was available. Then, turning to his left, where Pam stood, his face lit up. "My wife says, 'inappropriate circumstances,'" he concluded.

His manner for that brief moment evoked the lighthearted, friendly banter that often accompanied his interactions with both reporters and patients. The cheery, eyebrows-raised expression was a familiar one to those who knew his habits. To an unfamiliar and unamused national audience, it looked like a man totally disconnected from the seriousness of the setting. Widespread commentary concluded that Northam had been about to attempt to moonwalk, until stopped by his wife.

Both the governor and First Lady dispute that conclusion. Northam said he was trying to think of a snappy rejoinder and never contemplated attempting the long-forgotten dance step. Pam said her thoughts were directed at the cheeky reporter, not her husband. "I remember looking at him and thinking, 'I know that kid, because after many years of teaching, that's the kid in my fifth-grade class who's trying to get a rise out of somebody.' And it's interesting that people thought I was talking to Ralph. No, I'm talking to that kid who's being a smart aleck, and I'm saying 'No.'"

Tom King, a Northern Virginia media consultant who worked in all six of Northam's campaigns, watched the press conference from Bermuda while on an annual outing with six guy friends, two of them Black and four White. Their reaction? "It was not a good one, and they like Ralph," said King. "I thought he was fine until he talked too much." About Michael Jackson? Yes. Were there groans among his friends? Yes. And did the group think Northam started to moonwalk? "I did not, but everybody else did."

For Delegate Price, the press conference deepened the outrage. "I just could not believe my ears," she said, dramatically imitating Northam's words. "He was standing tall and projecting confidence, and I didn't see the remorse or the sorrow or the apology that we had seen the day before. . . . And also, the further revelation that, even if I don't know if it's me or not, I did do this other thing that had blackface. For me, it was either two times or one time, but either way, it was still a part of the event."

In contrast, Northam came away slightly buoyed by his performance. He had told the truth as he saw it. His conscience was cleared. "I'd answered the questions as best I could," he said. It did not take long for him to realize that in the minds of many others, the press conference had accomplished just one thing. He had sealed his fate.

THROUGHOUT THE DAY, BOTH BEFORE and after the media event, the calls for a resignation intensified. Top Democrats—Joe Biden, Bernie Sanders, Nancy Pelosi, and Hillary Clinton—weighed in, as did Democratic National Committee chair Tom Perez, Virginia attorney general Mark Herring, former Virginia governor Doug Wilder, and Gov. Gina Raimondo of Rhode Island, then chair of the National Governors Association. Northam had been something of a poster child for the organization because of his leadership in 2017 in turning the Virginia legislature from a Republican stronghold to a body on the brink of Democratic control.

Reaching out to Raimondo, he urged: "Please don't put a statement out until we figure out what's going on." Too late. A statement already was being prepared, she said.

The abandonment was starting to feel familiar. "I wasn't really angry. It was just disappointing," he said.

Watching the drama unfold from across the country, Brad Komar, Northam's former campaign manager, felt a sense of betrayal on Northam's behalf. "I was 1,500 miles away, but it felt like hell. It felt like a lot of knives in the back," said Komar, who had moved to Denver in preparation for running former Colorado governor John Hickenlooper's presidential campaign. "When you go through an election, you go to battle with these folks at your side, and Ralph is an extremely loyal person. These are your brothers-in-arms. And all of that brothers-in-arms loyalty was gone in an instant."

Mercer affirmed: "I didn't get a single call from an elected official offering to help."

Then came the call that Northam remembered most from a dizzying twenty-four hours. Virginia's three leading Democratic officials, other than himself— Senator Mark Warner, Senator Kaine, and Representative Scott, the dean of the Virginia congressional delegation—phoned the mansion together.

Each in turn told Northam some version of how they appreciated his service but believed he had lost the moral authority to lead. There was no productive way forward for Virginia other than his resigning, they said. The trio had drafted a statement. They would hold off for an hour before releasing it. If Northam resigned before the hour was up, the statement never would see daylight.

To casual observers, Northam can appear to be something of a mild-mannered Mister Rogers. With children, in his medical practice, he often was. But he also is competitive and driven. His track record in winning every office he has ever sought speaks for itself. He had not come this far without a measure of steel in his spine, and an ultimatum from his peers did not sit well. "Well, don't sit by your phones," he bristled at the threesome, "because I won't be calling you back."

CHAPTER 3

A Fateful Decision

The truth-telling at the Day 2 press conference did little to lessen the anguish of Day 3. Behind the scenes, as the nation readied for the nighttime Super Bowl extravaganza, Sunday proved to be the day when Northam came closest to resigning.

At Pastor Jones's urging, Ralph and Pam traveled the two hours from Richmond to Capeville on the Eastern Shore for Sunday morning services. In Washington media elites already had reached a verdict on Northam's fate. "Is there any way Governor Northam survives this?" *Sunday TODAY* host Willie Geist asked *Meet the Press* moderator Chuck Todd, who was appearing on the early morning show. "No, there's not," Todd replied authoritatively. "It's clearly a matter of when he leaves office. Is he going to have to be forcibly removed or is he going to finally see the light here?"

That verdict had yet to reach First Baptist Capeville, a simple chapel with a white spire and blue-and-mauve stained-glass windows, sitting beside a busy highway. Inside, a deep purple carpet and purple-and-gold pew cushions create an enveloping warmth. Northam had joined the predominantly Black church a decade or so earlier after he and the pastor became friends during his first state senate race.

Pam Northam remembered the February 3 visit as a brief ray of light on a dark landscape. "At one point, the pastor asked for us to come up and anyone who wanted to, to come up and pray with us. And so these folks, who had little or no reason to, other than just out of grace, came forward and gave us that great gift that I will never forget." Surrounded by kindness, Northam also absorbed a dose of strength. For a moment, the calamity awaiting him back in Richmond seemed less real. What mattered were the ordinary people reaching out to shake his hand or touch his sleeve.

Coming away, he felt less alone. Back in Richmond that afternoon, the dark returned.

The Northams were not the only ones agonizing over what had occurred. Staff members also were in shock. "It had been just a very confusing forty-eight hours for everyone," said Mercer, whose attention was focused not only on the governor but also on the dozens of people working for him and his cabinet. "The entire building was surrounded by reporters and cameras. Everyone's phone had hundreds of text messages. The phone 24-7 going off with international reporters, national reporters, Twitter."

Mercer had grown up in Alexandria, attending T. C. Williams High, the school depicted in the Disney film *Remember the Titans*, where he stood out as senior class president and as a White football player on a majority Black team. After graduating from Yale, he worked in an assortment of policy and political jobs before connecting with Northam while helping with debate prep during his 2013 race for lieutenant governor. They had been together ever since. Mercer was a bit more liberal and a lot more extroverted than his boss, but both were task-oriented and committed to achieving a policy agenda now in peril. Arriving home well after midnight on the first night, Mercer found himself weeping as he looked in on his young children. "My son and daughter idolize him," he said. "They call him Mr. Ralph. My son's very perceptive, and how am I going to talk to him about what we're dealing with?"

Throughout Saturday and into Sunday, Mercer's concerns grew. "Everyone calling for his resignation. People thinking that he wasn't going to be governor anymore. There's a whole universe of action behind the scenes related to that. Well, what if he's not governor? Who would be governor? And who would that person have sitting in these offices?" One Black staffer reportedly was warned by a prominent national Black Democrat that she would not work in Democratic politics again unless she resigned. Rumors were rife that various staff members planned to quit in protest.

Sober and saddened, Mercer privately joined the ranks of those recommending to the governor that he leave office. The chief of staff promised to stand with Northam, whatever his decision, but Mercer thought he owed both Northam and the staff unvarnished candor. With the likelihood that the office was about to start hemorrhaging workers, it was hard for Mercer to see how the administration could survive.

Northam recalled the searing moment: "Clark said, 'I don't see any way out of this for you. The entire cabinet's going to walk out.'" In that instant, his defenses came close to crumbling. "I said, 'You know what, I guess you're right.' And that's when I said, 'Let's go ahead and work on a statement.'" On the verge of defeat, Northam called his former colleague in Norfolk, Dr. Svender Toor, and asked if there was a spot for him back in the practice. "I called him and said,

'I'm in a situation here, and you all know what it is, and can I have a job?' And he said, 'Absolutely.'"

Still, as Northam pondered a step that would have been inconceivable a week earlier, things in his mind did not line up. He knew who he was. He was the kid who attended integrated public schools when many White families were switching to private academies on the Eastern Shore. The cadet who held the prestigious presidency of the Honor Court at VMI, one of the highest distinctions in a school centered on a strict code of honesty. The doctor who headed a frontline trauma unit at Landstuhl Army Medical Center, near Landstuhl, Germany, treating sometimes thirty-five to forty seriously injured Operation Desert Storm evacuees per day. The pediatrician who cared for tens of thousands of children, large numbers of them Black, with seizures, brain tumors, cerebral palsy, and other dire conditions. The volunteer who for some twenty years served as medical director at a Portsmouth hospice for dying and gravely ill children. The governor whose electoral success and bipartisan ties had ushered in an expansion of health-care opportunity to some four hundred thousand Virginians, many of them poor, many of them Black.

Thinking of all that, "it's like, How can someone just rip my life away from me, all the things I've done, because I dressed up as Michael Jackson? It didn't balance out for me."

Even so, much of the nation thought he had committed a worse sin than imitating a Black singer. He could not explain the shocking yearbook entry. And he was hearing from almost every quarter that his delay in resigning was causing deep pain for many Virginians. The most straightforward way out of the torment was to leave.

DAVID CARY, PAM NORTHAM'S CHIEF OF STAFF, had spent much of Sunday afternoon wading through hundreds of voice mails, hoping to unearth a caller with actual knowledge of the yearbook photo. Finally he took a break and biked for an hour. A disturbing message awaited his return. The governor was on the verge of resigning. Black and Brown members of the staff were being brought into the office for a summit. Cary quickly phoned Virginia's First Lady with the news.

Poised, introverted, a dedicated child advocate and an arts lover who quotes Mary Oliver poetry and Ocean Vuong essays, Pam Northam did not flinch. While she had not ruled out the possibility that resignation might eventually be the best course, she never had the slightest doubt that the man in the blackface photo was not her husband or that resigning in disgrace would leave him permanently scarred.

"Get him the hell out of there," she snapped before dashing to the Patrick Henry Building to intervene herself.

THE GOVERNOR DID NOT RESIGN that night. Or the next day. Or the next. By then, events as bizarre and out-of-left-field as those that had engulfed him were scrambling the fortunes of the two men next in the line of succession. Late on February 3, Big League Politics scored another scoop. Vanessa Tyson, a professor of politics at Scripps College in Claremont, California, accused Lt. Gov. Justin Fairfax of having sexually assaulted her in 2004. Fairfax denied both that charge and one from a second woman, which surfaced several days later.

Meanwhile, Attorney General Herring, apparently on the brink of being outed by a news organization, admitted to reporters that as a nineteen-year-old in college he and friends had donned "wigs and brown makeup" to imitate rappers at a party.[1] It did not escape notice that four days earlier Herring had called on Northam to resign. "He asked me to resign knowing that he had done the same thing. To this day, I don't quite understand that logic," Northam said much later. Astounded Virginia Democrats, some of whom had vowed to force Northam from office if he did not leave voluntarily, were left asking themselves if they truly wanted to turn over the reins of government to the third in line, the Republican Speaker of the House of Delegates. Unsurprisingly, no, they did not.

The Sunday night meeting with staffers of color that Pam Northam had raced to join had not started out well. Many around the table thought Northam's administration should end. Several spoke to the personal pain the picture had caused. Others thought the damage was too great for him to withstand. The governor mostly listened. The weight that he had carried throughout the day remained. These were voices he wanted, needed, to hear, but the messages were crushing. It helped to have Pam at his side.

Late in the meeting, one respected staff member took a different slant. Rita Davis, Northam's in-house counsel, the first African American woman to hold that position, had joined by conference call. She remembered thinking, "Okay, I'm going to have to dive in and be the person who speaks contrary to everyone else." Stylish and smart, no shrinking violet, Davis had been a police officer, sometimes working undercover as a drug dealer or prostitute, prior to attending law school and signing on with a top-notch private firm. She was a person to whom others listened.

Over the previous three days, Davis had reignited her investigative skills, trying to unearth information about the picture. A dozen or so others had joined in that task, contacting an estimated fifty to sixty people from Northam's younger life. Not one thought he was the man in blackface, she said.

With that in mind, Davis urged the group to give Northam time. "If we turned tail, as my father would say, and ran, then that's it. That's the news story forever." In her view the governor deserved a chance to prove his innocence and, if not that, then at least the opportunity to make amends or a smooth exit. The room quieted. Northam appreciated the support, whether or not it would hold sway.

To a degree, staff reaction exposed a generational divide. Many of the younger group were outraged. "There's no redemption. There's no excuse. It's just horrible," Davis described that view. Some older members, like herself, seemed more disappointed than shocked. "We'd seen a Virginia where it would not be unheard of to have good people, truly good people, do bad things like this in a moment of bad judgment. We'd seen the progression of that Virginia." From her perspective, she said, "It would be contradictory of me to say that I couldn't forgive, that I couldn't allow for redemption, because if you're a Virginian and you're a person of color, you wouldn't be able to live in this state if you couldn't at least believe in redemption and second chances and people changing and things changing."

As rumors about Fairfax's problems began swirling in the political world late Sunday, the news gave Northam time to breathe. By Day 4, with mounting indications that some in the cabinet and staff were rethinking leaving, he found himself settling into a decision. He would stay, at least temporarily.

The sudden turmoil surrounding Fairfax was a motivation, but not the only one. He also was heeding the voices of those who thought he should take his time. Memorably, through acquaintances he reached out that Monday to Scott Miller, a strategic adviser based in Atlanta with a high-profile client list. Miller's recommendation, one that fit Northam's own growing inclination, was to move deliberately through a decision. He could leave—or not—in a month or two months, whenever, once a succession plan was in place and he felt clearer about what had happened.

At a Monday morning cabinet meeting, the governor made his case. "You know me. You know my commitment to a more equitable Virginia. Together, we still have much work to do," he urged, scanning the room for any nodding heads. Twenty-four hours earlier, it had been a safe bet that several in the group, maybe more than several, were poised to walk out the door. But events were in flux. Northam was still in charge. No one could say with certainty who should replace him if he left.

Moreover, he was contemplating a new and exciting idea. If he stayed, the remainder of his term could be devoted to addressing racial disparity in Virginia. That always had been a goal for the office. "But after this happened, it was just brought into better focus," Northam said. He had assembled a diverse cabinet, a group that once would have relished this opportunity. By making racial equity the priority, could he entice them to stay?

In that meeting Secretary of Education Atif Qarni was the only cabinet official still saying, at least to the governor's face, that he needed to resign. In the end no one left, not even Qarni. How the narrative would have changed had Fairfax and Herring not run into trouble is unknowable. "I think I could have continued to ride the storm out," Northam said.

It surely would have been a wild ride.

AS THE ADMINISTRATION INCHED forward, two questions stood out. Was Northam the man in the blackface photograph? And if he was not, why had he issued the damning apology? Two investigations, one internal, one external, would soon be commissioned in an attempt to answer the first question. Northam himself had no easy explanation for the second.

Skeptics may doubt a parallel, but anyone who has studied the nature of false confessions in the criminal justice system can see similarities. Common themes include shock, panic, the false security of listening to authoritative voices, and the promise of relief if one takes a simple, readily available course of action.[2] All of those conditions existed in Northam's office on the night of February 1. He was not in handcuffs or sitting behind bars, but he was being hammered by demands for a quick decision on which his future might hinge. Add professional miscalculation and personal pride to the mix, and it is possible to see how judgment warped.

Northam staffers who pressed the importance of quick acceptance of responsibility as a way to defuse the critics failed to account for the mood of Democratic Party leaders in 2019. Time would show that many African Americans, particularly older ones, were, indeed, willing to forgive Northam. But party leaders, a hunk of them running for president, had drawn inviolate lines against insensitivity toward race. Few wanted to come down on the wrong side of that divide and certainly not on behalf of a lame-duck governor, prohibited by Virginia's constitution from running for reelection.

"If you're surprised by these calls for Northam's resignation, you haven't paid attention to how the Democratic Party has changed in recent years," Geoffrey Skelley wrote on the website FiveThirtyEight four days into the controversy. The Pew Research Center had found that the share of Democrats considering racism a "big problem" had more than doubled between 2009 and 2017, growing from 32 percent to 76 percent.[3] In that climate taking ownership of the photograph was more perilous than smart.

Finally, given Northam's unwillingness to risk a denial that might be proven wrong, he had two choices—equivocating, which the experts adamantly opposed, or taking responsibility. Consistent with his military training, he chose the latter and bore the consequences. "It was disappointing to me that I had made a statement that I was in the yearbook and then, once I figured out what was going on, that I wasn't. So, one way or the other, it wasn't accurate information, which was not the way I would have wanted it," Northam said.

If he could replay the tape, he added, he would clear the room and have one or two trusted people sit with him while he thought through the situation. "I would have taken my time. I would have put a different statement out that this is obviously very painful for Virginia, it's painful for me, and right now, I need to figure out what happened thirty-five years ago. And that's not what I did that night, and that's on me. I take the responsibility for that."

In the simplest terms, he erred, almost fatally.

Northam came to the controversy not fully comprehending either the origins or the depth of raw anger exposed by a photograph of two anonymous figures, one in blackface, one in the robes of the Ku Klux Klan. But sitting with members of the Legislative Black Caucus on the night of February 1, he had seen one quality in which he needed no education: pain.

His personal and professional instincts led him to want to heal. Instinctively some part of him recognized that his own redemption might lie down that same path.

WHEN RALPH NORTHAM ELECTED to stay in office after the blackface photograph surfaced, he had attitudes and blind spots for which to atone. So did Virginia, the state that had shaped him.

Among the founding fathers, George Washington had led with exemplary fortitude. Thomas Jefferson wrote noble texts embracing religious freedom and egalitarian idealism. James Madison displayed strategic genius as he crafted constitutional principles. Yet such stellar attributes coexisted with their tolerance for—and, most damningly, participation in—the brutality and dehumanization of chattel slavery. Both they and the White generations that followed had willingly oppressed Black bodies in order to reap personal wealth from their labor. After losing a civil war that sought to embed slavery's atrocities in a new nation, the Virginians and other White southerners adopted constitutions and passed laws that accomplished much of what they had failed to win on the battlefield. Black people might no longer be legally enslaved, but throughout the late nineteenth and early-to-mid-twentieth centuries, they were denied educational opportunities, decent housing, high-paying jobs, and voting access. White officials maintained a cheap Black labor force for public works by exploiting their arrests for vagrancy and other petty crimes.

When the US Supreme Court in 1954 ordered public schools to desegregate, the Virginians led the South in throwing the full apparatus of the state behind preserving educational apartheid. And when the legal battles of the 1940s and '50s combined with the street battles of the 1960s to impose on America at least the veneer of a more just society, powerful White Virginians only grudgingly addressed the persistence of deep racial inequities. Many governmental structures perpetuating divides in housing, education, criminal justice, and the economy remained.

In 1989 Virginia had taken the forward-looking step of choosing the first African American popularly elected as governor in US history. Yet thirty years later there remained more Johnny Reb statues in the Old Dominion than in any other state. And while significant segments of the Black population had attained middle- and upper-class wealth and prestige, overall statistics on everything from educational achievement to maternal mortality to incarceration to personal wealth still divided many Black and White Virginians into separate and unequal worlds.

After February 2019 Northam no longer accepted ownership of the blackface photograph. Plenty of others were happy to do that for him. But he could own the legacy that had been handed down to him and others through generations. He could try to better understand how that legacy had shaped and benefited his life and the lives of tens of thousands of Virginians who looked like him. And he could resolve to create something better.

The way forward would include not only fallout from the blackface scandal but also a mass shooting tragedy, a global health pandemic, the subsequent economic rollercoaster, and a national racial awakening. Northam's polling numbers would first rebound, then fluctuate as he became bolder—triggering the removal of the South's most iconic Confederate statue, that of Gen. Robert E. Lee, from Richmond's Monument Avenue; spurring the demise of the death penalty in the state that had executed more Americans than any other; calling for legalization of marijuana, a drug whose legal penalties were far more likely to entrap Black users than White in the prison system; and much else. No one could have predicted in Northam's winter of despair that through the intersection of a newly empowered Virginia Legislative Black Caucus and his own tenacity, he would leave office widely considered to have been the most racially progressive governor in Virginia history. Others might match him in personal commitment to racial equity, but none outdid him in the scope or consequence of the changes he had overseen.

What would become clearer over time were the larger dimensions of Northam's reckoning. The story was about far more than one man. His response and that of those around him—enthusiastic at times, halting in others, both righteous and flawed, bold and inadequate—became a lens for examining deeper questions: How do we, all of us, "do the work" of dismantling barriers to racial opportunity and fair play ? What are the many pieces of that challenge, for individuals and for society? When is it helpful to the Black cause to have White allies? When is it not? An unprecedented series of events converged during the term of a single Virginia governor to propel change. Yet how permanent are the alterations? How vulnerable are they to whim and to the sort of steps-forward, steps-backward swings that have typified the nation's racial arc?

As the months passed, Marcia Price—the disappointed former cochair of Northam's gubernatorial campaign—began to recognize something that had not clicked with her initially. How was it that a blackface photograph had remained on that yearbook page for all those many years without anyone thinking it was worth comment? Hundreds of people, possibly thousands, must have seen it there. That they took it for granted, saw it as nothing extraordinary, said something important about how deeply White entitlement and White myopia penetrated the culture.

The photograph was emblematic of so many other Black and White disparities that had been ignored, accepted, reinforced, and even celebrated. Shame was forcing a White man who had been considered a Black ally to take off blinders he had not realized he had. She and many others began to wonder: What opportunity to do long-neglected work lay in the moment?

A BLUEPRINT FOR CHANGE

The ghostly, blue-gray hue that obscured the landscape from New York to Georgia on August 13, 1831, might have been the handiwork of volcanic ash floating thousands of miles across the continent. Or as Nat Turner, a charismatic and literate enslaved man in Southampton County, Virginia, would have it, the spectacle may have been the work of an angry God, instructing him to launch a Day of Judgment against the enslavers.

Eight days later, acting on what he saw as divine guidance, Turner swung a hatchet blade into the skull of his sleeping master, igniting the deadliest uprising by enslaved people in American history. Before the insurrection by Turner and an estimated forty followers ended two days later outside the village of Jerusalem (modern-day Courtland), some fifty-five White men, women, and children had been butchered.

Revenge-seeking White vigilantes retaliated by slaughtering scores of Black people, many with no link to the uprising. Estimates of the dead ranged from about forty to several times that. A panel of slaveholding White judges condemned thirty enslaved people, including Turner, and one free Black man to death. The governor later commuted twelve of the sentences, partly in deference to property values of the enslavers.[1]

Turner was hanged from a tree on November 11, 1831, in Jerusalem as White onlookers cheered.

The event at the edge of the Great Dismal Swamp had ramifications far beyond a secluded Virginia county. The carnage signaled a watershed moment in the protest struggle against Black oppression in the United States. As news and rumor spread, it sent panic through the breasts of thousands of White people, leading in Virginia to the most serious reconsideration of slavery in any southern state prior to the Civil War.

From mid-December to late January 1832, the Virginia legislature and its committees struggled with newspaper and citizen calls for an end to the practice that had caused so much grief.[2] A grandson of Thomas Jefferson, Thomas Jefferson Randolph, was among those urging emancipation and African colonization of the formerly enslaved. "It must come," he said. The only question was whether freedom would occur through laws or bloody revolution.[3]

Ultimately lawmakers gave up on abolition. Doubling down instead on efforts to prevent the emergence of another Nat Turner, Virginia lawmakers enacted harsh punishments against free Black people who learned to read and write, owned weapons, or participated in public performances.[4] The whip replaced fines for certain offenses, whether the offender was free or enslaved. Laws prescribed up to thirty-nine lashes per crime for any Black person who preached to an assembly, attended such a gathering, carried a firearm, sold liquor near a public assembly, or wrote a book pamphlet advising Black rebellion.

Even as treatment of Black people sank to new depths, something had turned in the national psyche. Nat Turner had supplied indisputable evidence of Black hostility toward White enslavers. The bloodshed countered false claims of slave contentment and further emboldened the abolitionist cause.

CHAPTER 4

Not a Quitter

First came Ralph Northam's resolve. Then came the harder part: the work.

In the days that followed, he struggled to regain his footing. He held onto a fragile equilibrium by focusing on next steps and by trying to tune out the voices still demanding his scalp. "I hit bottom basically. There was nowhere to go but up, and I just tried to navigate my way through how to do that," he said. The only real relief came at night when he looked forward to falling asleep. Even that respite often lasted only a few hours before he was awake, his mind racing, trying to process all that had occurred.

The idea of walking away still held some appeal. He could go back to being a doctor. Pam could resume her life, teaching or working in an environmental nonprofit. Neither of them had signed up for this kind of drubbing, especially Pam, who was happiest in nature or with small groups of family and friends. Her instinct was to shun the limelight. Sometimes she felt as if she was masquerading when she had to appear on camera or address a large group. The perceived unfairness of the situation stung. Northam calculated that he had dealt with as many as thirty thousand families, either as patients or though his hospice volunteer work. "And I never really judged people by their color or by their sexual orientation. That's why this hurt me so bad. Well, here I am, this racist now. That's not who I am."

If a picture is worth a thousand words, the picture in his medical school yearbook boiled down to one word spoken thousands of times: *racist*. Racist. RACIST.

Harry Lester, the former president of EVMS, came to visit him in the week after the scandal broke. "He said, 'Ralph, you should step down. You don't need to put yourself, your family through this,'" Northam recalled. The subtle pressure triggered his defiant streak. "I told him, 'If I do that, I'd be leaving here as a racist. I'm not. I'd also be leaving as a quitter. I'm not that either.'"

All his life Northam had met challenges with effort, sometimes herculean. As a student at the Virginia Military Institute and later at EVMS, he had often worked deep into the night to overcome academic deficits. Running for governor, he had sequestered himself in a borrowed apartment for months, performing the distasteful but essential task of dialing for dollars. Even something as mindless as a Fitbit step competition among legislators had stirred his competitive streak. He won a pot of money for charity by running five miles every morning and two every evening during one legislative session, dropping pounds from an already lean frame.

He was not a quitter.

Now he was facing perhaps the biggest challenge of his life. This time there was no blueprint to success. "I felt guilty, badly, however you want to put it, that I was putting Virginia through this. That was certainly not why I ran for governor, not why I get up in the morning," he said. "I knew I had a lot of work to do, and I was willing to do it."

But how?

He needed a plan.

WHEN JARVIS STEWART ARRIVED at Northam's office on Monday, February 4, he found an office mood so intense that "you could cut it with a knife." As a Black man, once a top aide to former Tennessee representative Harold Ford, the Bethesda crisis management consultant was uncertain of whether he wanted to engage in so ugly a racial controversy. But he knew some people in the office, and they had agreed for him to come.

The tension was not unexpected. "There were parts of the staff that felt like they did not want to believe it was the governor. There were other parts of the staff that were very suspect [about the photograph]. I totally understood that," he said.

Rita Davis had detected a generational divide in the office. Stewart saw a racial one. "I think there was ample anger with the Black staff, whether young or old. I think they felt embarrassed. I think they felt isolated, and all of those were justifiable." As he interviewed people over the next few days, he also saw a familiar pattern of silence among the older White staff. "Out of the fear of looking and sounding insensitive and not being thoughtful, you say nothing," he said.

A robust man, full of energy and moxie, Stewart sat down to negotiate terms with three people who would be key to any rebound: chief of staff Mercer, political consultant Bergman, and counselor Davis. As a plan of action emerged, each of the three played important roles in its development and execution, as did the governor and First Lady themselves.

Stocky and curly-haired, a forceful and detail-driven wagon master, Mercer would have the most pivotal role as the chief of staff. It would be up to him to bulldoze past opposition and keep everyone on track as the office laid out an equity agenda—including his personal passion, fair and affordable housing. It was unknown how his relationship with Northam would be impacted long term by Mercer's recommendation that the governor resign.

Bergman had the deepest personal connection to the governor. A Long Island native, the grandson of a prominent New Orleans rabbi who had been a powerful voice in the civil rights movement there, Bergman cherished that heritage. His strengths lay in strategic thinking and political messaging, skills that would be essential if Northam was to reconcile with legions of unhappy Virginia Democrats. Many were seething at the thought that the Democratic leadership scandals had ruined once-bright hopes of taking legislative control in the November elections.

Both Mercer and Bergman felt committed to the governor and to the equity work. If there was a distinction, Mercer's loyalty tilted slightly to the work, Bergman's to the man, his client.

Davis, a born leader, would be an important bellwether for the staff and also a conduit to the broader Black community. A product of rural, southside Virginia, the first of her family to attend college, she had worked for more than a decade in an upper-crust Richmond law firm before entering government. On scholarship as an undergraduate at Washington & Lee University, she had watched Kappa Alpha frat boys in Confederate uniforms march into the cafeteria, part of a ritual for securing dates to their annual Old South ball. "The Rita of today would never have just sat there," she recalled with a grimace. "I would have done something to try to protest that."

The Rita of today had become a confident, striking woman. People noticed when she walked into a room.

In that first meeting, Stewart had a brusque message: there was to be no double-dealing, no surprises. If crossed or misled, "I will burn this house down," Davis recalled his warning. If Stewart signed on to the team, his reputation would be on the line as much as theirs. Later that day, Stewart also sat down with Northam. Skeptical, he wanted to get his own sense of the man at the heart of the controversy. Growing up in Houston, playing sports, and attending college in the South, Stewart had many interactions with White men, young and old. As he and Ralph talked about Northam's upbringing, his attitudes toward race, and his values, Stewart saw a man with whom he believed he could work. He also sensed in Northam a quality he had recognized in past interactions.

Visiting aunts and uncles in a rural community outside Houston, he had seen Black and White people coexisting easily, often more so than in cities. They might not attend the same church, but they worked together and rooted together for high school football teams. They probably regarded each other as friends. And yet there was often heedless insensitivity, a lack of awareness of how offensive some comments or behaviors that had been passed down from generation to generation by White people could be to Black people. That might involve certain jokes or nicknames or references to foods like watermelon or fried chicken.

Derogatory. Clueless. Uninformed.

In Northam's case, it appeared to Stewart as they talked, blackface qualified as such a lapse.

Over several days, with input from staff, Stewart, and others, a hazy plan began to form. Matters divided into two categories: Northam's personal growth and the equity work that should be done within the administration.

Personally, Northam needed to read, to listen, and to think. As best he could, he should immerse himself in the experiences of Black people. He needed to hear from them how it feels to live in a society dominated at every turn by White institutions and people, some of them overtly hostile, many others subconsciously governed by racial stereotypes perpetrated and embedded across time. The group laid out plans for Northam to speak with dozens of prominent Black leaders and also to conduct a series of listening sessions with regular folks of color around Virginia. Stewart urged appointment of a state director of diversity, equity, and inclusion, someone with intimate knowledge of the grinding work involved in moving systems and cultures. Mercer planned to schedule personal meetings for both Northam and the staff with a local executive skilled at helping groups and individuals better understand their beliefs, attitudes, and behaviors around race.

Unquestionably, part of Northam's motivation in embracing that agenda was self-preservation. But he was not a duplicitous person. Another part of his purpose was a genuine desire to learn.

Even while learning, Northam needed to move forward on the policy front. Virginians were expecting as much. He instructed cabinet members to identify initiatives under their secretariats that could advance racial justice in Virginia. No one had to start from scratch. A number of such projects already were in progress. The intention, going forward, would be to make those ideas priorities. "I'd already been working on equity," the governor said. Medicaid expansion was the most acclaimed success but not the only such project. After the scandal "it was just brought into better focus. And that's the discussion I had with the cabinet secretaries. This is an opportunity for me to listen and learn. And I want you all to do the same. Let that guide the rest of our administration."

One subtle sign that Northam's intention to remain in office was sinking in came from a group branding itself the Virginia Black Politicos. "Our preference is that he resign," asserted Wes Bellamy, a fiery Charlottesville city counselor whose call to take down the Lee statue in that city had helped initiate months of protest in 2017. If Northam insisted on staying, then Bellamy and his allies wanted concrete, transactional proof of remorse.

Among their demands: remove Confederate statues and memorials from public spaces; create a "business equity fund" to boost minority-owned businesses; establish an executive office focused on minority concerns; decriminalize marijuana; commit to a staff including at least one-fourth people of color; and pledge $5 million to each of Virginia's historically Black colleges and universities. The list came with a threat. If Northam did not comply, Bellamy said, the group intended to make the rest of his term a living "hell."[1]

Prominent Black Virginians, including members of the Legislative Black Caucus, were coming to an important understanding. If the man sitting in the state's most powerful political position hoped to serve out his term with any degree of calm, he would need their help. And in return he would owe them much.

EARLY FEBRUARY SIGHTINGS of the governor proved rare. Going from the mansion to his office in the Patrick Henry Building, he stuck to the underground tunnel separating the two. Some national media still were camped out on the grounds. Pam Northam recalled peeping through the blinds each morning to see how many remained.

Clark Mercer awoke one day to find a couple dozen messages to his Twitter account calling him a racist. "One of the campaigns that was launched, if the governor didn't resign, we're going to go after the top staff. I said, 'I can do without this.'" For a time, he got off social media entirely. "It was tough. You've got friends who've been friends for a long time, didn't want to look at you, didn't want to engage with you."

Infuriatingly for Mercer, some of those on the right heaping scorn on Northam were privately far more reactionary on racial matters than the governor. "They use horrible language when it comes to race. They don't have a progressive bone in their bodies," he said. He also understood that many friends on the left were reeling, justifiably so. "It was very valid, how upset and disappointed and angry people were," he said.

On February 7 the First Lady surfaced for the couple's first public appearance. She kept a commitment to the annual conference of the Virginia Association for Environmental Education. "I put on my reddest dress. I put on my heels, and I screwed up my courage," she said. In a small act of defiance, she read during her talk from Mary Oliver's poem "Wild Geese": *You do not have to be good. / You do not have to walk on your knees / for a hundred miles through the desert repenting. / . . . Tell me about despair, yours, and I will tell you mine. / Meanwhile the world goes on.*

The battering did not abate quickly, either from the right or the left. On Tuesday of week 1, in his annual state of the union address, before Congress and a national audience, President Donald Trump singled out Northam for scorn. "We had the case of the governor of Virginia, where he stated he would execute a baby after birth," Trump asserted, debuting a rallying cry that would soon punctuate his presidential rallies. "Execute a baby. Execute a baby."

Two days later, civil rights evangelist Al Sharpton, appearing at Virginia Union University, a historic Black college in the heart of downtown Richmond, delivered a furious, twenty-two-minute rebuke. His right fist pounding the air, his left index finger jabbing what might have been Northam's chest, Sharpton described blackface as a Trojan horse of inequality. "They're trying to reduce this to an act of 'boys will be boys,'" he said. "No, it is deeper than that. It is that attitude that causes inferior schools, . . . that causes wholesale Blacks in prison, . . . that causes a disparity in health conditions. Because if you can mock us, then you can legislate and govern against us and nobody will care."

He had traveled to Virginia on a mission, Sharpton said, building to a climax that lifted the audience to its feet. "I've come to Richmond to tell the governor I'm not going to be your minstrel. I'm not going to accept your insult. . . . I flew out of New York to tell you that your political days are over. Go on to another life as a healer and as one that is committed to God's will."

Gradually, more quietly, other Black voices began to penetrate the clamor with a different message. Eight days after the scandal broke, the *Washington Post* handed Northam his first genuinely good news. A new poll showed Virginians overall almost evenly divided on whether he should resign. However, Black Virginians opposed resignation by a solid majority, 58 to 37 percent. Kelvin Jones's expectation of forgiveness had legs. The governor felt enormous gratitude and relief.

To their surprise, some of the Black public officials who had righteously called for Northam's resignation also encountered resistance. Mayor Stoney of

Richmond, first out of the gate, recalled attending a Valentine's Day event in the city's East End. "I was going up and down the aisle, and one of my seniors tugged on my coattail. I turned around. She said to me, 'Now, you don't go off and give governor a hard time for something that happened some thirty years ago.'

"I said, 'Excuse me?'

"'Oh, we saw what you did, called for the governor's resignation. But don't go be judging some person for something that happened thirty years ago.'

"I admit, I was taken aback."

CNN journalist Chris Cuomo seemed similarly bemused when guest Carla Savage-Wells, a former high school classmate of Northam's, defied the scores of officials urging resignation. A popular teacher in the Eastern Shore community of Nandua, Savage-Wells told the host of *Cuomo Prime Time* that she understood the disgust of fellow African Americans at the yearbook photo. What they failed to comprehend, she said, was that the Northam she knew, and knew well, would not lie about the fact that he was not in the picture. "If Ralph tells me he's not in that picture, I believe him."

As reporters from across the state and nation descended on the rural community where Northam grew up, the sense mounted that the man in the spotlight was no stereotypical, middle-aged, southern, White racist. Had he chosen to use the often-maligned defense "some of my best friends are Black," the statement would not, for Northam, have been false. In fact such friends existed from boyhood and beyond, and many of them were coming to his defense.

What would also become evident was that, for all the personal relationships and for all Northam's good work for Black and other marginalized communities as a doctor and as a politician, he had a marked lack of knowledge and understanding of the history and depth of racial injustice in America. The gap left him oblivious to the privileges that accounted in part for his own success and vulnerable to just the sort of mistake of which he was accused.

"I obviously knew about slavery and how it ended. I didn't know a whole lot about Jim Crow, the statues, all those things, far less than I know now," he said much later, after an immersion in racial awareness. Lynchings? "If you'd asked me, what did that mean, I probably could have told you, but I couldn't have told you any stories about it." Massive resistance? "I knew that there was an ordeal when they desegregated the schools, and there was massive White flight, which I saw on the [Eastern] Shore. But that was about the extent of that." Mass incarceration? White privilege? Systemic racism? All those were terms waiting to be unmasked.

It would be many months before Northam could say with conviction, from his gut, "Black oppression, it's alive and well today, just in a different form than it was when we talk about slavery."

THE GOVERNOR TEMPORARILY had stopped announcing his public schedule, but he could not remain incognito forever. Reporters—state, national, and international—were clamoring for interviews. Stewart recommended starting with two. First, Northam would sit down with Greg Schneider, a respected reporter for the *Washington Post*, known for his perceptive coverage of Virginia. Second, he would engage with Gayle King, cohost of *CBS This Morning*, who was expected to bring empathy as well as toughness to her questioning.

The Schneider interview came first.

In it Northam reiterated important points. He had overreacted in his initial acceptance of blame for the blackface photograph. He had directed cabinet officials to come up with ways to address ongoing racial inequities in areas including education, health care, mortgages, capital, and entrepreneurship. And he was committed both to staying in office and to learning from his mistakes. "It's obvious from what happened this week that we still have a lot of work to do. There are still some very deep wounds in Virginia, and especially in the area of equity," he said.

Schneider described the governor's bearing as "chastened and subdued" and his initial agenda for moving forward—sensitivity training for the cabinet, agency heads, and colleges—as modest.[2]

King arrived at the mansion a day later with a film crew and staff of more than a dozen. After chitchat and a brief tour of the historic residence, she and Northam sat down face-to-face in two chairs in a reception space on the first floor. His compact, fine-featured face, with its narrow seam of a mouth, dancing eyebrows, and direct gaze, revealed a man as unassuming and believable as Virginians had mostly known him to be. That was not what some observers remembered most from the interview.

"Well, it has been a difficult week," he began. "If you look at Virginia's history, we're now at the 400-year anniversary. Just ninety miles from here in 1619, the first indentured servants from Africa landed on our shores at Old Point Comfort, what we call now Fort Monroe."

"Also known as slavery," King interjected.

"Yes," Northam replied, his mood sinking. Later he described the feeling. "First sentence, second out of her mouth, and I said 'indentured servants' and she corrected me, and I said, 'Oh, boy, this has gotten off to a good start.'"

The backstory on that moment dated to a speech Northam had given some time earlier at Hampton University in which he spoke of the enslaved Black people first arriving on Virginia shores. Afterward Dr. William Wiggins, a historian with three decades of teaching experience at universities including Columbia and Hampton, told him that he had been incorrect in his reference. The term *slave* did not appear in Virginia law until decades later. The first Black people brought to Virginia were treated more like indentured servants, Northam was told.

While prepping for the King interview, Stewart had approved Northam's saying indentured servants, over strong opposition from Mercer. A headline in the next day's *USA Today* spoke to the more common understanding. "Virginia Gov. Ralph Northam slammed for referring to 'first indentured servants from Africa' instead of slaves," the headline read. The ongoing debate among historians over the correct designation played out in the story.

Using "words like 'Indentured servant' is how people try to erase the pain and horrors of slavery. It is how they think it harmless to wear blackface. @Ralph Northam is done. If he won't resign, he needs to be forced out," author Julissa Arce tweeted.[3]

Not so, countered Kurt Eichenwald, journalist and author. "Folks, learn your damn history, Northam is correct . . . There were no laws for slavery in VA til 1661."[4]

If Northam needed any reminder that his pledge to racial equity was about to lead him into a minefield of easy misunderstandings and deeply scarred emotions, his interview with King had provided it.

To navigate those hazards, he would need to start with a cold, hard look at Virginia's history and at his own.

CHAPTER 5

Man in the Mirror

Ralph Shearer Northam was born in 1959 into a geographic treasure. The seventy-mile-long peninsula known as Virginia's Eastern Shore remains central to his identity. Bordered to the east by the Atlantic Ocean, the west by the Chesapeake Bay, and the north by the remainder of the three-state Delmarva Peninsula, the Shore was for centuries accessible only by ferry, boat, or a circuitous car or train ride through southern Delaware and Maryland.

Ralph was four years old when the 17.6-mile engineering marvel known as the Chesapeake Bay Bridge-Tunnel opened, connecting Shore residents to Virginia Beach and a more contemporary life. For many, the Northams included, tradition trumped modernity. Occasional trips to a doctor or a shopping mall across the water only slowly penetrated a world defined by the rhythms of nature—planting season for fields of tomatoes, corn, and sweet potatoes in the spring, crop harvesting in the fall, oyster shucking or clam digging when the time was right.

Even today, as an influx of "come heres," folks distinct from the "born heres" and the "from heres," have created a smattering of bistros and vacation rentals, a weathered, stark quality remains. Wide, flat fields punctuated by wooden farmhouses, dated motels, and stands of loblolly pines evoke an Andrew Wyeth solitude. Venture far off the Route 13 spine that conveys truckloads of vegetables and poultry north to urban markets and a traveler stumbles onto a warren of streams and creek beds tumbling into breathtaking shorelines of shimmering sea oats and shrieking gulls.

In the years since Ralph Northam left, eventually establishing a foothold across the bay in Norfolk and Virginia Beach, fortunes have improved on the Shore. Still, an ever-present poverty pierces the beauty in the peninsula's two counties, Accomack and Northampton. The economic disparity between Black and White residents remains stark. The year Ralph was born, income for non-White families (almost all of whom would have been Black) in Accomack

County was 30 percent of that for all families. In Northampton County the figure was 41 percent.[1]

Northam's sixth great-grandfather, John Northam, gave a deposition in Northampton County in January 1681, establishing his offspring's birthright at the apex of the Shore's ancestral hierarchy. Three centuries later the Northams remained among the region's leading citizens.

Ralph's parents—Wescott Northam, a lawyer and three-term commonwealth's attorney, and Nancy Shearer Northam, a homemaker and trained nurse —preached and lived the Protestant virtues of honesty, responsibility, and hard work. Economically they fit into the Shore's upper echelon, but there was little ostentation in their lifestyle. With revealing modesty, his parents nicknamed their property by the road sign nearest to the driveway: "End State Maintenance." Their home was comfortable but not showy, a plain-fronted farmhouse whose wood siding had been bricked over. The house, Wescott liked to say, was "old enough to be rundown but not old enough to be valuable." Even after he became a state court judge, he drove a worn, 1969 yellow Chevy pickup to the courthouse, where he never donned judge's robes. "He didn't do a lot of pomp and circumstance," said Tom, Ralph's older brother. "He never tried to impress anyone."

In contrast to her country-bred husband, Nancy Shearer grew up as a city girl, the daughter of a prominent Washington, DC, surgeon. The family lived in the affluent enclave of Wesley Heights, where life included live-in help and membership at the Congressional Country Club. Visiting the club as his grandmother's guest as a child, "I knew we weren't in Onancock," Tom said wryly. "It was a little bit uncomfortable."

More than a name, Ralph and Tom inherited a sense of place. Growing up on a pine-sheltered lane about five miles outside the fishing village of Onancock, they could look out their bedroom windows onto a finger of yard, bordered to the left by Parkers Creek and to the right by Finney Creek, two broad expanses of water that empty into Onancock Creek, which empties into the Chesapeake Bay.

The hours spent sailing those waters came back to Ralph during the blackface trials. "There's a nautical saying, 'I can't change the direction of the wind, but I can adjust my sails,'" he recalled. "A lot of things, you can't change, but you can modify." Appreciation for solitude, a lack of pretention, and an awareness of nature's abundant gifts and turbulent tests all transferred from the boy to the man.

Ralph's boyhood was steeped in outdoor passions. He paddled the creeks, perfected fishing skills, bicycled down country roads to buy popsicles and candy at a crossroads store, joined far-flung pickup games of basketball and football, learned to dismantle and reassemble car engines, and, as he grew older, joined in a bit of illicit drag racing on a secluded straightaway not far from home.

Clean-cut and sweet-faced, Northam was of middling height until his junior year, when a growth spurt pushed him past six feet and into a starting spot on the basketball team. "Anything I did, I wanted to excel," he said. From mastering a unicycle at age eleven to co-captaining the high school basketball team and leading various clubs, he remembers his youth as a largely unbroken string of setting goals, working hard, and achieving success. "I've probably got some obsessive-compulsive tendencies," he admitted. "Whatever I did, I just wanted to do it right."

His exactitude extended to rescuing a 1953 Oldsmobile from a junk heap and lovingly restoring it, the first of several such ventures. Even as governor, one of his greatest satisfactions came from lifting the hood of a car. "I like to go to the garage, go to Lowe's for tools and supplies. I miss that part of my life," he said. For a time he enjoyed shooting quail and duck. That ended on an afternoon in high school when, hunting alone, he winged a dove. The choice was to let it suffer or to wring its neck. He killed the bird by hand. "After that, it just kind of hit me, Why am I out here shooting an innocent animal that's minding its own business? That was the last time I hunted."

In the Northam home, slacking was not an option. "We worked very hard. It was just expected of Tom and me," he said. Only later would he start to see the degree to which family connections brought job opportunities. When those breaks arose, Ralph did his part by performing well, creating toeholds to a future. Ralph and Tom had their first real jobs at about eleven and thirteen, doing yard and farm work for a neighboring family. For $1 an hour, they cut grass, weeded, painted, and baled hay. By high school Ralph had graduated to bagging and stocking shelves at a local grocery. "The outgoing person that he was, he could tell you every person that had been in the store that day," his brother recalled.

The opportunity of Ralph's young lifetime came when one of the Shore's legendary charter boat fishermen, Capt. Ray Parker, hired him as a boat mate. Tom and their father had been visiting with Parker, a friend. The seaman had just lost a mate for his summer excursions. On the spot he offered the job to Tom, who had already committed to a summer job. Wescott Northam jumped in, "I have another son, and he'll do it."

Later, at age eighteen, building on the job born of his father's connection to Parker, Ralph climbed a step up the employment ladder. For a summer he captained a boat that daily ferried a paving crew to and from the island of Tangier during airport construction, making good money. That, he would come to realize, is how privilege works, one connection leading to another.

Ralph's nature seemed most patterned on his outgoing, service-oriented mother, Tom's on their more stern, reserved father. The Shearer connection also initiated awareness of medicine as a possible life calling. Trained at Johns Hopkins as a registered nurse, Nancy worked at least one day a week at the Shore's only hospital, then in Nassawadox, while her boys were growing up.

"My father is a smart man, a very fair person, but he didn't reach out to help others like my mother did. Looking back, my desire in life was to be successful, and my definition of success is to be able to help other people," Northam said. One trait that surfaced in the blackface scandal might be more attributable to his father. "Ralph is a very humble person. Oftentimes, people think humble people are not resolute, firm, decisive," noted Senator Kaine. But "once Ralph has made up his mind about something, he has definitely made up his mind, even to the point of stubborn."

It came as no surprise to Kaine that, in the face of enormous pressure, Northam refused to resign.

CENTRAL TO THE NORTHAM FAMILY narrative is the story of Thomas Long Northam, Ralph's paternal grandfather. A colorful figure who worked as a professional gambler before settling down and becoming an Eastern Shore judge, the elder Northam died in 1938, leaving his son as the man of the house at just fourteen years old. A few years later Wescott and his mother were forced by hardship to sell property that had been in the family for four generations. While conducting a title search in hopes of reclaiming that land, Wescott stumbled onto records documenting the family's slave-owning history.

According to the 1850 and 1860 censuses, Ralph's great-grandfather and Thomas's father, Levi Jacob Northam, in 1860 enslaved an eighteen-year-old female and a twenty-four-year-old male. Levi's father, James, was recorded as owning nine enslaved persons in 1850 and eight on the brink of the Civil War. Records showed that he also freed two individuals in 1858 and another in 1863.[2]

That discovery, surfacing in the course of Ralph's 2017 race for governor, prompted remorse from the candidate. "The news that my ancestors owned slaves disturbs and saddens me," Northam told the Richmond Times-Dispatch. Noting that Virginia once had the largest number of enslaved individuals of any state, he added, "My family's complicated story is similar to Virginia's complex history."

Delve a bit deeper into the family story and its complexity grows. Thomas's wife, Ida May Brownlee Northam, who died before grandson Ralph was born, had a far stronger connection to slavery and the Confederacy than Thomas. Born in Abbeville, South Carolina, she was the granddaughter of John A. Brownlee, a leading Abbeville citizen who was described in the local newspaper at his death as "high tone, pure minded, generous hearted and patriotic." He also left behind some four dozen enslaved men, women, and children whose value was recorded as ranging from $2,500 to $500 each. Further cementing his Confederate credentials, Brownlee had been one of five leaders in the Abbeville secession meeting of November 22, 1860, in which citizens adopted an ordinance of secession and selected delegates to a state convention. The event was one of the first formal actions leading to the Civil War.[3]

Ida May's father, John Ewing Brownlee, was a Confederate veteran who continued the White supremacist tradition. His obituary proudly noted his connection to the Red Shirts, a Reconstruction-era terrorist paramilitary movement dedicated to reasserting White control over freed Black people, sometimes through violent intimidation, including beatings and even murder.[4]

WHATEVER THE PREDISPOSITIONS of their ancestors toward race, when confronted with the moral test of their own generation, Wescott and Nancy Northam opted to stand on the right side of history. The US Supreme Court in 1954 had called for the desegregation of public schools, a mandate met in Virginia with fierce resistance. Initial responses included school closings and the use of public dollars to fund private White academies. Later Virginia had inched its way into token compliance by adopting a so-called freedom of choice plan, in which Black and White citizens theoretically could opt to enroll in each other's schools. Only a handful of Black students were allowed into previously all-White classrooms, however. Essentially no White students requested admission to the formerly Black schools.

In 1968 in a Virginia case, *Green v. School Board of New Kent County*, the High Court finally lost patience. Fourteen years after *Brown v. Board of Education of Topeka* ordered desegregation, the justices demanded that New Kent— and by extension, the rest of the South—live up to the mandate, providing "a plan that works to dismantle the segregated system in their district."

For many White Virginians, not only on the Eastern Shore but across Virginia and the South, particularly in areas with large Black populations, the ruling had a clear result. White parents who could afford to pulled their children out of the public schools and enrolled them in private segregation academies. On the Eastern Shore, the alternative of choice became the Broadwater Academy in Exmore. A contemporary of Ralph Northam's, whose parents had selected the private school earlier based on academics, recalled the impact of the New

Kent ruling on her fourth-grade class. "Enrollment exploded," she said, with class size doubling from about thirteen to twenty-five that year. "Ralph's parents never pulled him out, which was unusual for the folks in our social crowd," she said. "It was a big deal."

Not so, to hear the Northams tell it. There was never any doubt, said Wescott Northam in an interview when he was ninety-six, that Tom and Ralph would continue in public schools. "Life isn't all academics," he said. "You also have to deal with people." In the public-school arena, "you get an exposure" missing in a more homogenous, white-bread setting. In a frugal family where both boys were expected to pay their way through college and graduate school, the lack of tuition payments also appealed. Neither Ralph nor Tom recalls any conversation about the decision. They simply assumed, as their parents did, that they would continue where they were, in the public schools.

AS IS TRUE IN MUCH OF THE SOUTH, the story of race on the Eastern Shore from the arrival of the first shackled Africans in 1619 to the school integration reckoning of 1968 blends both cruelty and occasional enlightenment with the ordinary rhythms of day-to-day life. Even if Northam knew little of that history, he and his contemporaries were products of it.

The most celebrated early Black resident on the peninsula was Anthony Johnson. Possibly one of the first Africans arriving in 1619 at Point Comfort, Johnson had by 1640 immigrated to the Eastern Shore. There he prospered. Gaining his freedom, he raised a family and acquired some 250 acres of land and other property, becoming himself an enslaver of Black people. Notably, Johnson was not unique in gaining his freedom. Historians T. H. Breen and Stephen Innes estimate that as many as 30 percent of Black residents on the Eastern Shore were free in 1668, a figure that plummeted as the Virginia colony's enslaved population multiplied in the late seventeenth century. The lives of those early free Black people, Breen and Innes argue, represent "a road not taken," one where American society might have been defined more by class than race.[5]

If there was a pre–Civil War distinction to the Eastern Shore on race, it lies in the considerable interest in Black freedom. Preference for an end to slavery was not a majority White view. Far from it. Still, relative to many other sections of the state and region, a degree of anti-slavery activism flourished.[6] In the early nineteenth century, the number of freed Black men and women grew, even as the state legislature meeting in Richmond enacted harsh penalties for those still shackled and strict controls for those already freed. In 1860, on the cusp of the Civil War, the northernmost of the peninsula's two counties—Accomack—had almost as many free Black people as enslaved, 3,418 to 4,507.

Even in Northampton County, home to larger plantations and the accompanying demand for a larger workforce, roughly one in five Black people was free.[7]

In many ways the war that followed was a short-lived affair on the Shore. Determined to secure supply lines to Fort Monroe across the bay and to smother Confederate sympathies in eastern Maryland, Union forces made a preemptive strike on Virginia's Eastern Shore in late 1861. By November the territory was securely in Union hands. As a result, when President Lincoln issued his Emancipation Proclamation on January 1, 1863, local Black residents were unaffected. The proclamation applied only in Confederate territory. Adoption of a new Virginia constitution on April 11, 1864, finally brought the despicable practice to a close on the Shore.[8]

The low point of race relations on the peninsula in the postwar years was a race riot on August 10, 1907. White vigilantes upset by Black demands for better wages and by rumors of intended violence torched two Black-owned businesses in Onancock. "Notices were posted throughout Onancock informing the 50 Negro families who reside here to leave town," the *Daily News* of Frederick, Maryland, reported on August 13. "The streets are patrolled by white pickets." The governor sent troops to restore order. Compared to devastating early twentieth-century riots in places such as Tulsa, Oklahoma, and Wilmington, North Carolina, the Onancock outbreak serves as a historical footnote. But the attitudes that fostered it—fear of Black advancement, determination to maintain White control—paralleled those propelling bloodier outbreaks.[9]

As the twentieth-century school integration struggles and ongoing twenty-first-century economic disparities attest, "the end of slavery was not the end of the story," wrote Kirk Mariner, author of *Slave and Free on Virginia's Eastern Shore*. "Not of the racism in which it had thrived, nor of the inequality on which it had depended, and not of its lingering impact on the economic, cultural, political, and personal lives of people of all races on the Eastern Shore."[10]

SUCH HISTORY BARELY PENETRATED the closed world of Ralph Northam as he came of age in the 1960s and '70s. Just eight years old when Martin Luther King Jr. was assassinated and in his mid-teens when the Vietnam War wound to conclusion, he has few memories of world events outside his home turf. "It's not a good excuse," he said. "It just wasn't a priority of mine." While they had no way of knowing at the time, Nancy and Wescott Northam's school choice for their sons had long-lasting consequences. As a result of that decision, Ralph Northam possibly had the most integrated childhood of any Virginia governor. The interaction began at an early age.

For a time in elementary school, even before the *Green* decision brought significant school desegregation, Ralph's best friend was Black. He and Elvis Pratt traveled back and forth to each other's homes, a fact still remembered for its oddity by another Black friend, Robert Garris. Ralph's spending the night in a trailer home in a predominantly Black area of the county, and vice versa, was not standard practice for the Shore in the 1960s, said Garris, a retired postal worker and traveling minister. Robert was younger than Ralph, but he often joined in pickup games at the Northam home. Occasionally he and other Black players stayed for dinner. As adults the two reconnected when Garris's three-year-old son had a stroke and wound up in Norfolk under Northam's care. A gregarious man with many acquaintances, Garris pays Northam high tribute: "I only have five, six real friends, and he's one of 'em."

Pratt, whom Northam recalls fondly, traveled to New York to work in theater after high school and died of AIDS in his twenties. "I was just saddened for him. He was a wonderful person," Northam described his reaction to his friend's death.

At Onancock High School, Ralph's class of 1977 included about seventy-five students, roughly half Black and half White. Intermingling rarely extended to interracial dating. "It was frowned on by the general community, also homosexuality," Northam recalled. On the inside cover of his senior yearbook, two couples silhouetted against a marsh sunset are clearly delineated by race. One couple is obviously White, the other obviously Black. In retrospect Northam realizes that a teacher who sometimes cooked gourmet dinners for guests and hired him to serve as a waiter was gay. "It's just not something I recognized at that stage of my life," he said. In the conservative world of the Eastern Shore, "it was frowned upon and not talked about a lot."

Neither Ralph's choice of college nor of medical school did much to broaden his worldview. Both VMI in the late 1970s and EVMS in the early 1980s were socially conservative places. Northam's focus on science further limited discussion of broad societal issues. By the second decade of the twenty-first century, at least some southern medical schools were teaching about the ways Black people had been experimented on and abused for years by the medical establishment. That was not part of the curriculum four decades earlier.

Northam's transition from Onancock to VMI was anything but smooth. Soon after arriving at the then all-male school, a formidable fortress steeped in tradition and harsh discipline, one of Northam's high school friends died in a car accident. That tragedy, coupled with the deliberately abusive "Rat Line," in which first-year cadets are subjected to an endless stream of demands from upperclassmen, soured Northam on his college choice. He had also been accepted at Davidson College in North Carolina, and a quick call confirmed that he could still enroll. "I went home at Thanksgiving. I'll never forget, we were sitting around the Thanksgiving table. I said, 'Father,' I called him *Father* or *Judge*, 'I'm miserable at VMI. But I've made arrangements to transfer to Davidson in January.' He's a man of few words. He said, 'No, you'll be going back to VMI.' And that was the end of the discussion. I went back."

As he would do during the blackface scandal, Northam committed to making the best of an unwelcome situation. His grades steadily improved. Most impressive, in his senior year, he rose to First Battalion commander and president of the Honor Court, one of the school's most prestigious student posts. The court investigates and rules on charges of violations of VMI's rigid honor code, which demands that "a cadet will not lie, cheat, steal, or tolerate those who do." Under Northam's leadership, the court drummed thirteen violators out of the corps his senior year. None of the complaints or actions had anything to do with race-related misconduct. It would be years before racial harassment became a recognized offense at the school.

In yet another way, VMI stood in stark contrast to Onancock High School. Of 261 cadets pictured in Northam's senior class, only 8 were Black. When he arrived, the school had been admitting African Americans for only a decade. It was the last public Virginia college to do so. At the time he paid scant attention to school traditions that would come under fire in a more racially aware era. Deification of Confederate symbols, such as the mandatory saluting of a statue of Confederate general Stonewall Jackson, was simply a given. "It's not politically correct to say that I didn't see color, but I didn't see it. I didn't see homosexuality, any of that," he said. "Maybe it was the way I was raised, maybe being naive."

Decades later he would recognize with chagrin the added psychological strain shouldered by Black cadets in that setting. "Looking back at it, knowing what I know now, man, it must have been a very uncomfortable environment for African Americans," he said.

NORTHAM HAD PAID FOR COLLEGE in part through a navy flight program requiring postgraduate military service. When a failed eye exam squashed those plans, he switched to an army medical school track. Entering Eastern Virginia Medical School in Norfolk in the fall of 1981, he again found himself academically challenged. Focused on classwork, he barely noticed that his class contained only a smattering of Black students.

In the late spring and early summer of 1984, he was winding up a rotation at Brooke Army Medical Center in San Antonio and preparing to start a pediatric residency there in the fall. A blip on the radar—publication of the school year-book—barely registered with him, if at all. Thirty-five years later, a high-profile investigation would conclude that EVMS yearbooks of that era, including the 1984 product, repeatedly included instances of blackface as well as "other content that could be offensive to women, minorities, certain ethnic groups, and others."[11]

Northam could not comment. He had no memory of ever seeing those publications.

Settling into the busy pace of treating army dependents in San Antonio, Northam also found time to socialize. That was the fall he entered a dress-up contest, donning blackface to enhance his appearance as singer Michael Jackson. His imitation of Jackson's moonwalk glide cemented his victory. The previous winter and spring, the Reverend Jesse Jackson had galvanized progressive Black and White voters nationwide, winning several Democratic presidential primaries, including Virginia's. For Northam there was no connection between such rising Black pride and his use of shoe polish to blacken his face. He saw the Michael Jackson costume as, if anything, a compliment, not a cause for remorse.

The following May the *San Antonio Express-News* picked Northam as one of the city's most eligible doctor-bachelors. A month later he met the woman destined to end that bachelorhood. Pretty and petite, Pam Thomas captured Ralph's attention at a friend's pool party. He overheard her telling friends that she had just rescued a cat with a kitten that was too weak to nurse. More interested in the University of Texas–trained occupational therapist than in the kitten, Northam offered to help.

"So, I went and rigged up a little syringe," he recalled. "I took a piece of surgical tube and rigged up a little nipple and took some formula and started nursing this kitten at her apartment. One thing led to another." Smitten, he proposed three months later, and they married on July 5, 1986. Among the qualities that attracted him were Pam's caring nature and her open-mindedness. "She sees a worm, literally a worm, on the sidewalk on a hot day, she'll go and put it back in the dirt. That's the kind of person she is," he said. Pam's circle also exposed him, for the first time, to friendships with openly gay individuals and couples. "It just kind of opened my eyes," he said.

The marriage, more than anything in his previous life, pushed him to view the world around him through a wider lens.

Meanwhile Northam was realizing that a steady diet of childhood ear infections and tummy distress was not for him. An opportunity to check out pediatric neurology revitalized him. "I went and did this elective for a month, and I loved it," he said. The caseload was a challenging and fascinating blend of seizures, headaches, muscular dystrophy, brain tumors, cerebral palsy, developmental delays, and other conditions. Finishing in San Antonio, he and Pam moved to Silver Spring, Maryland, where he completed additional training in pediatric neurology at Walter Reed Army Medical Center and worked for six months as a chief resident in child neurology at Johns Hopkins.

From there he was assigned to the Landstuhl Army Hospital in southwest Germany, and his horizons again expanded. It was supposed to be a two-year tour of duty, which by army rules meant that Pam and their toddler son, Wesley, could not accompany him at government expense. Sign up for another year, he was told, and the family could come along on the military's dime. Tapping his mulish streak, Northam saw that as a form of blackmail. Pam was pregnant with their second child, and they were not about to be separated for two years. Nor did he intend to be coerced into extending his service beyond the two-year commitment. At their own expense, the couple secured German housing, a small cinderblock house that was the best they could afford.

Shortly before Pam was due to deliver, Operation Desert Storm launched, on January 16, 1991. The fighting closed the Landstuhl hospital, the main destination for war casualties, to civilian use. As a result daughter Aubrey's birth was an international event—a German hospital, a Greek doctor, and an Iranian roommate for Pam.

For Ralph the weeks of Desert Storm were a blur of traumatically injured patients, many mangled from explosions or jeep accidents, others suffering anxiety disorders and panic attacks. Charged with overseeing neurological services, he had to sort out physical from emotional injuries. Army protocols called for returning anyone with psychiatric injury to the battlefield as quickly as possible. Failure to return to one's colleagues would create greater emotional damage than reentry, so the thinking went. Interaction with soldiers and, from a distance, their families, convinced Northam otherwise. "I got to the point where if someone wanted to go back to the arena, we'd help them. If they wanted to go back to the States, we would ship them back home," he said.

Listening to what he was being told by the patients themselves came to trump official policy in his mind. He was elevating people and their stories to the center of his decision-making, again stretching boundaries.

WHEN THE TOUR ENDED, NORTHAM was ready to go home. Settling the family in Virginia Beach, with the bonus of proximity to the Eastern Shore, he and four other men formed a practice in pediatric neurology. He also joined the medical school faculty. Later, that group and some two dozen other doctors created

Children's Specialty Group, offering a host of pediatric subspecialties. He continued with that team, which is affiliated with the Children's Hospital of the King's Daughters, until leaving to serve as governor.

In the decade and a half between the army and entering politics, Northam's focus was on the thousands of children who filtered through his practice. Elective politics barely penetrated his radar. He voted twice, in 2000 and 2004, for Republican George Bush for president. "Back at that stage of my life, I just thought he would do the best job," he said. When he decided to run for the state senate in 2007, he had to think hard about why he was doing so as a Democrat. The answer had to do with helping people and with his concern over the deterioration of the Chesapeake Bay. It also reflected the fact that a Republican incumbent already held the seat. It would be easier to challenge him under the Democratic Party banner. Mostly Northam saw himself as a centrist, concerned about solutions, not labels.

In the wake of the blackface scandal, he would see two ways in which his years in medicine benefited his recovery. First, he had developed an ability to listen, the most critical part, he believes, of both medicine and politics. Second, time spent with seriously ill and often dying children gave him a clear perspective, one that steadied him in the excruciating months of national criticism. "The hardest thing in life has to be the loss of a child. I don't think it gets any tougher," he said. "I always told folks, if you think you're having a bad day, let me take you with me and show you what a family is going through when a child is sick or dying." Bad as his circumstance felt, he had lived alongside far worse.

He also had seen what sustains people through trials: not necessarily the achievement of the most desired outcome but finding the strength to shoulder the burden. That, too, spoke to the personal trauma he underwent. "The most important thing when you talk about a dying child is to never give up hope. I've always taught that when someone loses their hope, they lose their will to live. The hope might not necessarily be that you're going to get better or that you're going to survive this, but the hope might be that we're going to keep your child comfortable and the remaining days are going to be at home."

The goal of working for racial equity—for reducing structural, race-based barriers to opportunity—gave him that sort of focus and purpose.

THE HOPE NORTHAM GAVE HARRY MEARS, one of countless parents he has counseled, was that Mears could have six to seven years with his infant son. The assessment turned out to be correct. Born with cystic fibrosis, intractable seizures, and an assortment of other problems, Taylor Mears was delivered at a hospital in Salisbury, Maryland, and airlifted almost immediately to Johns Hopkins in Baltimore. There he was given three weeks to live.

Harry, manager of Shore Tire and Auto in Onley, Virginia, had grown up with Ralph, riding the school bus together. He telephoned his old friend, who had the baby transferred to King's Daughters. Northam predicted that with medication and treatment, Taylor could have a life. Mears's appreciation for the years that followed remains profound. "There was not another person who came close" to Ralph in support, he said, recalling that the Northams insisted on his staying at their home during regular medical trips to Norfolk from the Shore. He also believes that Northam was instrumental in stopping the bank from foreclosing on his home, although he does not know how.

Over a long career, there are many such stories, growing in part out of Northam's once-a-month commitment for many years to travel across the Chesapeake Bay Bridge to treat underserved children through an Eastern Shore rural health clinic and to his twenty-year volunteer service as medical director for the Edmarc Hospice for Children in Portsmouth. The latter, Northam said, was "probably the best experience of my life." He resisted taking the job because of the certainty of attendant grief. The sadness, as it turned out, was offset by the reward of "having those families put their trust in me at a very difficult time."

The tools that assisted Northam in handling the weight of life-and-death responsibility resurfaced in the months of peril for his own well-being. Regularly he slipped on his running shoes and headed down Capitol Hill toward the James River, two of his protective unit state troopers running alongside. Crossing a pedestrian suspension bridge to Belle Island, which housed some thirty thousand Union prisoners during the Civil War, he followed the trails, glimpsing the ever-changing patterns of the James, reclaiming for a moment the serenity of a youth spent navigating the tributaries of the Chesapeake Bay. "I go running. That helps. If I can get out on the water in a boat, that helps. Obviously, Pam. She understands," he said. Friends, prayer.

Those were Northam's anchors as he headed into the next phase of the storm.

CHAPTER 6

Diving into White Privilege

Ralph Northam's rehabilitation rumbled along three tracks: policy, politics, and personal growth.

The work of Virginia could not pause on account of his problems. The 2019 General Assembly was in session through February, and there were legislative priorities to monitor, bills to shape. Staff needed to remain focused on that work. In numerous meetings with cabinet members and agency heads, Northam stressed that the first order of business was to keep calm and carry on. He spent more time dropping into the offices of the staff than he had in all his previous thirteen months as governor. "I said, 'We've been elected and you have been put in position to do the work of Virginia, to help people.' And I said, 'While I'm working through all this, you all need to keep doing your jobs.'"

The Legislative Black Caucus felt similarly beset. When members showed up for work on the Monday after the blackface scandal broke, legislative dynamics had not changed. "We had bill presentations. We had fights. The Republicans were still in the majority," Delegate Price recalled. Normally an exuberant swirl of energy, she, like others, felt mentally and emotionally whipped. Drawing on her philosophy degree from Spelman College and her masters in religious studies from Howard University, two historically Black institutions that helped shape her activism, Price weighed the conflicting voices in the Black community.

"I heard, 'Forgiveness, that's what Christians are supposed to do.' I heard, 'Well, what do you expect?' I heard, 'Now we're in a position to get what we've needed for years.' And that is the one that resonated the most with me, because my motto is "Be the change; do the work." Separately, the governor's office and the Black caucus were galvanizing around a similar theme: proof of reclamation would lie in the work.

Politically Democrats had hoped to take control of both houses of the legislature in upcoming fall elections for the first time in a quarter century. Many worried that the three top Democrats, beginning with Northam, would act as albatrosses, dragging the party to defeat. In normal times a governor serves as the party's chief fundraiser, filling the coffers for so large an undertaking. Who was even going to answer the phone now when Northam dialed?

The governor had personally committed to a deeper understanding of racial inequity. If that promise was to be more than empty words, he would have to invest time, lots of it, in reading, listening, and evaluating. "I knew I had a lot of work to do, and I was willing to do it," he said. Speaking at graduation ceremonies, Northam had often said that people make mistakes and that the key is to grow from them. He reminded himself regularly of his own advice.

Guided by Jarvis Stewart and others, Northam dived into race-related readings. For a time the office looked almost like a lending library. "There would be books from people to the governor, saying, 'I think you should read this, and you should read that,'" recalled Rita Davis. Copies were left out for others in the office to read as well. Two books with messages that resonated were *Why Are All the Black Kids Sitting Together in the Cafeteria?* by Beverly Daniel Tatum and Robin DiAngelo's *White Fragility: Why It's So Hard for White People to Talk about Racism.*

Tatum defines racism not just as individual prejudice but as "a system involving cultural messages and institutional policies and practices." In the United States, she writes, White people often defend racial advantage—access to better schools, housing, and jobs—even when they do not embrace overtly prejudicial thinking.[1]

Northam had never thought about racism in terms of such broad, underlying systems.

DiAngelo accentuated the message: "We are taught to think about racism only as discrete acts committed by individual people, rather than as a complex, interconnected system." The focus on individual acts makes it easier for White people to deny or fail to see their own complicity in housing, schooling, and economic policies that disadvantage people of color, she writes. When legal authority and institutional control prop up collective prejudice, it transforms into systemic racism, a "far-reaching system" independent of individual intentions or actions.[2]

Terms such as "White supremacy" and "institutional racism" had not been part of Northam's vocabulary. Gradually they gained traction and meaning.

Meanwhile Northam scheduled telephone conversations, many of them, with Black farmers, educators, officeholders, and ministers, seeking their counsel and favor. He scheduled one-on-one office meetings with prominent Black legislators. "It was like drinking from a fire hydrant," he recalled the pace.

Two conversations with lawmakers stood out.

State senator Jennifer McClellan gave him much-needed clarity about why blackface is so offensive. The youngest member of the Legislative Black Caucus when she first won election in 2005, McClellan had by 2019 emerged as an authoritative voice on both policy and Black history. With her short, sculpted hair, classic dresses, and clout as a corporate lawyer, the Richmond lawmaker emitted an air of level-headed competence. Meeting with Northam shortly after the scandal broke, she asked, "Do you understand about minstrel shows?" "Never heard of 'em," Northam replied. He learned from McClellan that minstrelsy, which dated to the early nineteenth century, was a peculiarly American form of entertainment in which performers through skits, dance, and exaggerated makeup mocked Black people as shiftless, dim-witted, and comical. Typically the entertainers were White people who blackened their faces. Even as the practice faded in the mid-twentieth century, some of the stereotypes it had encouraged clung.

How had Northam gotten to be fifty-nine years old without ever hearing of minstrel shows? Other than to say that his focus had been elsewhere, he could not explain it.

For her part McClellan was still in shock over a man she'd considered a family friend. The blackface image, she said, had for her "triggered four hundred years of shit that has been heaped on Black people in America." Now she zoned in on Northam's startled face as he asked, "Why didn't I know that?" Somewhat to her relief, "I remember thinking to myself, 'He's not racist. He's race ignorant.'"

Northam also held onto the words of Delores McQuinn, the most vocal member of the Virginia Legislative Black Caucus in urging him not to resign on February 1. "Take this lemon," she had told him then. "Make lemonade, lemon chess pie, lemon bars. You make everything you can to sweeten this outcome." For McQuinn those words were not some breezy banality. As a minister she had worked for years on teaching herself to look past anger and betrayal to possibility. "You can go back and be a doctor," she had said. "Or you can take this and learn from it and then begin to help teach others."

To Northam, that vision made sense, as did her advice during a couple of subsequent meetings in his office.

When McQuinn first saw the yearbook photo, her reaction had been no less stunned than those of the legions demanding that Northam resign. She felt a visceral shock, propelling her back to childhood and a day in the 1960s when Klansmen firebombed a small, Black-owned grocery store in her tiny, segregated suburban Richmond neighborhood. "They did a cross burning and distributed propaganda all through the neighborhood. I remember to this day the horror in my father's eyes," she said. The store never recovered.

That memory was augmented by another: being shaken from sleep after midnight by her father and, along with her mother and eleven siblings, being sent to shelter in the family station wagon. He had heard a ticking sound and feared a bomb. The noise turned out to be from a malfunctioning appliance, "but he woke all of us up, got us quickly out of the house, and then bravely went out with a gun in one hand, a flashlight in the other. It had something to do with the era, what had been happening across the nation," she said.

Whereas Ralph Northam was horrified that the blackface photograph was on his yearbook page, Delores McQuinn was horrified by the picture itself. The distinction spoke to the gaps in their lived experience. As they met later, McQuinn encouraged Northam to see possibility in those differences. Blackface, she told him, was part of a culture, a system, threading American democracy from its origins. Now, whether as someone who had participated in that system or simply as a White male of his time and place, he had an opportunity through his powerful position to help trigger a paradigm shift. "I thought that this experience gave him a unique opportunity to look at a culture and rebuke that culture. He could go places and sit in places, board rooms, bankers, realtors, you name it, that many of us would not have an opportunity to be exposed to," she said.

Advising Northam, she offered two instructions. First, impossible as it would be for him to fully grasp the Black experience, he needed to try. "I walk out of the door. I'm Black. I can never, ever rid myself of that, even as for White America, there's a system that says, 'Just being birthed, you're superior.' Because of my skin color, I am inferior, I am less. You've got to be intentional in wanting to understand that, you've got to be very intentional," she said.

And second, Northam needed to be bold. "In your boldness, so much will be accomplished," she said. He should understand also that the blowback was certain to be fierce. "As you are opening doors and opportunity for people who've been left out of the equation, know that not everyone is going to applaud you for it. But the end result will be a better commonwealth and a better America."

Unsurprisingly, others had a less exalted notion of Northam's prospects. If he wanted to learn all about racism in America, fine, some said. Let him do it on his own time, out of office. "It seems implausible that a well-educated white man would have such ignorant views on race in 2019, and it's frankly inexcusable," wrote Peter Wade in a *Rolling Stone* article. "If Northam wants to read *Roots* and [Ta-Nehisi] Coates, he is free to do so, but he should not do it on the public's dime."[3]

Northam tried not to wallow in such criticism. He was not some White-supremacist yokel, he reminded himself. He had cared about and cared for Black friends and patients all his life. If he had failed to understand the depth of their experience, then he could not possibly be alone. There must be many other Virginians who shared a similar or even a greater degree of myopia. Yes, there was self-interest in redemption. There also was a larger mission that might come of the work he was doing. "It kind of awakened me that I'm in a situation now that I have a lot to learn, but I can also contribute a lot as a White person who will have a better understanding of systemic racism and Black oppression and White privilege," he said.

He could find ways to share newfound knowledge with other White Virginians, and through his search he might arrive at strategies to reduce disparity. If successful, he suddenly grasped, that would be the most important contribution he could make to the state that had elected him governor.

UNDERGOING A STEEP LEARNING CURVE, Northam had much to absorb. The looming four hundredth anniversary in August of the 1619 events at Jamestown and Point Comfort highlighted the complexity of Virginia's racial history. A Depression-era government study titled *The Negro in Virginia* had summed up the relevance of the state story to the nation's: "It is appropriate that the first [Works Progress Administration] State book on the Negro be produced in Virginia; for here the first African natives were brought and held in enforced servitude, and here also, more than two centuries later, freedom for some 5,000,000 of their descendants was assured on the surrender grounds at Appomattox. In a real sense, the story of the Negro in Virginia is also the story of the American Negro, for the roots of more Negro families were nurtured in Virginia than in any other State."[4]

After Congress ended the nation's participation in the transatlantic slave trade in 1808, Richmond became the largest market for enslaved humans in the Upper South, second nationally only to New Orleans. That shameful enterprise operated as Virginia's largest industry. The journeys of those trapped in the trade are recorded in chilling detail in the annals of the city's slave auctioneers. An 1860 circular distributed by Betts and Gregory, a prominent city firm, noted that "Boys and Girls five feet in height" were selling for $1,100 to $1,250. Those standing four feet commanded prices between $500 and $600. Children of that tender age and size could be, and often were, purchased separately from their parents.[5]

Partially as a result of the need to defend the Confederate capital in Richmond, the war that erupted in 1861 would see more battles fought on Virginia soil than that of any other state. When freedom came, the Old Dominion had the largest population of enslaved Africans of any state, almost half a million.[6] A brief flowering of Black political participation—thirty-three Black men served on Richmond's city council between 1871 and 1898, for example—did little to interfere with an ingrained racial separation. A system of universal public education was born segregated, and an 1878 state law set the penalty for an interracial marriage at two to five years in the penitentiary.[7]

The arrival of the twentieth century erased any illusions about the continued segregation and enforced inferiority of Virginia's Black citizens. Delegates arriving in Richmond in 1901 to rewrite the 1870 state constitution that had enfranchised formerly enslaved individuals aimed unabashedly at White domination. One delegate affirmed his purpose as "at any cost, to secure White supremacy," while another noted that "I am a White man and propose to represent White interests." Carter Glass, a future US senator and secretary of the treasury under President Woodrow Wilson, summed up the plan: "Discrimination! Why that is precisely what we propose . . . with a view to the elimination of every Negro voter who can be gotten rid of, legally, without materially impairing the numerical strength of the White electorate." When the dust had settled on the convention's handiwork, the number of registered voters in a typical Black precinct, Richmond's Jackson Ward, had collapsed from almost three thousand to thirty-three. The 1902 constitution would remain Virginia's governing document for seven decades.[8]

The demand of White people for racial segregation produced a host of so-called Jim Crow laws, the name drawn from a fictional character created by a White actor who donned blackface to mimic a shambling Black slave. Long-standing custom and laws such as the Virginia Public Assemblages Act of 1926 segregated public spaces in buildings, restrooms, elevators, swimming pools, trains, and buses. The 1896 US Supreme Court decision in *Plessy v. Ferguson* had decreed that separate must be equal, but any notion of equality in public facilities was a farce. Meanwhile the 1902 state constitution dictated that public schools in Virginia remain strictly segregated. When the Supreme Court struck down that mandate in 1954, Virginia senator Harry F. Byrd spearheaded Southern opposition. In Virginia his obstinacy led to the closing of all or parts of school systems in Warren County, Charlottesville, Norfolk, and Prince Edward County. In the latter, a rural expanse southwest of Richmond, the public schools remained closed for five years, the longest such enforced denial of education to children in modern America.

While fewer lynchings occurred on Virginia soil than in states farther South, White Virginians excelled at breaking the spirits of those who dared challenge their supremacy. Lutrelle Palmer, a nationally recognized principal in Newport News, possibly the state's most acclaimed Black educator in the 1940s, offers a telling example. Palmer was stripped of his job after he committed the unforgiveable sin of advocating for equal pay for Black teachers. His son believed the rejection contributed to his father's early death.[9] Meanwhile frequent executions of Black defendants turned that vehicle into a form of legal lynching.[10] In one notorious case, seven men known as the Martinsville Seven were executed in 1951 for the rape of a Martinsville housewife, even though they participated unequally in the crime and some likely not at all. Evidence uncovered during the trial revealed that all forty-five men electrocuted for rape since the state assumed death-penalty record keeping in 1908 had been Black.[11]

AS NORTHAM REVIEWED SUCH HISTORY, *13th*, a 2016 documentary by filmmaker Ava DuVernay, jolted him into a much clearer awareness: racial oppression did not end with the 1960s civil rights movement. That truth would be driven home repeatedly over the next months. DuVernay's work, named for the constitutional amendment abolishing slavery, provided a critical starting point. He watched the film at the suggestion of Alena Yarmosky, his twenty-nine-year-old press secretary. Armed with a master's degree in public policy from the University of California, Berkeley, Yarmosky had joined Northam's staff just two months before the blackface scandal. Like others, she found the episode disturbing, but she brought a bit of personal context to the mix.

Not long before, she had discovered that her father, so committed to racial justice that he had given her sister the middle name "King" in honor of Dr. Martin Luther King Jr., had worn blackface to a Halloween Party in the 1980s. "He mentioned it casually," Yarmosky recalled. Shocked, "I said, 'That's so bad.' He said, 'What?'" She had watched *13th* with her father, and "it had really resonated with him. The governor was reading a lot, learning a lot at that time, and I thought it would be a powerful thing." They watched it together one morning.

"Of all the things I've listened to or read, that was like, 'Now I get it,'" Northam described his reaction. The eye-opening film, drawing heavily from *The New Jim Crow: Mass Incarceration in the Age of Colorblindness*, a book by Michelle Alexander, traces the growth of the US prison population from 357,000 in 1972 to 2.3 million in 2014. At the time of filming, the United States had 5 percent of the world population and 25 percent, or one in four, of the world's prisoners. Black men constituted 6.5 percent of the nation's population and 40 percent of the prison population. Whereas one in seventeen young White men might expect to spend time in prison over the course of their lifetimes, the number soared to one in three among young Black males.

"This didn't just appear out of nothing," the film explains. "This is the product of a centuries long historical process," starting with the mass arrests of Black men after the civil war on vague charges such as loitering or vagrancy. Their enforced labor helped rebuild the southern economy, even as cultural touchstones such as D. W. Griffith's blockbuster film *The Birth of a Nation* created a narrative of "rapacious, menacing Negro male evil."

Over time, crime began to stand in for race as a political call to arms. A war on drugs, in which abuse was treated as criminality rather than a health issue, brought much tougher sentences for crack cocaine, which predominated in African American communities, than for the powder cocaine preferred by White drug users. President Bill Clinton and other centrist Democrats, looking to regain political strength in the suburbs, joined Republicans in supporting tough crime measures such as mandatory minimum sentences and three-strikes laws. The private prison industry grew, incentivizing incarceration. The result is "a presumption of dangerousness and guilt that follows every Black and Brown person wherever they are," says author and social justice advocate Bryan Stevenson, founder of the Equal Justice Initiative in Montgomery, Alabama, in the film.

After watching the documentary, Northam saw racial oppression in the criminal justice system through clearing eyes. "A lot of people who look like me think Black oppression ended or doesn't exist because slavery ended," he said. "[They think] 'it was a bad thing, but that's behind us.' What they don't realize is that you had the Jim Crow era and then massive resistance and now mass incarceration and the police brutality that we've seen. So the point I'm making, Black oppression exists, just in a different form. And that's what a lot of people who look like me don't realize."

Before, he had assumed, more or less, that people who wound up in prison belonged there. Now he was starting to see how differing arrest standards, grossly inadequate legal representation, and the snare of a criminal record could trap lives in an almost inescapable vise.

NORTHAM'S EDUCATION EXTENDED beyond books, movies, and private conversations. More formal interactions included several sessions with Jonathan Zur, the president of the Virginia Center for Inclusive Communities. Zur's organization, formed many years ago as part of the National Conference of Christians and Jews, since rebranded, advises schools, businesses, and communities on issues of inclusion. He met with Northam several times, as well as with staff.

In his work, Zur said, he encounters individuals who through their identities and backgrounds see racism as pervasive and central to how society functions.

"And then there are other people who may have close friendships with people of color, may work closely with people of color, may think of themselves as being nice people, who say, 'Well, I didn't see that at all.' And that is in some ways where the governor was, trying to make meaning of 'How could I be fifty-something years old and, certainly, intellectually know that racism exists and has an impact, but also be realizing how there may have been things that I didn't understand, or didn't understand how impactful they were until this moment?'"

Northam's strengths in the sessions, Zur said, were an earnestness about learning and an openness to self-reflection, also a fairly unique background for a White leader in the extent of his youthful associations with Black people. And yet it was clear to Zur that "even with those relationships, he had not had a significant number of conversations about race." The question bore asking: "If these folks were friends with the level of depth you thought, how is it that this information is such a surprise?"

One incident occurring during their time together tested the limits of Northam's learning. A thirteen-year-old Black girl and her mother accused Pam Northam of gross insensitivity while conducting a tour of the mansion for a group of young people who were ending their service as senate pages. According to a letter from Leah Dozier Walker, while in the kitchen the First Lady had singled out three African Americans students, including her daughter, handed them raw cotton bolls, and asked them to imagine what it would have been like, as slaves, to pick cotton all day. Her daughter was "deeply offended," she said.

Coming on the heels of the blackface incident, the complaint quickly became national and international news. A partial list of outlets reporting the comments included the *New York Times*, *USA Today*, *Newsweek*, *Time*, the *Guardian*, CNN, ABC, CBS, NBC, and the BBC. The *Washington Post*, whose initial story had prompted the surge of interest, followed up a day later with a more nuanced account. The newspaper contacted ten additional pages who had taken Pam Northam's tour, both Black and White, four of them in the same group as Walker's daughter. According to the account, "in all ten cases, the pages or their parents insisted that the first lady—a former science teacher—conducted their tours with sensitivity and with no special focus on the black pages." Walker, however, stood by her daughter's "perception of what occurred in the moment."[12]

Most media outlets did not bother to do a follow-up when the second story appeared.

For the Northams the episode was another lesson in the easy misinterpretation of intentions in matters of race. Pam Northam had enthusiastically advanced a project begun under the McAuliffes to ensure that the once-ignored kitchen and the enslaved workers who toiled there were made part of the mansion's story. She had seen passing the bolls around as a hands-on way to make history more real. Devastated by the criticism, the First Lady found herself in tears for the first time since February 1. The notion that she would embarrass a child hit her at the core. "I'd been strong through most of this stuff," she said. "It was tough for me personally to think that people felt so strongly negatively about us that they would suspect me of doing something so heinous. That was a real low point for me."

Zur urged the Northams to look at the incident in a broader, less self-protective way. He saw it as illustrating the power of perception, the reality that there can be truth in multiple perspectives. "It wasn't about right or wrong or guilt or shame," he said. "It was about, 'How can two people see the same exact interaction and situation from completely different lenses, and how might a person in a position of leadership like the governor consider that in making decisions?'"

Senator McClellan also counseled the couple. "You still have a lot of work to do to educate yourself, because you're not there yet," she told the governor. The episode illustrated a message of DiAngelo's *White Fragility*: White people, from your privileged position, be strong enough to set aside your perception of being unfairly criticized to hear a Black person's truth, whether or not their perception dovetails with your own. Whatever the First Lady's intentions, a Black girl had felt herself singled out in a negative way.

"Your tendency is to want to be very defensive," Pam said later. After steadying, her ultimate response was to redouble efforts to locate descendants of the mansion's early staff and to ensure that their voices helped decide how the mansion's story should be told. "Who is allowed to hold those stories? Who is allowed to tell those very important stories?" she asked herself. The First Lady delved also into the concept of "blood memory," the belief that the traumas of one generation can be passed on to the next though DNA, and of a taboo in Native American culture against allowing outsiders to speak of tribal pain. "That belongs to them," she said.

What she came to better understand was that "involving the descendent community was very, very important and what we should have done first." Two years later the kitchen had become the first stop on mansion school tours rather than an afterthought. The agricultural products greeting children were oyster shells, peanuts, and gourds.

Chief among Zur's prescriptions was one to which Northam already had committed: listening. "Most critically, those of us who have benefited from historical injustices must listen deeply to those who have been most aggrieved," Zur wrote in a newspaper op-ed at the time.[13]

The primary vehicle for Northam's listening would be a series of gatherings, more than a dozen, stretched over the next six months and spanning much of the state. In each setting groups of fifteen to twenty people, African American leaders and citizens, agreed to meet with Northam for an unscripted conversation about the present moment and the future. Traci DeShazor, a Black woman serving as deputy secretary of commonwealth, overseeing restoration of rights, pardons, and multiple other duties, and Yarmosky the press secretary, who is White, did much of the organizing. They and Northam envisioned three purposes for the sessions: rebuilding trust, providing an opportunity for accountability for the governor, and informing the office policy agenda going forward. "Community-driven policy is always the best type of policy. It felt if we were going to do this in a way that is legitimate and impactful, it had to be something that was informed by those who were most harmed by the policies," said Yarmosky.

Northam worried that DeShazor was among the staff members who had been deeply hurt by the blackface photograph. He was unsure whether her agreement to be involved derived from support for him or her commitment to Virginia. Either way, she was widely credited in the aftermath of the sessions as a major force in their success. "I always say, 'She saved the state,'" said Wes Bellamy, the Charlottesville activist who had promised hell if Northam did not adopt an aggressive policy agenda after the blackface scandal. Bellamy, who in 2020 became head of the political science department at Virginia State University, a historically Black school, said DeShazor helped spur his forgiveness of Northam. "She saw to it that the work wasn't just talk," he said.

Even as they recognized the importance of the listening sessions, some in the administration also were mindful of their risk. "Time and time again people who want you to resign are going to say mean things about you to your face, say things that have probably never been said to a governor," warned Clark Mercer at their inception. "If you're willing to listen to those things and truly dig in and work," important change could occur. As the weeks passed, Northam "took some tough conversations, and he kept taking them. There would be peaks and valleys in his fortitude to keep going with this, but that was kind of the deal, the commitment he made."

Pam Northam also weighed the potential toll on her husband—physical and mental. "I was worried about him, I've got to tell you," she said. "There's only so much physically that a human being can hold for people in that painful space. And he was holding a lot of that. There's so much inequity to hold there and great sadness, and so many stories of people's personal experiences to this day. It was his choice, and privilege honestly, but it is a lot." She saw his training as a doctor as critical to his safely navigating an onslaught of face-to-face criticism.

Still others looked skeptically at the entire project. "I didn't like the idea. I felt like it was so generic. It didn't feel authentic—like somebody on his team said, 'You need to do this,'" said Lamont Bagby, the black caucus leader. "I wanted him to focus on, how can you deliver on this stuff?"

Northam launched the first listening session on March 20 in Danville, near the state's North Carolina border. The city served as the last capital of the Confederacy after Jefferson Davis escaped there during the April 1865 Confederate collapse. Before the meeting the governor toured two sites connected to Black history. That pattern would continue in future locations, bringing visual images to his awareness of Virginia's fraught racial past.

The first site commemorated what has come to be known as Bloody Monday. On June 10, 1963, during weeks of protest, more than three dozen civil rights demonstrators were arrested there. That evening, during a prayer vigil for the detainees, police joined by deputized garbage workers attacked the assembled group with billy clubs and fire hoses, injuring forty-seven. The moment remains a painful scar in the city's history. From there Northam proceeded to the headquarters of First State Bank, more recently called Movement Bank, one of Virginia's oldest Black-run financial institutions. A tour reinforced awareness of the long struggle of marginalized Virginians to gain access to wealth and financial stability.

With those underpinnings Northam arrived at the first meeting. He was unsure what to expect, but he knew the potential for explosive anger. Yarmosky recalled the mood in the room as the session began. "The first one was scary for everyone involved, including the governor," she said. Almost two years later, "now you go into a room and it's, 'Oh, good, the governor's here.' It was definitely not that vibe. It was serious, and I think there was a feeling of, certainly, interest, but also a real need to be heard and to share. In some cases, anger. In some cases, disappointment, or hope, or frustration at him or with the whole situation. Walking into the room was, like, heavy in almost all of these."

Northam opened the meeting by saying he knew it was wrong of him to have dressed up as Michael Jackson. He understood blackface was hurtful, and he apologized. By conscious choice, he avoided trying to excuse or defend his actions. "I want to learn more and take actions to do better and move Virginia forward," he told the group. Many people "were very forgiving when they didn't need to be," he said later. The attitude was not universal. "There were some that needed to get it off their chest, if you will, and let me know how offensive what I had done was. And I said, 'I understand that, and I want to do better.'"

When it came to discussing the blackface episode, a pattern emerged. "Folks would start off pretty formal, a little hesitant," Yarmosky said. "Then, usually, there was one person who would say, 'Let's talk about the elephant in the room.'" They would point either to the scandal or to the racist roots of the problems being discussed. "Usually, when that would happen, the conversation would open up in a way that was deeper. I always personally liked it when that happened because it gave him an opportunity to respond directly. I think it made people feel like we weren't just dancing around issues."

Northam remembered vividly an NAACP official at a gathering in Norfolk angrily lecturing him at length. His response to the hammering? "I just try to understand where they're coming from," the source of the anger, he said. Bellamy, who attended several of the sessions, held a frank conversation with Northam prior to a gathering in Charlottesville. "I told him, 'You can't joke. Saying, like, you're going to do the moonwalking and all that. This isn't something to joke about. This is very serious.' I think he understood that. He just took it." During the listening tour, Bellamy said, "People were frank. You heard people saying, 'How can we trust you?' He was just asking people, 'What do you want to see? How can we move forward?'"

Over and over, as the sessions continued, Northam heard stories about Black men stopped by police for inconsequential reasons and treated badly, of parents petrified of potential police encounters when their children went out at night. He heard about the racial disparity in arrests for marijuana use and the almost unscalable obstacles facing previously incarcerated men as they tried to reestablish their lives. Parents told him of children who learned almost nothing of the Black experience in America in history classes or were fed the false narrative that the Civil War was primarily about states' rights. He learned of financial struggles, the challenges of getting home mortgages or financial loans or of starting businesses. Food insecurity and food deserts proved a regular theme, as did the scarcity of affordable housing and the presence of zoning restrictions that separated families of modest means from the best school systems. To his surprise, he heard the skepticism some felt in dealing with White doctors or other White professionals. He absorbed stories of terrible health outcomes for pregnant Black women and others, of how lack of an automobile or driver's license squelches job prospects, and more.

Sharp statistical divides reinforced the personal narratives. On matters from high school graduation to home ownership to loan approvals to incarceration to accumulated wealth to life expectancy itself, the numbers told of two Americas. Black citizens sat largely on the losing end. Northam saw the absurdity in imagining that the gaps reflected personal inferiority. More and more, he recognized the ways in which privilege rewards its own. Yes, some Black people escaped the thicket of marginal education, substandard housing, limited access to capital, and criminal-justice double standards. Far too many did not. Once again, statistics buttressed the case. As a Brookings Institution analysis laid out two weeks after the blackface scandal broke: "Not only is birth too often destiny, so too is race. . . . On every rung of the income ladder, black children have worse prospects of the American Dream than white children."[14] As schools and housing resegregated and as wealth divides persisted, the promise of merit-based advancement had become a myth. "It is now quite clear that improving economic mobility in the U.S. will be virtually impossible without a dramatic alteration in the trajectories of black children, and black boys in particular," Brookings concluded.

Both Ralph and Pam, who sometimes accompanied him to the sessions, found themselves changing. "I thought of myself as growing up very progressive, which sounds funny coming from a little place in Texas," the First Lady said. "But I had to look with a very close lens at my own prejudices that I didn't even realize were so deeply ingrained in my own privilege. Subtle judgments about people. I was complicit in not seeing things." She remembered, for instance, considering the option of taking one of their children out of a public school that had a poor physical plant. "I wasn't stopping anyone, but I personally had the privilege to consider that I had options that others did not," she said.

What the couple heard most as they traveled the state, Pam added, was "'Do the work. This is an opportunity for you to do the work. You are in a unique position. The burden shouldn't just be on us as African Americans. It should be on you too.'

"Ralph really heard that, and he said, 'Then let's get to work.'"

THE GOVERNOR'S INTROSPECTION WENT BACK to his youth on the Eastern Shore. He had not been a coddled youth. He had had to rebuild a car almost from scratch to have his own wheels. He had to earn every penny of college tuition himself. "Everything I've done to get where I am, I worked hard," he said. Having worked hard and achieved much, he had thought of life as a simple equation: goal plus effort plus determination equals success. Now he was encountering lives for whom that was not true. Two plus two did not always equal four (or, in his fortunate case, sometimes five). For some others it might add up to three or two or zero.

"And so, I didn't realize that someone even working hard, there were breaks for me along with it because I'm White," he said. "And there are a lot of African Americans that have worked hard also that haven't been able to get where they'd like to be because of their color. And I never looked at it that way before. There are a lot of people out there who look like me who still think like I used to. 'I'm working hard, so why isn't everybody else working hard?' Well, they are, but they haven't had the breaks that you've had."

Even White people who had not had other sorts of opportunities still had the advantage of their skin, the unspoken kinship born of a shared racial identity. Many of the breaks in his own life were subtle—walking into a grocery store and being recognized as the son of a local official, so he was given a job. Using that job to progress to the next and then the next. Having well-connected people advise him on career choices and write letters of recommendation. Never knowing true insecurity when it came to such basics as food or shelter or health care. He thought of the Black friends who had spent time at his home or who he'd given rides after school. "I had opportunities that these people didn't have. They didn't have the connections to get into college, didn't have the connections to get into medical school or to start a residency or a fellowship or start a business or get a loan."

He had done his part by working hard at each stage of his life, but connections, camaraderie, and assumptions of competence attached to his Whiteness had smoothed the journey. "So that is something that existed, but I never really understood until I listened and learned."

Probably the most overt act of White privilege in his life, he saw, came when he applied to the Eastern Virginia Medical School. When Northam sought admission to medical school, he had decent grades and slightly subpar medical school entrance-exam scores. A family friend arranged for him to meet with the EVMS dean of admissions. After reviewing his credentials, the dean told Northam that he should spend a year taking graduate courses and improving his test scores, then reapply. After leaving EVMS that day, Northam went straight to another meeting, also arranged by the family friend. This one was with Vince Thomas, then the mayor of Norfolk, and Dick Welton, an owner of one of the city's major department stores, Smith and Welton. Two of the region's most powerful White men, Thomas and Welton were graduates of VMI, Northam's college. The trio met in Welton's office. There were hunting and fishing pictures on the wall, so they chatted about those pursuits. "After about fifteen minutes, Mr. Thomas asked me, 'How did your interview go?'" Northam told them the part about returning after a year. They nodded. He said goodbye and went on his way.

"Well, a week later, I got a letter from the medical school inviting me for an interview for early admission. I filled out my application, and the next thing I knew, they said, 'You're accepted.' So, if you want an example of White privilege, that's about as good as it gets."

Privilege also surfaced in his initial foray into politics. His frugal father contributed just under $260,000 to his first senate campaign, far and away the largest sum for any individual. Few, if any, of his Black contemporaries on the Eastern Shore could have received such a windfall.

In one other unexpected way, the blackface scandal added to Northam's deepened compassion for Black lives. For years he had prided himself on being able to say truthfully that he did not see race. A large portion of the thousands of patients he had seen over the years were children of color. Their race played no conscious role in his care. To the best of his ability and knowledge, he treated everyone the same. In January 2019, a few weeks before the blackface photograph surfaced, Northam had conducted an interview on the Eastern Shore that spoke to that intention.

A local communications firm was completing a video documentary about Sam Outlaw, a renowned blacksmith in Onancock who was Black. Asked for an interview, Northam recalled visiting Outlaw's shop as a young person and bringing in a shovel or a wheelbarrow for repair. Then he turned to racial awareness. "The way we were raised, my brother and I, we didn't see color and I don't think he [Mr. Outlaw] saw color either. He just treated everybody as human beings, and I think it's a lesson everybody needs to hear."

Alena Yarmosky, his young office guide, had suggested at the time that he might want to rethink that statement. He had not understood why. After months of meeting with Black Virginians, studying their history, and being shown evidence of racial disparity in almost every aspect of American life, he understood. To see a shared humanity was essential, but to see no difference was to ignore the systems and the deep-seated, even unconscious, personal biases that continue to oppress. To impose a veneer of sameness was to deliberately ignore the vast gaps that split Black and White Americans in almost every measure of quality of life. Once he had adjusted his focus, "Oh, my Lord," he said. He saw race-based difference everywhere.

"The eyes can't see what the brain doesn't know," he became fond of saying. "Well, once you are educated and understand, talk to people, then it [racial inequity] is all over the place. It's everywhere you look."

CHAPTER 7

Starting the Work

Policy and politics could not wait for Northam's personal growth. A little over two and a half years remained in his term. If he intended to make bold change, the work needed to ramp up quickly. The outcome would depend in large measure on his political clout, or lack of it, so his political recovery needed attention as well.

"February was god-awful," said Mark Bergman, the political strategist, returning to the days immediately following the scandal. Fortunately, he said, General Assembly members did not transfer disdain for Northam to his staff. Government business largely went on as usual. "They'd ask the governor's staff and governor's cabinet what they thought on bills. That never changed. But the General Assembly would have nothing to do with the governor, and they kept pounding him in the press."

Not a micromanager, Northam saw his initial policy role as challenging the cabinet to serve up a broad prescription for social healing. His awareness of possibilities had grown as he traveled the state, listening to Black voices. He thought of roles for each of his cabinet secretaries. For the secretary of agriculture, "I say, 'How do we help minorities get into farming, agriculture, and forestry? How do we help them get loans?' I go to my secretary of transportation and say, 'Shannon, not everybody has a car. We need to put more emphasis on rail and transit,' which we're doing. I go to my secretary of commerce who oversees SWaM [small, women-and-minority-owned businesses] and say, 'Brian, we need to get out there and listen to people and help with business opportunities, how to get capital.' You go to education, say, 'We've got a problem right now with access to education and schools that are falling into the ground.' I go to the secretary of health and say, 'Dan, we need to deal with infant and maternal mortality, need to make sure we have more diversity in our medical schools, more providers that look like society.' You go to the secretary of the commonwealth, and you say, 'There's too many people of color in our prisons and too many people that don't have their voting privileges, and so you work with her on that.'"

Northam was not a newcomer to equity ideas. Even so, the scandal had created an opportunity to go at them full tilt. His top ten priorities after the scandal were probably the same as his top ten before, said Mercer, the chief of staff, "but we reordered them." Brad Komar, Northam's former campaign manager, added context. "I cannot sit here and say that Ralph Northam ran for office for racial reconciliation and equality to be 'the' defining issue." He ran for office as a problem-solving, results-oriented doctor. Because of the blackface scandal, he evolved. Before, Komar said, Northam saw his challenge as "'how do I improve people's lives?' Now, it's 'how do I change a broken system, a systemically broken system that is rigged against African Americans and Latinos and others in Virginia?'"

Conscious of the emotional Tilt-A-Whirl the staff had endured, Mercer copied a page from a book that he often read to his young children. He distributed it to the cabinet and staff. In the story a family goes on a bear hunt, encountering numerous obstacles—a deep, cold river; a dark forest; a whirling snowstorm; and a narrow, gloomy cave. In each case they confront the danger with a simple refrain: "We can't go over it. We can't go under it. Oh, no! We've got to go through it!"[1] In the months that remained in Northam's term, both the governor and the staff that stayed with him had a single option, Mercer told them. They would have to go through whatever lay ahead, come what may.

He drew also from one of his favorite movies, *The Shawshank Redemption*, in challenging staff to recognize the next months as a unique time, ripe with opportunity. In the movie Red, played by Morgan Freeman, describes his friend Andy's prison escape after patiently digging a tunnel, inch by inch, over many years. "Geology is the study of pressure and time," Red says. "That's all it takes, really . . . pressure . . . and time." That, and "a big goddam poster," he adds, referring to a poster of Raquel Welch covering the entrance in Andy's cell to the escape route.

Mercer saw the "pressure and time" quote as matching up with political scientist John Kingdon's theory that change occurs when three streams—problems, policies, and politics—converge. Through Northam's trials the administration had a chance to address problems that had festered for generations. They just needed to be relentless in applying pressure, and they must hope that the politics would align.

Pressure would not come from Northam's resolve alone. Black lawmakers and activists had no intention of letting up in their insistence that the governor atone for past sins with concrete actions. In mid-February the Virginia Legislative Black Caucus tested the governor's commitment. Privately the group handed him a list of six priorities that they believed were being seriously underfunded in the Virginia budget. If Northam truly was resolved to show remorse, he could do so by pressuring House and Senate budget committees to prioritize those equity issues. When Northam complied—pressing for additional funding for schools in poor communities, eviction prevention services, women's access to health care, and other VLBC priorities—the action offered early proof of the caucus's elevated status.

The maternal-health funding particularly delighted Delegate Price. The previous winter she and Delegate Lashrecse Aird of Petersburg had pushed the administration to confront an abysmal disparity in Black maternal mortality. Black women in America are two to three times more likely to die during pregnancy than White women. Several high-profile Black women, including Serena Williams and Beyoncé, had just undergone dangerous deliveries. The response from Health Secretary Daniel Carey in late 2018, as Price recalled, had been, "It's not the year for that. It will have to wait."

After the blackface scandal, priorities transformed. By fall the administration had committed to a frontal assault on maternal-health disparities. "I felt like his team was, for the first time, prioritizing the voice of Black leadership and our input," Price said. The shift did not silence rebukes. When Northam touted his equity budget priorities at a February 14 breakfast at the mansion, Delegate Luke Torian of Prince William County, the only Black budget negotiator, boycotted the event. Further, when the General Assembly session ended on February 23, tradition called for a small delegation of legislators to walk to the governor's office to inform him of the departure. Northam was waiting in his office to receive the group. In a deliberate snub, no one came.

AS SPRING ARRIVED NORTHAM HIGHLIGHTED bill signings and vetoes that reflected his new priorities. He turned a thumbs up on bills creating an African American advisory board for his office, curtailing Virginia's embarrassingly high renter-eviction rates, and ditching a Jim Crow–era law exempting jobs such as shoeshine boys, newsboys, and theater ushers from the state's minimum-wage law. Simultaneously he announced creation of a commission assigned to unearth any vestiges of Jim Crow segregation in the state legal code. He turned thumbs down on bills undercutting the Affordable Care Act, hindering voter registration drives, and requiring local police departments to help enforce federal immigration laws.

Citing his recent community conversations across Virginia, he vetoed two bills creating mandatory minimum sentences and announced in an op-ed in the *Washington Post* that he would sign no more such bills as governor. "Piling on mandatory minimum sentences has contributed to our growing prison population over the past few decades, to the point that the United States has the highest rate of incarceration in the world," he said. Already more than two hundred such laws existed in Virginia. Halting or reversing that number was one step he could take "to make our commonwealth fairer and more equitable for communities of color."[2] The lessons absorbed in watching *13th* were bearing fruit.

Still, some skeptics were asking: Where was the bold equity agenda Northam pledged? A group of educators from Norfolk State University rushed to help fill the void. Led by Dr. Cassandra Newby-Alexander, the group in March requested a meeting with Northam to talk about Black history. A historian and dean of the College of Liberal Arts and an offspring of a great-great-grandfather who in 1859 was one of the first graduates of Ashman Institute (later Lincoln University), Newby-Alexander for years had fumed over the inadequate and inaccurate ways history was being taught in Virginia. "I remember when the SOLs [Virginia's content teaching standards] had four questions on the exam about Betsy Ross, all of which was mythical," she said. "They were teaching it like it was factual." Ross was the least of it.

Slavery had been prettied up and glossed over. Textbooks barely grazed the multiple ways Black citizens had been oppressed in Virginia since the end of the Civil War. Not only noted individuals but also important concepts such as Black agency or self-determination had been ignored. "People have been fed—and especially in the White community—these lies for generations, and it's hard to move away from a lie. It's hard to move away from a concept that Black people, as a whole, are not like everybody else. That somehow we are less than, that we're different."

Northam scheduled a meeting with the group. He appeared to welcome the interaction. "We took a chance," Newby-Alexander said of the visit. Within months she had started to see concrete payoff.

A BOOST TO THE NORTHAM'S CREDIBILITY as a functioning governor came in early April when the General Assembly reconvened to consider his proposed changes to the lawmakers' winter handiwork. Two victories signaled that he might yet emerge from the political netherworld. The first lined up well with the commitment to racial equity.

For years Virginia had stripped drivers' licenses from people unable to pay court fines. Such punitive action perpetuated a cycle of failure. Northam had prioritized nixing the practice when he opened the 2019 legislative session in January, but the idea had floundered. In late March, at the urging of a rural Republican senator, Bill Stanley, Northam announced that he would revisit the matter through a budget maneuver at the reconvened session. When the House backed reversing the policy on a 70–29 count and the Senate by 30–8, Northam celebrated a victory in both policy and politics. A whopping 627,000 low-income Virginians had just been given a dose of hope.

A second triumph stemmed from Northam's resurrection of long-sought funding for improvements on I-81, an overcrowded and dangerous demolition-derby course stretching the length of western Virginia. Heading into the January session, Northam had spearheaded a $2.2 billion bipartisan plan using tolls for improvements, but the fix had collapsed amid legislative wrangling. For the reconvened session, Northam proposed a combination of fees and taxes, with much of the burden falling to heavy truck operators. The plan's adoption was unrelated to racial equity, but the solution to a long-standing policy migraine led the *Washington Post* to opine: "The scandal-tainted Democrat still has sway in the Capitol."[3]

As if Northam could be allowed only so much good news at any one moment, a poll released a few days later by the Wason Center for Civic Leadership at Christopher Newport College reported that the governor's popularity statewide had plummeted by 19 percentage points since a December survey. At 40 percent, his approval rating trailed even Donald Trump's 44 percent. A slight majority of those polled, 52 to 48 percent, thought Northam should stay in office. Just under three in ten Democrats thought he should resign. However, a surprising 23 percent of voters were unaware of the highly publicized scandal, a snippet of a silver lining.[4]

ON THE POLITICAL SIDE, BERGMAN ENTERED MARCH with trepidation, un-sure whether Northam's political action committee, The Way Ahead, could raise substantial money to help Democrats win in the fall. Northam was not requesting donations, and almost none were coming in unsolicited. Two de-velopments helped Bergman's confidence rebound slightly. No matter what the public polls might show, he knew Northam had done well in private polling by some state delegates in April and May. "It was very clear that he was popular inside the party, even if the politicians were still considering him toxic," Berg-man said.

An ongoing series of phone calls to major donors confirmed that a criti-cal mass had not abandoned Northam either. Continued backing among the monied elite, or at least some of them, undermined the primary political charge leveled at Northam: that he must resign because he could not garner the back-ing necessary to lead. On April 17, Robert Hardie, a Charlottesville investor and businessman, became the first donor to write a significant check after the blackface scandal. That ten-thousand-dollar gift signaled that the governor still had moneyed friends.

Another step in Bergman's recovery strategy called for testing whether Democratic candidates were willing to campaign with and take money from Northam. The consultant was pleased when five legislative candidates accepted a total of thirty-five thousand dollars from the governor's PAC in late winter. The totals might be paltry by normal standards. Still, tiptoeing back into circulation was preferable to being at a dead stop. In light of the scandal, Bergman was most pleased that one of the early recipients was Joshua Cole, an NAACP official and minister from Fredericksburg seeking a seat in the House of Delegates. Cole's acceptance of a five-thousand-dollar gift in February and another ten thousand in June signaled that Northam was not a pariah with Black candidates.

The governor's first plunge into the campaign circuit in mid-April on behalf of a friendly delegate from Richmond, Betsy Carr, went smoothly; the second, anything but. When word spread that Northam planned to attend a campaign kickoff barbecue for Senator Dave Marsden in Fairfax County, a sprawling locality just south of Washington, DC, the president of the local NAACP responded angrily. "He should not be allowed to be touring around the state, doing fundraisers, or doing anything, because he has hurt a lot of people and shown no remorse for that," fumed Kofi Annan, the official, to news outlets. NAACP leaders from Fairfax and Loudoun Counties promised protests if Northam appeared.

The state Republican Party joined the chorus. "Northam is trying to sneak back onto the scene after putting our commonwealth in a very embarrassing spotlight," piggybacked a GOP spokesperson. Holding true to those messages, protesters outnumbered Marsden supporters at the community-center event. The object of their wrath was nowhere to be seen. Northam had canceled due to what campaign officials called "safety concerns." The governor had no intention of subjecting himself or his supporters to unproductive rage.[5]

It did not sit well with either Northam or Bergman, as they struggled to rebound, when Terry McAuliffe dropped out of contention for the Democratic presidential nomination later that week, pledging to save Virginia Democrats from their tribulations. "They're desperate down there," he told CNN's Chris Cuomo, essentially kneecapping his successor. "Ralph only raised $2,500 in the last quarter."[6] The comment further fueled Northam's sense that people he had considered personal friends—McAuliffe high among them—had, in his words, "thrown me under the bus."

BY REPUTATION AMONG THE LEGIONS who had worked in multiple Virginia gubernatorial administrations, Northam's anger had a much longer fuse than that of predecessors such as McAuliffe or Mark Warner. That did not mean he had no limits. When he had had enough, people knew. The primary emotion he expressed toward those who had called for his resignation was disappointment, not anger. Valuing loyalty, he went over in his mind many times the way he believed he would have responded to a friend, a son, or a daughter who found themselves in trouble. "I would say, 'So and so, you've done something that you shouldn't have done, but I'm going to try to help you through this, not pull the rug out from under you.'"

When something similar did not happen for him, "that's kind of what hurt about that." He still did not see how all the good he had done as a person and a politician could have been wiped out so instantaneously for so many, especially those who knew him as more than the caricature being portrayed. As McAuliffe's lieutenant governor, for instance, when they disagreed or when McAuliffe was faced with an FBI investigation into campaign finances that eventually evaporated, "I never spoke publicly, never said a word against what he was doing." When Wes Bellamy, the Charlottesville firebrand, had gotten into trouble a couple of years earlier over racist and misogynistic tweets, as Bellamy himself described, Northam "reached out, brought me to his office, said, 'We've got your back.'"

Northam voiced his sense of betrayal when he met with Senator Kaine in the governor's office in late May. Kaine had requested the meeting because Northam was due to bring the cabinet to Washington in a few weeks for an annual meeting with Virginia's congressional delegation. The senator did not want unspoken tensions between them. "We had a very candid sharing of our points of view, our strong feelings, and our continued emotions about the situation," Kaine described the meeting. "For me, at least, it was a very cathartic opportunity to be very candid but also to listen."

"Look," Kaine began, he was not backing down on what had occurred between them in February, "because I thought I gave you good advice and you didn't follow it." The result had hurt Virginia. Still, Kaine voiced two regrets. He wished he had turned his car around and gone directly to Northam's office on the night of February 1. In retrospect he thought the situation might have turned out differently if he had. Second, he believed he should have delivered his message to Northam face-to-face. For that, he apologized.

Northam had his say, as well, describing his sense of betrayal from people he had considered to be his friends, including Kaine. "He was very candid that what I had done had been hurtful to him because of our relationship," Kaine said. From the senator's perspective, the aggravating factor in the episode was racial injustice, the original sin of Virginia. "When an issue comes up that kind of gets into the painful realities of racial insensitivity, you've got to be really careful." Lack of sufficient care snowballed into an untenable situation on the weekend of February 1.

Both men said later that they were grateful for the interaction. Of the dozens of people who called for Northam's resignation, Kaine was the only one who requested a follow-up meeting to try to talk through what had occurred and who acknowledged second thoughts about his actions. Lack of similar response from others taught him a hard-earned lesson, Northam said. There is a difference between political friends and true friends. "I don't burn bridges. If I'm upset with someone today, I may need their help tomorrow, and that's just the way politics is." Indeed, two years later Northam endorsed McAuliffe in a five-person primary for the Democratic nomination for governor, believing him to be the candidate most likely to withstand a Republican challenge.

"But there's a difference between those relationships and what true friends are. I understand that a lot better than I used to," he continued. "I forgive, but I don't forget, never will, what I went through."

For his part McAuliffe said that, as "a big fan" of Northam's, he would not have called for his resignation if the governor had told him on the night of February 1 that he was not in the picture. "If he had told me Friday night he wasn't in it, I never would have asked for him to resign. Craziest thing I ever heard. I don't know what happened in twelve hours," he said.

Over time many of the broken connections gradually mended without any real conversation or accounting. Most of those who challenged Northam "just kind of move on," he said.

On one other occasion, it struck Northam that apologies for mistakes ought to run in two directions. That summer the Northams hosted a dinner at the mansion honoring individuals recognized for community service. "It was just a great evening and then someone came up to me at the end and said, 'We've got a problem.' And I said, 'What's wrong?' And they said, 'A couple of people were offended and have reported to one of the senators that there's cotton in the floral arrangements.'"

Though cotton and tobacco had long been used in mansion decorations because of the historic link to Virginia agriculture, the practice had been discontinued some years before due to the association with slavery. "And I said, 'Well, let's go take a look. I'm sorry that that's the case.' And I went and looked at the floral arrangements. Well, it was pussy willows. It wasn't cotton. This is the world we live in now, and everything that Pam and I do is under a microscope.

And nobody ever came back and said, 'Ralph and Pam, you know what, I apologize for making a disturbance.' And I didn't ever say anything, but if you're so intent on these types of issues, if you don't know the difference between what cotton looks like and what pussy willows look like, then we've all got a lot to learn."

CHAPTER 8

Blackface Investigations

Two reports on the origins of the EVMS blackface photograph, anxiously awaited, landed with a thud.

Neither an inquiry commissioned by the medical school for about $300,000 nor an almost $250,000 investigation paid for out of Northam's political funds answered the questions: Who was in the photograph? How did it originate? Why did it show up on Northam's page?

"We weighed all the evidence that we had, and based on that, we cannot conclusively identify either person in the photograph, and that includes Governor Northam," said Richard Cullen, a partner in the Richmond law firm McGuire-Woods and a former US attorney for the Eastern District of Virginia, speaking at a May 22 press conference at the medical school. Cullen, a Republican, had overseen a team hired to probe both the photograph and the broader school culture that had allowed it.[1]

Similarly the investigation by Alston & Bird commissioned by Northam's political arm struck out. "Ultimately, despite considerable time, effort, and resources committed to this investigation, our team was unable to definitely answer any of these questions," the never-released report concluded. Alston & Bird said the failure was "principally due to the passage of 35 years since the subject photograph was published in the 1984 EVMS yearbook, the lack of conclusive documentary evidence, and the inability to conduct a conclusive forensic examination of the subject photograph due to its poor image quality."[2]

Interviewed in April 2021, Edward "Ted" Kang, lead investigator on the Alston & Bird report, said the result was "unfortunate but not entirely surprising," given the passage of time. A former federal prosecutor, Kang in 2019 was cohead of Alston & Bird's white collar, government, and internal investigations team. He and his colleagues posited a variety of theories about the photograph. "At the end of the day, we weren't able to definitively conclude that one was more likely than others," he said.

The company that produced the yearbook no longer existed. The photograph was of too poor quality for facial imaging either to rule out or to establish connection to Northam. In the several dozen interviews completed by each team, no one identified the photograph or who was in it. Internally the Cullen team split on whether or not it was Northam. But, as was also true for those in Northam's camp, a belief one way or the other was based more on intuition than hard evidence.

Both investigations confirmed that assembling the 1984 yearbook had been a disorderly affair, raising the question of whether the picture might have wound up on Northam's page mistakenly. "Chaotic and often frustrating," the EVMS report described the endeavor. "Pretty chaotic, unorganized," echoed Kang. However, neither side found evidence of photographs winding up mistakenly on anyone else's page.

The person considered most likely to have answers, yearbook editor Pam Kopelove, did not speak to either team. The Alston & Bird investigators reported that "we made multiple attempts to reach the editor-in-chief, but were ultimately unable" to make contact. Kopelove "appears to be actively avoiding contact with reporters and our investigators," they wrote. Similarly a woman thought by some to have possibly been the figure in the KKK robe, a practicing physician in Hampton Roads, avoided investigators.

Reached by the author in January 2022, Kopelove said she had no real memory of the blackface photograph. Disappointingly, but not surprisingly, given the time-lapse, "I can't recall any of the events around that picture," she said. A surgical first assistant living in New Jersey, Kopelove agreed with investigators that assembly of the yearbook had been challenging. "I was promoted without having any real experience," she said. Her memory was clearer of Northam himself. "I do remember that Ralph was a really good guy, a very upstanding person," she added. "I never knew him to be racist or sexist. He would be one of the last who would do anything to hurt another person."

For a time Alston & Bird considered a man who had attended both VMI and EVMS to be a prime candidate for the figure in blackface. Some comments he had made in a telephone conversation with Rita Davis, the governor's counsel, were tantalizingly coy. Both groups spoke with the man, however, and came away believing that, at least in his own mind, his denial of involvement was truthful. Some medical issues might have contributed to a loss of memory, Kang said. The author's encounter with the same man, a resident of South Hampton Roads, was equally unilluminating. Another possible candidate was ruled out by the Cullen team when he turned out to be about five feet, five inches tall, too short for the figure in blackface.

One rarely mentioned fit between the photograph and the text on the page involved beer. Sophomorically, Northam's quote reads: "There are more old drunks than old doctors in this world so I think I'll have another beer." Both figures in the blackface photo appear to be holding beer cans, as does Northam in another of the four pictures on the page.

Conversely those who persist in the belief of Northam's guilt need to confront one weakness in their argument. When Northam said that his credibility and reputation would be forever ruined if he denied guilt and was then proven wrong, he was correct. When he went before a national audience and proclaimed his innocence regarding the blackface photograph, he was putting that premise to the test. Had he been lying, he would have been taking a huge, potentially fatal gamble. At least two other people—the second person in the photo and the photographer—could have come forward, exposing him as a liar. That would have destroyed more than his political career. His reputation for honesty also would have been in shambles. It is not proof of innocence that no one challenged his claim, but the absence weighs in that direction.

As the days passed, one fact became clear, abundantly so. Blackface in the 1984 EVMS yearbook was not an anomaly. As reporters began to review college yearbooks of the era, blackface seemed almost as prevalent as spring formals and intramural basketball games. The Republican leader of the Virginia Senate, Tommy Norment, had edited a VMI yearbook in 1968 that included multiple blackface photographs, although none of himself. Astonishingly, a popular Black student at the University of Richmond showed up in a snapshot in the 1981 yearbook with a beverage in one hand, a lynching rope around his neck, and five members of the Sigma Alpha Epsilon fraternity hovering nearby in KKK robes. He was grinning.

A USA Today investigation published in the wake of the Northam scandal uncovered more than two hundred examples of offensive or racist material in yearbooks during the 1970s and 1980s at 120 colleges in twenty-five states. Casual racism among White students, sometimes with go-along-to-get-along Black participation, was no anomaly. It was a norm.

That attitude still prevailed when Rita Davis arrived at Washington & Lee in the early 1990s. One of perhaps a dozen Black students in a class of several hundred, she encountered a community "where people would feel comfortable coming into your space in a Confederate uniform, completely oblivious or maybe just not caring." The chagrin and discomfort that caused was echoed throughout the USA Today report. For Black students "it was, quite frankly, 'let's just put our heads down and get through this,'" she said.[3]

One other race-tinged question shadowed Northam. His senior-year VMI yearbook listed two nicknames: Goose and Coonman. Given broad recognition of "coon" as a derogatory term for Black people, "coonman" was taken as further evidence of Northam's racial insensitivity. Unanswered in the rush to judgment were two questions: How did the nickname originate? What did it mean? Richmond mayor Stoney paused over the latter. "Obviously, the word 'coon' is offensive to me and to Black Virginians. But you have to ask, what does it ['coonman'] mean? I've heard the word 'coon,' but never 'coonman.'"

Possibilities: Someone who ridiculed and/or disliked Black people. That emerged as the dominant view in press coverage. But also someone who was perceived as being unusually friendly with Black people. Or a southern good ol' boy. Or something unrelated to race. Northam thought the nickname might have stemmed from a stretch as a boy when he captured some baby raccoons. Fearing ridicule, his team advised against offering that as an explanation.

Robert Leatherbury, who runs an accounting firm on the Eastern Shore and who grew up with Northam, likely is the individual who carried the nickname to VMI. "I did used to call him that, absolutely," said Leatherbury in a telephone interview. "I won't say I made it up." As a teenager, "I think I heard it was what some people called him. I thought it was kind of funny."

Leatherbury declined to say whether the nickname carried racial connotation —arguably an indication that it did. "I don't know," he replied. "High school kids, you joke around about things."

He did offer clarity on another matter. Was he aware of Northam's having had negative ideas about Black people? A Republican, with no political motivation to defend the governor, he replied, "No, he wasn't that kind of person."

CHAPTER 9

A Tragedy and Its Aftermath

Personal and political concerns evaporated in an instant in the staccato clip of gunfire as a veteran city engineer, wielding two semiautomatic handguns equipped with extended ammunition magazines, moved from floor to floor in a Virginia Beach municipal building on the afternoon of Friday, May 31. By the time DeWayne Craddock was shot dead in a gunfight with police, he had killed twelve people and wounded four others. The victims reflected a spectrum of skin colors, ages, ethnicities, and sexes, a swath of life cut short in a resort city known for sand dunes and surf, not bloody carnage. Virginia Beach joined Pittsburgh, Aurora, Charlotte, Parkland, and scores of other American cities in the dread register of mass shooting sites.

At face value the horrific moment had nothing to do with the racial reckoning Northam was undergoing. Eventually the connection would become clear.

Within hours of the shooting, the governor climbed out of a state police cruiser, tight-faced and somber, brushing past reporters and cameras as he arrived to confer with city officials. His air was professional and level, that of the good doctor. Unfolding before him was a scenario he had long feared. It was impossible to watch the ever-mounting toll of mass shootings nationwide without imagining having to confront one nearer home. Now the horror had struck in his own backyard. "This is just a horrific day," he repeated several times before disappearing into the building. Earlier he had tweeted, "My heart breaks for the victims of this devastating shooting, their families and all who loved them."

Over the next several days, he would attend prayer vigils and briefings, pay hospital visits to victims recovering from wounds, console grieving families, and renew his conviction that America's fascination with guns had become untenable, too destructive for a sane society to endure. As a doctor he had seen too many gun victims, some felled by accidents, some by deliberate or random violence, some by acts of war.

"I was raised with them," he said of firearms, but he could not ignore the human toll. "Whether hunting or serving in the military or taking care of children that have been shot, I just know that they're dangerous," he said. Assault weapons in particular, he had concluded, did not belong in civilian hands. "I don't see any reason for assault weapons to be in our society, and especially open carry of assault weapons because it's nothing but intimidation."

Three days after the Virginia Beach shooting, he announced plans to convene a special session of the legislature later in the summer to consider a package of gun-control bills. "I will be asking for votes and laws, not thoughts and prayers," said Northam, surrounded by Democratic legislative leaders at a press conference.[1]

His resolve was driven by more than the Virginia Beach events. Nine-year-old Markiya Simone Dickson of Richmond had died just five days earlier while at a cookout with her family in a Richmond park. Northam attended her heart-wrenching funeral. Markiya had been caught in the gunfire among a group of men unconnected to her family. "We weren't even nowhere near the basketball court" where the shots were fired, said Mark Whitfield, her father. "That just shows you bullets have no names on them. They just flying at people."[2]

The story was hauntingly familiar. Year after year Northam had treated children—often toddlers—accidentally shot by themselves or their siblings. He still grieved one heartbreaking gun death, that of a young mother shot by her husband in a fit of rage. Northam had cared for the victim since she was a toddler suffering intractable seizures. She had grown into a beautiful young woman. "I took that call" from her mother, post-midnight, "and it was one of the toughest calls I ever took," he said.

Gun-rights advocates accused Northam of playing politics with tragedy, but the charge seemed more rote than right. Backing for gun controls had been one of the defining issues of his 2017 gubernatorial campaign. And just months before, prior to the blackface scandal, he had pressed for a comprehensive package of gun bills in the legislature, only to see his goals obliterated by a Republican majority. "It's an emergency here in Virginia," Northam said. "Every one of these pieces of legislation will save lives." The weekend tragedy had instilled a new level of urgency to act, he said.

As Northam stood shoulder to shoulder at the June 4 press conference announcing the special session with Mark Herring, Justin Fairfax, and key Democratic lawmakers, the portrait revealed an evolved reality. Many in the group had spent recent months distancing themselves from him. Now here they were, joined in a united front. Not for any reason the governor wanted or relished, events had accomplished something months of behind-the-scenes strategizing and maneuvering had not. "At that moment," said Bergman, "he was the leader of the Democratic Party for the first time since February."

CAPITOL SQUARE TOOK ON THE APPEARANCE of an outdoor theater as hundreds of sign-waving, slogan-chanting citizens descended for the start of the July 9 special session on guns. Defying the summer heat, women in red "Moms Demand Action" T-shirts queued up or faced off with men in camouflage, some shouldering assault rifles or wearing holstered handguns.[3] A healthy sprinkling of posters decorated with a blown-up image of Northam's blackface yearbook photograph peppered the crowd, blaring the message "The man behind the sheet wants your guns."

A protestor hoisted a flag with a picture of a black-and-white assault rifle and the message "Come and Take It." A huge banner countered, "End Gun Violence Now."

Passage of significant gun-control legislation was a stretch in a legislature narrowly controlled by Republicans. Nonetheless Northam hoped that the violence in Virginia Beach might have caused some soul-searching. And he figured that no matter what happened, his party stood to come out the winner. The gun issue galvanized Democrats. If the Republicans did little or nothing, disappointment could be a unifying force in the fall campaign.

Settling in for what promised to be a long afternoon, the gubernatorial watch party in Northam's office listened as Democrats opened with impassioned speeches about the need for stricter gun laws. "We're ready to act; we're ready to vote," urged Delegate Chris Hurst, who had run for office after his girlfriend, television journalist Alison Parker, was shot to death on live television in Roanoke in 2015.

Then, some ninety minutes into the session, in preplanned coordination before a single vote had been taken, Republican leaders in the House and Senate rose and made nondebatable motions to adjourn. Onlookers exchanged shocked glances. Stunned Democrats scrambled futilely for a way to block the procedural move. None existed. Given the political makeup of the chambers, the special session on guns was over before it had barely even begun.

Speaking to reporters afterward, House Speaker Kirk Cox promised that a legislative commission would review gun-law proposals after the upcoming fall elections. Northam's call for a special session had been nothing more than "an election-year stunt," he said.

Northam was as surprised by the GOP action as most everyone else. Initial anger at the audacity morphed quickly into "we're not going to let 'em get away with this." Instinctively he felt certain that the maneuver would backfire. "It was a very arrogant approach that they took, and it was a politically risky approach," he said. "I knew that when I saw it. I knew from just listening to people around Virginia and some of the polling we'd done that they were walking down the wrong path, staying here for less than ninety minutes."

Turning to Mercer and other aides watching the legislature disband, Northam said matter-of-factly, "They're going to wind up paying for that."

His warning doubled as a promise.

Ralph Northam takes the oath of office as Virginia's seventy-third governor on January 13, 2018. Office of Governor Ralph Northam, photographer Pierre Courtois.

The Northams recite the Pledge of Allegiance at his inaugural ceremony. Office of Governor Ralph Northam, photographer Pierre Courtois.

Chief of Staff Clark Mercer listens to remarks at the August 2019 commemoration of the Jefferson Davis signage removal at Fort Monroe. Office of Governor Ralph Northam, photographer Jack Mayer.

Rita Davis speaks at the March 2021 signing of the bill abolishing the death penalty in Virginia. Office of Governor Ralph Northam, photographer Jack Mayer.

Mark Bergman chats with Governor Northam prior to his January 2019
State of the Commonwealth speech. Office of Governor Ralph Northam,
photographer Jack Mayer.

Ralph Northam's page in the 1984 Eastern Virginia Medical School yearbook.

Delegate Delores Mc-Quinn speaks in July 2019 at a Richmond rally denouncing gun violence. Office of Governor Ralph Northam, photographer Jack Mayer.

Senator Jennifer McClellan speaks at a January 2020 press conference outlining equity and justice priorities for the upcoming legislative session. Office of Governor Ralph Northam, photographer Jack Mayer.

Delegates Lamont Bagby, Marcia Price, and Jeff Bourne gather on the floor of the Virginia House of Delegates in February 2109 for the reading of a proclamation honoring a notable Black Virginian. Courtesy of Lamont Bagby.

Members of the Virginia Legislative Black Caucus gather before the Kehinde Wiley sculpture *Rumors of War* at the Virginia Museum of Fine Arts during the 2020–21 session. Courtesy of Lamont Bagby. Front row (*l to r*) Delegate Marcia (Cia) Price, Delegate Jeion Ward, Delegate Lashrecse Aird, Senator Jennifer McClellan, Senator Mamie Locke, Senator Louise Lucas, Senator Lionell Spruill, Delegate Jeff Bourne, Delegate Luke Torian. Back row (*l to r*) Delegate Hala Ayala, Delegate Jay Jones, Delegate Sam Rasoul, Delegate Clint Jenkins, Delegate Lamont Bagby, Delegate Josh Cole, Delegate Alex Askew, Delegate Don Scott.

CHAPTER 29

How the Negroes Lived under Slavery

treatment
and the
that som
treated
upon ha

A fe
slaves i
Winche
to Libe
and th
boy at
call th
were v
Th
slaves
his se
he be
tears
depa
S
speal
me.
toge

Above: Page from a Virginia seventh-grade history textbook in use into the 1970s. *Left:* The cover of that textbook celebrated Gen. Robert E. Lee.

Dr. Janice Underwood joins celebrants as Fort Monroe is designated as a UNESCO Slave Route Project site in February 2021. Office of Governor Ralph Northam, photographer Jack Mayer.

Cynthia Hudson stands against a mural of acclaimed Richmond entrepreneur Maggie Walker during the January 2022 presentation of the final report of the Commission to Examine Racial and Economic Inequity in Virginia Law. Office of Governor Ralph Northam, photographer Jack Mayer.

PART III

ABOUT FACE

Pinch-faced and white-haired, with owlish glasses and a mouth that drooped to match his mustache, Walter Ashby Plecker served for decades as the keeper of Virginia's racial-purity flame. From passage of the Racial Integrity Act of 1924 until his retirement twenty-two years later, the director of the state Bureau of Vital Statistics worked tirelessly to prevent mixing of the races. Even a single drop of non-Caucasian blood might taint the White race, according to Plecker and state law. Any interracial couple electing to marry faced a year in jail.

A letter to a Lynchburg mother who, Plecker claimed, had duplicitously listed her new baby's Black father as White captured his tone and technique. "This is to give you warning that this is a mulatto child and you cannot pass it off as white," he scolded. "You will have to do something about this matter and see that this child is not allowed to mix with white children. It cannot go to white schools and can never marry a white person in Virginia.

"It is an awful thing."[1]

To Plecker's annoyance, Virginia had carved out one exception to the draconian act. Descendants of Pocahontas and John Rolfe might pass as White, but only if Native American blood accounted for no more than one-sixteenth of the total. Convinced that many were trying to scam state enforcers under the exclusion, Plecker rebranded much of the state's Indigenous population as "colored."

Two years later lawmakers went further, mandating racial separation in public spaces including "public halls, theaters, opera houses, motion picture shows and places of public entertainment and public assemblages." The 1926 Virginia Public Assemblages Act, soon a model for other southern states, originated in the outrage of a Tidewater newspaper editor and his wife after they were seated next to Black patrons at a Hampton Institute dance recital. The law separated Black and White Virginians for the next forty years.[2]

Yet a third law illuminated Virginia's obsession with racial purity, although its dragnet captured poor White people as well as Black people. The Virginia Sterilization Act (1924), born of the false science of eugenics, decreed than anyone deemed a "mental defective" could be sterilized by the state. No less a luminary than Oliver Wendell Holmes wrote the infamous 1927 Supreme Court ruling upholding the law. It would be "better for all the world," he declared, if those so "manifestly unfit" never gave birth.[3]

At the Nuremberg trials, lawyers defending Nazi doctors responsible for hundreds of thousands of German sterilizations cited the Holmes decision. More than eight thousand Virginians, White and Black, were sterilized under the law before relevant parts were repealed in 1974. Late twentieth-century investigations concluded that Carrie Buck, the impoverished White girl who was the first victim of the law, had likely been raped. Her intelligence appeared to fall within normal range.[4]

Virginia's felony ban on interracial marriage stood until 1967 when the Supreme Court in Loving v. Virginia overturned both it and the Racial Integrity Act.[5] The interracial couple bringing the lawsuit, Mildred and Richard Loving, had been sentenced to one year in prison, suspended if they would leave Virginia for twenty-five years and never again live as a couple in the state. The Lovings complied with that mandate for five years before summoning the courage to resist through legal action.

CHAPTER 10

Lessons Learned

More than the failed effort to strengthen weak gun laws occupied Virginians in the summer of 2019. August marked the quatercentenary of the arrival of shackled Africans at Point Comfort and the first exercise in democracy at Jamestown, both in 1619. For a governor enmeshed in his own struggle to better understand the effects of those conflicting events in American life, the milestones were an opportunity to address his personal growth since the blackface scandal the previous February. He was eager to showcase the results.

As planners prepared for events that they hoped would shine an international spotlight on Virginia's history and progress, Northam continued to unveil projects that spoke to his commitment.

In April he had urged directors of the authority overseeing the Fort Monroe National Monument in Hampton to dismantle a fifty-foot wrought-iron arch honoring Jefferson Davis. The facility is located at Old Point Comfort where imprisoned Africans first came ashore. The former president of the Confederate states had spent two years incarcerated at Fort Monroe, then a US Army base, while awaiting trial for treason after the Civil War.

The United Daughters of the Confederacy had paid ten thousand dollars to erect the archway in 1956 as southern opposition to desegregation of public schools raged. With his expanded focus on Virginia history, Northam knew exactly what that had been about—celebrating White supremacy in the face of Black ascendency. At the governor's request, members of the authority's board voted unanimously to begin dismantling the arch.[1]

Meanwhile he signed executive orders aimed at addressing two of the most troubling statistics referenced time and again as he spoke with Black Virginians. The maternal mortality rate for Black women giving birth in Virginia was more than twice as high as for White women. Also women- and minority-owned business struggled to a far greater degree than those owned by White men. The executive orders were largely aspirational. Others had shown that goals were easier to set than to achieve. Still achievement without goals was even more unlikely.

Northam set a target of eliminating the maternal mortality disparity by 2025, and he directed executive branch agencies to push to procure 42 percent of discretionary spending from certified small businesses. He ordered concrete steps toward meeting those goals, starting with updating data on the amount of government work going to female- and minority-owned firms. The most recent such disparity studies in 2004 and 2011 had found that the numbers were shockingly low, 1.27 percent in 2004 and 2.82 percent in 2011.

He progressed also on fulfilling one of Jarvis Stewart's recommendations: naming the state's first director of diversity, equity, and inclusion. After a vetting process that identified thirty finalists and included joint interviews by the governor and First Lady, the Northams settled on Dr. Janice Underwood. Underwood's Italian American mother had been beaten by her father and shunned by most of her family for marrying a Black man. As the offspring of that interracial union, Underwood grew up believing that her life mission was to bridge cultural divides. She taught high school biology, working to bring more minority students into STEM classes, then sought to expand the minority pool in science and math education classes at Old Dominion University in Norfolk. Most recently she had been assigned the task of expanding racial diversity and equity on the campus.

Committed to radical reform, unafraid to be bold and even blunt, Underwood cemented the deal with the Northams when, during their interview, Pam mentioned reading *Citizen: An American Lyric* by Claudia Rankine, and Underwood pulled the book out of her purse. *Citizen* seeks to expose racism in everyday acts through poetry, prose, and images. The First Lady was attracted also to Underwood's phrasing of how she might respond to a racially offensive comment. "How can I say this to you in a way that we can continue to ride in this car together?" she said, envisioning a possible scenario.

Even as the Northams were interviewing her, Underwood said later, she was scrutinizing them. "They wanted to know, was I good enough for them? And I wanted to know, were they good enough to have me?" *Good enough* in her mind meant sincerely committed to learning and growing themselves, while giving her the access, the support, and the team she would need to penetrate entrenched government systems.

She rapidly realized that Northam's commitment to creating the position did not mean that he—or others in the administration—had a concrete plan for the job's execution. During multiple interviews she found herself vacillating. "It was not that I didn't think I could do the job. It was because no one even knew what the job was." She would, she saw, be walking into a vast, uncharted space between intention and implementation.

The challenge and the opportunity finally overrode the doubt in her mind. Accepting the appointment, Underwood laid out the terms of her agreement. "He hasn't always gotten it right," she said of the governor. "But what I respect the most is that he is willing to learn and do the work."[2]

Months later she smiled at her own naivete—not about Northam per se but about the enormity of the task. "Sometimes you don't know what you don't know. If I had to go back to talk to Janice Underwood before I was offered the position, I would probably tell her, 'This is going to hurt.' This has been the heaviest lift. This has been the hardest thing I've ever had to do."

Republicans made sure that Virginians did not lose sight of the blackface controversy presumed to be the genesis of such actions. "It doesn't matter if Northam is vetoing or signing legislation, he is still a racist that's doing everything he can to stay in power. It's embarrassing to all Virginians," said John March, spokesman for the Republican Party of Virginia, in early summer.[3]

THE FIRST OF TWO MAJOR COMMEMORATIVE EVENTS occurred on July 30, the anniversary of the first meeting of burgesses at Jamestown. The celebration included a midmorning speech by Northam at the restored church on Jamestown Island. Flanked by Senate Majority Leader Norment and House Speaker Cox, two of the many Republicans who had demanded the governor's resignation just six months earlier, Northam urged a full accounting of the state's history. "We have to remember who it included and who it did not," he said, alluding to the Native Americans, Black people, and women excluded from the 1619 gathering.

Then he delivered a soft punch to the day's headline speaker, President Donald Trump, who would arrive later. "Our doors are open and our lights are on," he said. "No matter who you are, no matter who you love, and no matter where you are from, you are welcome in Virginia."

Not entirely, as it turned out. The political and racial tensions in the state were on full display as Trump landed in southeastern Virginia. Fresh off a weekend tweet-bash of Baltimore as "disgusting, rat and rodent infested" and long-time congressman Elijah Cummings as "a brutal bully," just days removed from a rally in Greenville, North Carolina, in which Trump's mocking of Minnesota representative Ilhan Omar prompted chilling chants of "Send her back," the president adopted a civil tone for Jamestown.

Trump urged listeners to "honor every sacred soul who suffered the horrors of slavery" and stressed an imperative to nourish and protect the nation's "hard-won culture" of democracy. "Self-government in Virginia did not just give us a state we love. It gave us the country we love," he said.

State delegate Ibraheem Samirah of Herndon may have agreed with the message. He had nothing but contempt for the messenger. Midway through Trump's speech, the twenty-seven-year-old offspring of Jordanian-Palestinian immigrants, newly elected and the youngest member of the General Assembly, sprang to the front and hoisted signs reading "Deport Hate" and "Go Back to Your Corrupted Home."

Stunned organizers had Samirah quickly removed, but he was not alone in the presidential shunning. Members of the Virginia Legislative Black Caucus had collectively boycotted the event. "We offer just three words of advice to the Jamestown-Yorktown Foundation," fumed leaders incensed by recent news stories about the poor treatment of families seeking asylum at the Mexican border. "Send him back."

A few decades earlier, that display for a sitting president would have been unthinkable in staid, proper Virginia. The impassioned reception sent as clear a signal as might be imagined about a state that voted for Hillary Clinton and twice for Barack Obama after supporting only one Democratic presidential contender, Lyndon Johnson, in the half-century between Dwight Eisenhower and George W. Bush. A contentious new day had dawned in the incubator of democracy.

AS THE SECOND COMMEMORATION, that of the first landing by Africans at Point Comfort, approached on August 24, work progressed on removing Jefferson Davis's name from the Fort Monroe arch. Structural complications dictated against removing the arch altogether, but Davis's name could go. Not only was it inappropriate, in Northam's view, that the state should honor an American traitor, but also the fort and the location told an ennobling story of Black courage and self-determination early in the Civil War. That story deserved more attention than Davis.

On the night of May 23, 1861, under cover of darkness, three enslaved fieldhands—Shepard Mallory, Frank Baker, and James Townsend—stole a small boat and rowed it across the James River to the fort, which remained in Union hands. There the escaped men petitioned the Union commander, Maj. Gen. Benjamin F. Butler, to grant them shelter and protection. The men, who had been forced to help construct a Confederate battery across the harbor, had learned that they were about to be banished to North Carolina by their owner, Confederate colonel Charles King Mallory. They would be put to work building more Confederate fortifications. Loath to leave families and their familiar world for so ignoble a task, they opted to risk life and limb in a bid for freedom.

When Mallory demanded return of the three under the Fugitive Slave Act of 1850, Butler refused. Since Virginia had seceded from the Union, he was under no obligation to honor the statute on behalf of a rebellious enslaver, he said. Instead Butler accepted Mallory, Baker, and Townsend as "contrabands of war." President Lincoln and his cabinet discussed the matter and elected not to intervene. The men spent the remainder of the war at the fort, working as brickmasons.

Federal support for such action later was cemented in two Confiscation Acts, approved in August 1861 and July 1862. The first made all property used in support of the rebellion "subject to prize and capture." That included enslaved people. Indeed Fort Monroe soon became known as a haven for fleeing Black fugitives, earning its nickname, "Freedom's Fortress." According to historian Ervin Jordan Jr., eight more enslaved people arrived at Fort Monroe a few days after the first three. The next day, fifty-nine appeared, their ages spanning three months to eighty-five years. And by July 30, 1861, the number of Black refugees at Fort Monroe totaled about nine hundred.[4] Eventually, across the South, tens of thousands of Black people sought Union refuge under the acts.

In early August, between the two historic commemorations, Northam invited Lamont Bagby to join him and Mercer on a trip to Northern Virginia to visit the Freedom House Museum in Alexandria, once home to the nation's largest domestic slave-trading firm. From the slave pens of Franklin and Armfield, thousands of men, women, and children plodded by foot or by ship toward their sale in Natchez, Mississippi, or New Orleans. The setting had a profound effect on Northam. Deeply moved by notes written by some of the slaves to spouses and children from whom they were separated, he shook his head. "If that doesn't get your attention, then you need to see a doctor."

A different incident on the trip stood out for Bagby. As they drove north, Mercer shared a snapshot that had just been sent to him on his cell phone. It showed workers dismantling Jefferson Davis's name from the archway of Fort Monroe. For Bagby it was a breathtaking image, the first time he could recall such a prominent emblem of Confederate sympathy being removed in Virginia. "I was a bit shocked and extremely pleased," he said. The photograph affirmed to him that Northam's commitment to change was real. It went beyond rhetoric. "It said to me that he's unapologetic in making sure that we remove these symbols of what we believe is hate."

A FEW WEEKS LATER, NORTHAM returned to Hampton Roads for the sober commemoration of the arrival of the first Africans at Point Comfort. Both he and his staff viewed the event as an ideal opportunity to give a candid update on his personal evolution. Shouldering past the awkwardness of sharing a venue with Warner, Kaine, and Scott, the trio of top state Democratic officeholders who in February had questioned his ability to lead, Northam launched into one of the most important speeches he would ever give.

Shoulders thrust back and feet slightly spread, he looked out solemnly on hundreds of listeners. A slight sea breeze stirred the humid air, and a hush of anticipation quieted the crowd. "We are here today for a commemoration—and a reckoning," he began.

That reckoning, he said, was both for a nation and for himself. Through 246 years of slavery and 100 years of Reconstruction, Jim Crow terror, and discrimination, the government failed to represent African Americans. "In many ways, it struggles to represent them today." The way out of that morass, however, began not in the halls of government but at a more human level. Ida B. Wells, the valiant Black journalist and civil rights activist, wrote that "the way to right wrongs is to turn the light of truth upon them," he noted. "If we are going to truly right the wrongs of our four centuries of history, if we are going to turn the light of truth upon them, we have to start with ourselves."

Of rude necessity, he said, that was where he had begun. Since February he had cast an unsparing eye on his own history. He had listened intently to scores of Virginians of color. In the face of those conversations, as he traveled the state, "I have had to confront some painful truths. Among those truths was my own incomplete understanding regarding race and equity." He had come to recognize, in a way he had not previously, that racism continues "not just in isolated incidents, but as part of a system that touches every person and every aspect of our lives, whether we know it or not."

The importance of the ground where he stood had been illuminated by Ed Ayers, a Virginian and a nationally known historian of the American South, Northam said. Ayers had cited General Butler's contraband decision as "the greatest moment in American history."[5] The intersection of Black people bidding for their own freedom and Butler's decision to put the imprimatur of the federal government on that quest was a glorious moment. Yet it also was one scarcely recognized in a flawed and incomplete teaching of American and Virginia history.

How is it that children, parents, and teachers know the names of Robert E. Lee, Stonewall Jackson, and J. E. B. Stuart—men who were willing to tear apart a country in defense of slavery—but not the names of Mallory, Baker, Townsend, and Butler, men whose actions illuminated a far different vision? Which of those groups better reflects the aspirations of the nation's founding documents? No mystery. The elevation of Jefferson Davis and his accomplices and the obscurity of three enslaved Black men and a White Union officer reflect the power and prejudice of those White leaders who wrote the history and held society's reins.

Later that day, Northam announced, he planned to sign an executive order creating a state commission to review and improve the teaching of African American history in Virginia. The seed planted by Dr. Newby-Alexander and her colleagues five months earlier when they pressed Northam to see that schoolchildren learned a truer, fuller Virginia history had borne fruit.

"Virginia is the place where enslaved Africans first landed and where American representative democracy was born," he continued. "Virginia is the place where emancipation began and the Confederate capitol was located.

"Virginia is the place where schools were closed under Massive Resistance, rather than desegregate and allow Black children to attend, and it is the state that elected the nation's first African American governor.

"Virginia is a place of contradictions and complexity. We take a step forward and, often, a step back. And we have to acknowledge that. We have to teach that complexity to our children, and often to our adults. We are a state that for too long has told a false story of ourselves. . . . We memorize dates, but not connections. We don't teach the themes that appear in our history over and over again. We often fail to draw the connecting lines from those past events to our present day. But to move forward, that is what we must do."

He paused. "We know that racism and discrimination aren't locked in the past. They weren't solved with the Civil Rights Act. They didn't disappear—they evolved. They're still with us, in the disparities we see in educational attainment and school suspension rates, in maternal and neonatal mortality for Black and White mothers, in our courts and prisons, and in our business practices. . . . And if we're serious about righting the wrong that began here at this place, we need to do more than talk. We need to take action."

Then Northam allowed himself the familiar slight smile. "I also learned that the more I know, the more I can do." After months of hard listening and self-examination, "I know more, and as your governor, I will do more."

The speech served as Northam's manifesto going forward. The full measure of what he could do had only begun to take shape.

CHAPTER 11

The Road to Richmond

Northam's ability to reform Virginia hinged in no small measure on elections seventy-three days away. Securing Democratic control of the legislature would be the challenge of the next two and a half months. The difference between what he could accomplish with a Democratic majority and his likely fate without one was night and day. His racial-equity platform hinged on erasing a slim Republican advantage of 51–49 in the House and 20–19 in the Senate.

The governor had launched his own political career a dozen years earlier with a state senate bid against a two-term Republican incumbent, Senator Nick Rerras. Republicans held the edge in a district centered in Norfolk and Virginia Beach, but the addition of a Democratic favorite son from the Eastern Shore provided an intriguing wild card. Bolstered by a dose of cash from his father and a reassuring white-coat, stethoscope-around-the-neck television image, as well as a healer-warrior resume, he won his political debut in an impressive upset, 54 to 46 percent. Four years later he was reelected by an even wider margin.

Hailing from a family that rarely talked politics, Northam was something of an accidental Democrat. "I didn't grow up as one or the other," he said of the major parties. For much of the mid-twentieth century, Virginians voted in state elections in line with the conservative, Democratic machine controlled by former governor and US senator Harry Byrd, a fiscal and social arch-conservative. In presidential contests they tilted Republican. Northam assumed his father had done much the same, despite having as a law partner a former maverick Democratic lawmaker, Senator Bill Fears.

Northam recalled his father's advice when he entered politics: "'I'm not sure I'd recommend it. But if you run, you're going to need to run as a Democrat.' I don't think he saw a path running against a Republican [incumbent]." For his part Northam didn't much care about parties. Motivated by his complaints over managed health care and the decline of the Chesapeake Bay, "I just wanted to run," he said.

On finances and government red tape, he tilted conservative. On some social issues, the Democratic Party was a more natural fit. "He's always been pro-choice. That's what he believes. He was pro–gay marriage in 2007," said Tom King, Northam's longtime media consultant. As for racial issues, "he was always just a Democrat, not out front, but he was Democrat. The first time I met him he was at a clinic. His practice had a clinic in Newport News, and it was only Black kids. I don't think he was one of those guys who said, 'Oh, I should do this because it's the right thing to do.' I think he just saw people."

Entering the legislature, Northam quickly made friends on both sides of the aisle. He and three other centrists—two Republicans and a Democrat—formed an informal caucus that, in a closely divided senate, could sometimes sway decisions. Such alliances spurred talk over the years that Northam might switch parties or, when the blackface scandal arose, become a political independent. Neither was ever a deep consideration, he insisted.

The hallmarks of Northam's legislative career included early work on protecting young athletes against concussions and, in 2009, helping pass a ban on smoking indoors in bars and restaurants. In a state whose economy had long centered on tobacco, the Kaine-spearheaded victory signaled a seismic cultural shift. Northam's ability to speak authoritatively to the hazards of smoking had made him an ideal person to carry the legislation in the senate.

In 2012 Northam cemented a position in the major leagues of Virginia politics courtesy of a Gatorade bottle. The setting was the floor of the senate chamber. The topic was pre-abortion ultrasounds, and the passion was fierce. All across America, energized abortion foes were finding new ways to complicate access to the procedure. Virginia Republicans were on the front lines of the drive.

Legislation moving forward in the Senate required women seeking an abortion to first undergo a fetal ultrasound. Similar bills were wending their way through legislatures in several states, including Alabama, Idaho, Pennsylvania, and Mississippi. In the Virginia model, a doctor or radiographer must offer the woman an opportunity to view the image, which must then be retained in her medical file for at least seven years.

Democratic leaders, resisting what they saw as intimidation of women at a vulnerable moment, looked around for someone to lead the floor fight in opposition. Their sights settled on the doctor. Northam's understanding of just what such a procedure involved proved key.

As members of the mostly male Senate squirmed, Northam made clear that fetal ultrasounds occur in two ways: one, the jelly-on-the-belly variety familiar to many prospective parents or, two, the transvaginal, inserting a probe into a woman's vagina. In the early months of pregnancy, when most abortions occur, option one would show nothing, he said. Then, waving a Gatorade bottle that had been sitting on his desk, Northam memorably asserted: "I might as well put the ultrasound probe on this bottle of Gatorade. I'm going to see just as much."

Be forewarned, he said. The Senate was getting ready to mandate a vaginally invasive procedure for thousands of Virginia women. The labeling reverberated nationwide. Comedians from Jon Stewart to Amy Poehler picked up the refrain. "I love Transvaginal," Poehler deadpanned on *Saturday Night Live*. "It's my favorite airline. I've got so many miles on Transvaginal that I always get upgraded to Lady Business." In Richmond female protesters clambered onto the capitol steps. Police in riot gear hauled off thirty-one in a single swoop. Across the nation lawmakers loath to find themselves in a similar mess backed down. So did Virginia governor Bob McDonnell, a Republican. He quickly insisted that the bill be amended to erase any prospect of a transvaginal mandate.

Meanwhile Northam collected a prominent mention on the pages of the *New York Times* and his first serious consideration as a possible candidate for statewide office.[1]

NORTHAM'S AMBIVALENCE ABOUT A STATEWIDE BID almost cost him a spot on the 2013 Democratic ticket.

Party leaders had courted him, as well as some other candidates, to run for lieutenant governor. The position entails only one real task: presiding over the state senate. Otherwise it amounts largely to a ribbon-cutting, résumé-building way to run for governor. Northam dallied until Aneesh Chopra, an Indian American and the nation's first chief technology officer during the Obama administration, had a solid head start.

A pivotal moment for Northam's surge came at the annual Saint Patrick's Day Fete hosted by Congressman Gerry Connolly, serving Northern Virginia's Eleventh District. The event includes a straw poll on whatever upcoming election is in season. As expected, Chopra did well in his Northern Virginia home base. Still, a Northam speech drew unexpectedly positive reviews. He spoke passionately about gun control and about his role in defeating the transvaginal ultrasound bill. Aides were encouraged when multiple people said they'd have changed their straw-poll vote if they'd heard Northam speak first.

The response proved a harbinger as Northam swept past Chopra to a 54–46 statewide victory. In the voting Northam held his own in Northern Virginia and swamped Chopra in South Hampton Roads. As would prove true in Northam's gubernatorial bid four years later, much of the media coverage had centered on Chopra, whose history-making résumé offered a more colorful story.

In the general election, Northam scored an easy victory over Republican E. W. Jackson, a flamboyant Black minister from Chesapeake who accused Democrats of exploiting African American voters. While Northam made no racial appeals, he had risen by leaping past two men of color.

Positions reversed in the Democratic primary for governor four years later. After Attorney General Herring opted not to wage a gubernatorial bid, Northam appeared a shoo-in for the nomination. Then, unexpectedly, in early January, a challenger emerged. Tom Perriello, a Yale-educated progressive, had served just one term as a congressman from Virginia's Fifth District before being defeated for reelection. His 727-vote victory in the 2008 blue wave that elected Barack Obama had proved unsustainable in a mostly conservative rural district. Still, despite a few votes in Congress that ran counter to the narrative, he entered the gubernatorial contest as a liberal darling.

The previous fall Northam had taken a sabbatical from his medical practice and essentially moved into a borrowed townhouse in Northern Virginia for the duration of the campaign. With his usual resolve, he was putting his whole being into the effort. An opponent, especially one who soon garnered the backing of progressive senators Bernie Sanders and Elizabeth Warren as well as more than thirty members of the Obama administration, was an unwelcome wrinkle.

Northam's team believed that Connolly's annual March gathering once again altered the outcome. Speaking to a crowd fuming over Donald Trump's election as president a few months earlier, Northam used an off-the-cuff phrase that would quickly become a campaign staple. As a doctor he believed Trump qualified as a "narcissistic maniac," Northam said, drawing laughter and cheers. The term was not polite. "Maniac" is an offensive designation within the mental health community. But, in Northam's view, the "narcissistic" part of the phrase was medically correct.

"When he was running, I knew. I knew he was sick, and I knew he was dangerous," Northam said. He had seen a disturbing lack of empathy in Trump's mocking of a disabled journalist, the *Access Hollywood* tape in which he boasted of assaulting women, and the campaign-trail claim that "I could stand in the middle of Fifth Avenue and shoot somebody, and I wouldn't lose any voters, OK? It's, like, incredible."

Yes, indeed, Northam had thought as he and Pam watched the election returns on November 8, 2016. It was incredible that a man with such disregard for normal human decency had been entrusted with the care of American democracy.

The label resonated with Democratic voters. The most memorable ad of the primary campaign was titled "Listening." It opened with a smiling Northam tracking the heartbeat of a young Black boy, progressed quickly to his meeting with families of the 2007 mass shooting at Virginia Tech, and ended with the candidate speaking directly to the camera: "I'm listening carefully to Donald Trump, and I think he's a narcissistic maniac." A brief pause. "Whatever you call him, we're not letting him bring his hate into Virginia."

The only way the Northam team thought they could lose to Perriello was if the former congressman became broadly viewed as the anti-Trump candidate in the race. Northam's spontaneous phrase had staunched that danger. Northam emerged the solid victor, 56–44 percent.

One other blip from that campaign played a role in Northam's blackface scrutiny two years later. Asked on the campaign trail by Jonathan Martin, a *New York Times* reporter, about his voting history, Northam acknowledged his votes—not once but twice—for George Bush for president. That was not an admission likely to endear him to Democratic primary voters.[2] Later, supporters cited the episode as proof that Northam values truth. Bergman recalled pressing Northam at the time about why he had provided an unnecessary and risky answer. The candidate's response reflected a familiar political naivete. "Well, he asked me," Northam said.

THE GENERAL ELECTION FOR GOVERNOR pitted Northam against Ed Gillespie, a genial Washington, DC, lobbyist and former chairman of the Republican National Committee.

Race surfaced briefly in early June when reporters uncovered pieces of Northam's slave-owning ancestry. Delegate Price remembered the internal campaign conversation about how to respond. "I pushed hard to use the term 'White privilege,'" she said, smiling at the memory of herself as "this big ball of energy that could help people understand their footing through an intersectional lens."[3] The academic jargon of critical race theory and intersectionality, terms Price had absorbed at Spelman and Howard, fell flat. "I felt listened to. I felt valued," she said. "But I also understood people were only going to push themselves up to a certain point."

In 2017 in Virginia, among the Northam brain trust and with the candidate himself, calling out "White privilege" was a step too far.

As the campaign progressed, an unscripted episode upended advance planning. On August 11 and 12 in Charlottesville, a shocked nation came face-to-face with a grim reality. Domestic extremism was flourishing, cloaked in part by a distracted focus on foreign terrorism. Plans to take down a statue of Robert E. Lee in the city had incited a furious response from opponents, including organizers of a so-called Unite the Right rally. Hundreds of members of far-right groups, including neo-Nazis, Klansmen, White nationalists, and an assortment of militias, descended on the city. On Friday evening, August 11, scores of torch-bearing young men chanting White supremacist and neo-Nazi slogans strode the central lawn of the University of Virginia. The next day brought clashes between protesters and counterprotesters, ending in tragedy. James Alex Fields Jr., an alt-right sympathizer, rammed his car into a crowd of pedestrians, including counterprotesters, killing one and injuring some thirty others. Heather Heyer, a thirty-two-year-old paralegal, died. Fields later was sentenced to life in prison for the carnage.

Separately two members of the Virginia State Police assigned to assist in security for the rally died when their helicopter crashed southwest of the city.

In the aftermath Northam would take his strongest stand yet for racial equity, becoming the first major elected official in Virginia to endorse the removal of Confederate statues from public grounds. The stance was unplanned and unscripted. Asked by a reporter how he thought such statues should be handled, Northam did not duck. Put them in museums, he said.[4]

Close advisers were as surprised as anyone. "We'd always said he would never take down Confederate monuments, because how would he face his friends at VMI?" Mark Bergman said. "That was the first time he ever kind of resolved himself and stiffened his spine."

Northam had watched the weekend's unfolding events in horror: the violent confrontations, the open displays of intimidating weapons, and the three deaths. "It's like, you know what? If a statue caused this kind of unrest, and supremacists have come into a city like that, then these statues need to go," he recalled his thinking.

"It was just sickening," Northam said of the events.

At the time he knew very little of the history of Confederate monuments in Virginia. That learning would come later, in the wake of the blackface scandal. He did not yet know that the Lee statue in Charlottesville, like many of the scores of Confederate monuments scattered across Virginia in 2017, was not commissioned in the wake of the Civil War. It was born in a turn-of-the-century southern movement to reestablish White supremacy after Black progress during Reconstruction. The sculpture was dedicated in 1924, the same year as passage of the Virginia Racial Integrity and Sterilization Acts.[5]

Northam's off-the-cuff statement prompted in-house angst. The campaign staff worried that it would prove costly in a tight race. Some thought he should walk it back. In reality a state law prevented localities from removing war memorials. As long as that was in place, unless courts ruled otherwise, the statues would stand. Despite his advisers' concerns, a formal statement released on

Wednesday morning, August 16, cemented Northam's position. Confederate statues "should be taken down and moved into museums," he said. "As governor I am going to be a vocal advocate for that approach and work with localities on this issue."

The statement put him at odds with Gillespie, who favored keeping statues in place but adding "historical context." To Northam's surprise, it also left him crossways with Terry McAuliffe.

Driving to a meeting with a group of Richmond business executives shortly after releasing the statement on statues, Northam answered his ringing cellphone. The governor was on the other end. What followed, Northam said, was "the worst cussin' I ever had." The conversation lasted about thirty seconds, and "I would say the F-bomb came out at least ten times." By one interpretation McAuliffe was angry that Northam had gotten ahead of him on the issue. Not so, McAuliffe said in a later interview: "I thought it was great that he did it." What infuriated him, he said, was having been in the dark about Northam's statement when he went into a press conference with scores of national and state reporters immediately after Heather Heyer's funeral. "I could have been blindsided. . . . My only anger was that he put me in a very vulnerable position." Later that day, reversing earlier opposition, McAuliffe endorsed removal of statues as well.

The possible political price for Northam became apparent a few days later in a private campaign survey by Public Policy Polling of Raleigh, North Carolina. After likely voters were informed of Northam's position on statues and recent statements on Trump, his advantage in the poll dropped from six percentage points to one.

By election day Democratic resolve to send a message to the man in the White House outweighed any lingering cost of the statue debate. Other hot-button issues, ranging from sanctuary cities to MS-13 gangs to Confederate flags, as well as more substantive ones involving health care and education, seemed dwarfed as well. Once again belying expectations of a close race, Northam swept to a nine-point victory, 54 to 45 percent. Washington pundits had not let up in their disregard for a man who still dropped his g's on words like *comin'* and *goin'* and preferred open-collared shirts to more formal attire. "Everybody on both sides of the aisle said this guy [Northam] ran one of the worst closing campaigns they had seen in recent memory," said Joe Scarborough on his *Morning Joe* program the next day. "Last night wasn't as much about Ralph Northam as it was voters—Republicans, moderates, Democrats, and women—sending a message to Donald Trump."

That argument did not explain why, among Democrats winning the state's three top offices, Northam had the largest margin of victory. "If you watched MSNBC, you'd think Ralph was losing," Tom King said in the aftermath. "Whereas, what I saw, when he speaks, people like him and believe him."

Satisfying as the top-three victory might be for Democrats, the 2017 election had accomplished an even more remarkable feat. It had almost erased a 66–34 seat advantage for Republicans in the House of Delegates. The gap had shrunk to 51–49. Save for a lost draw when one tied seat was resolved by picking a film cannister containing a candidate's name out of a decorative blue bowl, the House balance would have been 50–50.

The House margin as the legislature entered the 2018 session, combined with a similarly close 21–19 Republican edge in the senate, led to what was then, and to some degree remains, Northam's greatest racial-equity victory: expansion of Medicaid coverage under the Affordable Care Act.

While he did not yet view such matters through the lens of systemic racism, Northam knew firsthand the havoc that unpaid medical bills could play with families and individuals. McAuliffe, throughout his time as governor, had sought futilely to convince a GOP-dominated legislature to support Medicaid expansion, bringing medical coverage under Obama's Affordable Care Act to hundreds of thousands of uninsured Virginians. Dozens of supportive groups had helped McAuliffe lay the groundwork for success. With near parity between parties in both chambers, and given his good relations with several members of the GOP caucus, Northam believed he could make that last critical step happen.

The hope proved founded. Chastened by the November losses, several key members of the GOP House caucus, including Speaker Cox and House Appropriations chair Chris Jones, signed on to a compromise that traded endorsement for work requirements, copays, and other conservative restrictions.[6] Four Republican state senators, including the pivotal Emmett Hanger of Staunton, voted for the measure as well, leading to a 23–17 victory there. The final House count was 67–31.

The action extended to four hundred thousand low-income Virginians what for many amounted to a lifeline. Northam had been at the forefront of that change.

CHAPTER 12

Election Rebound

Two years later Northam's name was not on the November 2019 election ballot. His reputation was.

With the confessional at Fort Monroe and the aborted special session on guns behind him, Northam suddenly looked more like a team leader than an injured player. The *Washington Post* took note in a September 6 article. No one mentioned resignation when Northam attended Congressman Bobby Scott's annual Labor Day picnic in Newport News, the newspaper reported. No one protested when the governor attended a seminar at predominantly Black Virginia Union University the prior week. And when Northam delivered his mea culpa at Fort Monroe, there had been no boos, only a standing ovation. "Northam is still wounded by a blackface scandal that almost cost him his job in February. But with campaign season in full swing during a crucial election year, he is far from the pariah that most people expected," the newspaper affirmed.[1]

The *Christian Science Monitor* agreed: "His ability to recover even partially from what seemed to many a career-ending incident speaks to both his constituents' capacity to forgive and his own willingness to learn."[2]

Northam had not regained the standing he held before the controversy, but he was showing a hint of luster. His approval rating in a series of public polls conducted between August and October ranged from a low of 37 percent to a high of 51 percent. The numbers improved as the fall progressed.[3] A *Washington Post*-Schar School poll identifying gun control as the most important issue in the campaign pointed to why. In the aftermath of the Virginia Beach shooting and the aborted special session, guns were at the forefront of Northam's message as he kept up a solid schedule of campaign events through the fall. They were foremost in the minds of many voters as well.[4]

Democrats reaped the rewards on Election Day. Flipping six House seats, they emerged with a 55–45 advantage in the House and a 21–19 edge in the state senate, gaining control of both chambers for the first time in a quarter century. The working majority that Northam needed if he wanted to make substantial change on racial equity was in place.

Multiple people and forces contributed to the victory. McAuliffe campaigned hard throughout the fall, as did the state's Democratic senators and congressmen. Court-ordered redistricting of several House of Delegates seats found to have been racially gerrymandered created openings for Democrats. Disdain for President Trump continued to galvanize Democratic voters. And demographic trends underway for years continued a steady erosion in the influence of rural conservatives in western Virginia while deepening Democratic inroads into once solidly Republican suburbs in the state's eastern half.

Northam also deserved credit, however. He had raised $1.3 million during the year to contribute to the Democratic effort, besting the $824,000 raised by McAuliffe during the period. Perhaps most significantly, his emphasis on gun control inspired more than $2 million in contributions to Democratic candidates from the personal wealth of former New York mayor Michael Bloomberg and affiliated groups, including Everytown for Gun Safety.[5] The money, the most from any nonparty source, proved crucial in buying television ads late in several Democratic campaigns.

The wisdom of focusing on gun safety in the wake of the Virginia Beach shootings had paid handsome returns. "Not only did it get the people behind me, but it got significant funding behind the people that were running for election," Northam said in the aftermath. "I don't sit here and take credit for a lot of things," but starting with his campaign for lieutenant governor and continuing through races in 2015, 2017, and 2019, he had played a significant role in powering Virginia's blue wave. "I've helped to build that," he said. He had.

NORTHAM'S AUTUMN WORK INVOLVED MORE than wooing voters. It included tangible steps toward creating a more inclusive Virginia, although the results would not be evident overnight.

He had appointed a distinguished group of educators and historians to the Virginia Commission on African American History Education announced at Fort Monroe, including Newby-Alexander as one of three cochairs. The group was poised to launch a series of public panels and community hearings beginning in December. True, what was being taught to Virginia children about the African American portion of American and Virginia history was less outrageous than the lessons contained in a series of three textbooks distributed to every fourth-, seventh-, and eleventh-grade Virginia student from the 1950s to the early 1970s. Even so, it did not take commission members long to start identifying misrepresentations or omissions in current prescribed teachings.

The earlier texts, published by Charles Scribner's Sons and developed with extensive input by historians and politicians steeped in a Lost Cause point of view, had fabricated a happiness myth around bondage. A chapter in *Virginia: History, Government, Geography*, the seventh-grade text that Ralph Northam studied, illustrates the approach. Titled "How the Negroes Lived under Slavery," the chapter opens with a drawing of a fantasized Black family arriving by ship. The females were neatly attired with petticoats and bonnets. The father wore a long coat and black pants, a portmanteau at his feet, as he shook the welcoming hand of a distinguished-looking White man. Accompanying text asserted: "A feeling of strong affection existed between masters and slaves in a majority of Virginia homes." Masters "knew the best way to control their slaves was to win their confidence and affection. . . . Many Negroes were taught to read and write. . . . They went visiting at night and sometimes owned guns and other weapons."[6]

Never mind that at times the enslaved could have been lashed or worse for any one of those acts—or that, before the importation of slaves to the United States was banned in 1808, those who survived a brutal passage set foot onshore in a wretched state, not as fashionable gentry.

A further passage titled "How the Slaves Felt" asserted that "life among the Negroes of Virginia in slavery times was generally happy. The Negroes went about in a cheerful manner making a living for themselves and for those for whom they worked." While "the Negroes had their troubles and problems," they "were not worried" by the furious abolition debates. "In fact, they paid little attention to those arguments," the textbook claimed.[7] All of which would have come as a surprise to Nat Turner.

Newby-Alexander saw such false teachings as "foolishness" and "brainwashing." Unfortunately, by 2019, inaccuracies had not evaporated. In a course titled Virginia Studies, for instance, one of the "essential understandings" under state guidelines included this sentence: "Because of economic differences, the North and the South were unable to resolve their conflicts, and the South seceded from the United States." Years after most historians' study of personal letters, official documents, and transcribed speeches had identified the clash over slavery as the indisputable primary cause of the Civil War, the word *slavery* did not come up in an "essential understanding" about the source of the conflict. Instead the moral schism over human bondage was reduced to "economic differences."

The commission unearthed many more such distortions as its work progressed.

Another Northam-appointed group, the Commission to Examine Racial Inequity in Virginia Law, also was moving forward. In December members issued their first interim report, focused on outdated racist statutes and regulations remaining on Virginia lawbooks. Most if not all of those 1900–1960 laws had been effectively overturned by court rulings or practice. Still, the hundred or so statutes targeted for formal repeal offered a disturbing look at how government had fostered enduring prejudices. Examples:

A 1908 law let localities hire out vagrants for forced labor. Those individuals, many of them Black, could be transferred from one city or county to another, creating a source of cheap labor and criminalizing poverty.

A 1912 law approved cities and towns' creating "segregation districts." Allowing White and Black people to live in close proximity, the law said, endangered "public morals, public health and public order."

A 1920 law legitimized sending Black children to schools in neighboring counties, often at great distance, when no Black school existed in their own county. Racial segregation and cost-saving for localities trumped convenience for children.

A March 1924 statute forbade "any white person in this State to marry any save a white person, or a person with no other admixture of blood than white and American Indian." Racial purity was to be preserved at any cost.

In September 1956 lawmakers eliminated compulsory school attendance for any child required under *Brown v. Board of Education* to attend an integrated school. Receiving no education was preferable to an integrated one.

In 1959 lawmakers adopted a series of laws designed to thwart school integration. The statutes authorized the governor to close any public school facing forced integration through federal intervention, allowed state and local governments to fund private school tuition grants, and permitted teachers to repay state scholarships by teaching in private schools.

"My god, where would we be by now as a society?" asked commission chair Cynthia Hudson, if the same level of resolve had gone into planning an inclusive Virginia.

The report urged Northam to authorize a next step far more consequential than removing old laws from the code. Members hoped to begin ferreting out not just historical discrimination but also current laws that perpetuated inequity, even if those statutes appeared nondiscriminatory on their face. That bold task, which Northam approved, might spur true transformation in Virginia.

On yet a third front, Janice Underwood had begun setting up an office focused on confronting discriminatory practices embedded in state government by those centuries of discrimination. As the nation's first cabinet-level chief

diversity officer, she would be carving a path in the wilderness. Her mission included promoting fairness in hiring and promotion while ensuring that a diverse
set of individuals participated in decision-making.

That was no small order for one woman with a six-hundred-thousand-dollar
budget approaching more than one hundred state agencies.

Attending the ceremony at Fort Monroe in August, Underwood had felt a
shiver when Northam spoke about "righting the wrongs that began here at this
place." His words, "the more I know, the more I can do," resonated deeply. "I
remember sitting there almost with a physiological sensation from our ancestors, saying, 'You have an amazing opportunity to make sure people know that
our lives mattered, and to undo some of the systems.' I remember sitting there
thinking, 'Don't waste this opportunity.'"

A hazel-eyed blend of African and European heritage, Underwood stood
more than a head shorter than her new boss, but there was nothing diminutive
about her message as she made the rounds. "I'm not here to bite you. I don't
bite," she emphasized. Even as she navigated a host of personalities and sensi-
tivities, she knew that success would depend on finding ways to hold individuals
and agencies accountable. The authority to make that happen did not yet exist,
and time was short.

As Underwood spoke to community groups, some questioned her judgment in joining an administration tarnished by the blackface episode. "Ralph
Northam is a bigot. Why would you work for him?" she was asked. Her answer
challenged the questioners to look at their own lives. "The reason I did not call
for his resignation," she said, is that "folks in my field know that everybody has
biases, everybody has an equity story, everybody falls short of the glory. Everybody makes mistakes. And if you are in that position, you want a restorative
path back for yourself, so why wouldn't you give it to someone else?"

Outside the top echelons, a range of staff reactions greeted her arrival. "It
was, 'I'm so glad you're here. We've needed this position so badly.' It was, 'Am I
allowed to talk to you? Let me share with you what's really going on that they're
not going to tell you about.'" To her astonishment, notes were slipped under her
door or handed to her surreptitiously in the elevator. Complaints and resent-
ments emerged like cicadas, freed after years buried in silence. "It was almost
like a contemporary, twenty-first-century Underground Railroad," Underwood
described the contacts.

"That weight was difficult," she added. "Nobody told me about that when I
was interviewing." From the man who had hired her, "I saw sincerity. I certainly
sensed commitment, but, like, not knowing what to do. I think he didn't know
how to support [me], other than to laud me publicly."

If Northam did not fathom the nuances of diversity, equity, and inclusion, he did recognize the challenge of bringing a prickly new mission to state government. One perfectly good finalist for the job struck him as slightly timid. That would not do. "I knew that this was something that was going to need someone to come in and be secure and take charge," he said. Underwood fit the profile.

Moving forward, the new equity chief identified her overriding goal: creating a template to guide the many individuals assigned, in one form or another, to expand diversity and build fairness into state government. One thing she knew for certain. She did not intend to be anyone's equity prostitute—her term for someone given a title to make an organization (or a governor) look good but without any real authority or consequence. With the November elections, she felt the prospects for success soar. "We won both houses, and it was like, well, we're about to do some really big things."

THE CHANGED OUTLOOK also energized Northam and the rest of his top staff. The election had opened the door to advances that, without a legislative majority, would have been impossible. The first concrete evidence of the new day lay in Northam's proposed 2020–22 state budget, crafted in consultation with members of the Virginia Legislative Black Caucus and other Democratic leaders. By early November much of the work on that document was already complete. There had been Plan A and Plan B versions, however, tailored to different election outcomes. Plan A could go forward.

In a $135 billion, two-year budget, covering everything from Medicaid reimbursements to highway construction to outlays for public schools, most of the spending was dictated by predetermined formulas and by state and federal law and regulation. Only a few billion could be considered discretionary—that is, money that a governor and a legislature might tailor to their personal priorities and preferences.

Still, that was no piddling amount. Sitting down with Clark Mercer, Secretary of Finance Aubrey Layne, and members of the policy and legislative teams, Northam signed off on items that would put his stamp on Virginia government as much or more than many higher-octane policy fights. Deep in the weeds of a five-hundred-page budget lay enormous power: the ability to recommend which programs and organizations might benefit from dollars and cents doled out across the commonwealth.

In Virginia's way of doing business, governors operate for their first two years under a budget largely conceived by their predecessor. The 2020–22 budget was the first purely under Northam's domain. Presenting that document to House and Senate money committees on December 17, Northam dubbed it "the most progressive in Virginia history." That was not hyperbole. His proposed investments dramatically stretched Virginia's commitment to historically neglected people and causes.

He targeted $22 million to help reduce maternal mortality rates among women of color, with plans including home health visits, extension of Medicaid coverage for at-risk mothers to a year after pregnancy, and investment in maternal support from doulas, professionals trained to provide physical and emotional assistance during and after pregnancy. For early childhood education, a passion of the First Lady and the focus of much of her staff's work, he proposed $94.8 million to boost preschool access for at-risk four-year-olds, to pilot a similar project for three-year-olds, and to improve teacher training and standards for those programs.

Another $92 million would address housing affordability, soaring eviction rates, and supportive housing. The Virginia Housing Trust Fund, which helps finance affordable housing units, would see its coffers boosted to record levels. Plans called for a hefty $1.2 billion boost to K-12 education, one of the largest such single-budget increases ever proposed in Virginia. The sum included $140 million for an "at-risk add-on" for precarious schools, balancing—however slightly—school funding strategies that, in practice, heavily benefit advantaged communities. The sum included money for teacher raises, additional school counselors at each grade level, and increased instructional support for English-language learners.

A $145 million proposed outlay went to tuition-free community college for low-and-middle-income students who pursued jobs in high-demand fields, a pet cause of Northam's. Known as the G-3 Program—"Get Trained, Get a Job, Give Back"—the plan funneled economically challenged students into health care, information technology, public safety, and several other tracks likely to guarantee employment.

Additional equity proposals included $2.5 million for a Black history and cultural center in Richmond, $7 million to support historic African American history and heritage sites, and expanded funding for two historically Black state institutions of higher learning, Norfolk State and Virginia State universities.

Finally Northam's budget recommended stripping away a long-standing annual budget commitment of $83,750 for the United Daughters of the Confederacy to maintain Confederate cemeteries. The money would shift to support of African American burial grounds.

Republicans lamented the largesse. "Santa Claus Northam is going to have to get a second sleigh to carry all of these presents and goodies that he wants to extend to the citizens," scoffed Senator Norment, soon to be demoted from majority to minority leader.[8] Some progressives took issue from the opposite direction. The proposed outlay for K–12 schools—however historic it might be in total—still fell well shy of recommendations from the state board of education. Much more would be needed to bring true equity to Virginia's most disadvantaged school districts. Environmental enthusiasts, in contrast, seemed elated with the commitment to their causes. Northam had addressed his deep personal dedication to the Chesapeake Bay and environmental matters with a proposed $733 million, a record investment in new funding for the environment and clean energy.

The reaction perhaps most valued by Northam came from Lamont Bagby of the Virginia Legislative Black Caucus, who termed the document "the best budget I've seen from a governor."[9] The coordination between the governor's office and the caucus was evident in a VLBC statement, released immediately after the budget document, citing almost two dozen items that the caucus had advocated for and that were recommended for funding: eviction prevention services, more school counselors, support for the Housing Trust Fund, expanded post-incarceration support, higher teacher pay, on and on.

As the year ended, a *Washington Post* editorial attested to Northam's post-blackface rebound. Headlined "How Ralph Northam Came Back from the Political Dead," it provided perhaps the governor's best holiday present. "The history of U.S. politics is full of second chances—of scandal-scarred, disgraced and irredeemable public figures staging improbable comebacks—but few back-from the-dead narratives have been as swift and sure-footed as the one Virginia Gov. Ralph Northam has managed this year."

The editorial counted the ways: seeking counsel from Black leaders; visiting racially important historic sites; hiring the state's first director of diversity, equity, and inclusion; establishing a commission to comb state lawbooks for racial language and intent; expanding access to state contracts for women- and minority-owned firms; establishing a commission to review the teaching of Black history; and, in mid-December, introducing a proposed state budget chock-full of proposals to help minority and low-income communities.

Now the General Assembly had a majority capable of turning that blueprint into reality.

BASKING IN THE ELECTION AFTERGLOW, NORTHAM joined family and friends for a celebratory evening at the theater. The national tour of the Broadway hit *Hamilton* had arrived in Richmond for a three-week stint on November 19, setting the city's cultural scene abuzz. The story of the West Indies immigrant who helped found the nation's financial system was all the juicier because of

Alexander Hamilton's enmity with two Virginia native sons, Thomas Jefferson and James Madison.

After weeks of intense budget preparation, the governor looked forward to relaxing with an evening of music and dance.

Arriving at Richmond's glittery Altria Theater, he nodded at friendly faces, stopped to exchange a few pleasantries, and then froze.

From across the way had come an unmistakable shout: "There's blackface."

The derision, the embarrassment seemed unending. Was it his fate to wear sackcloth forever?

CHAPTER 13

New Day, Old Battles

Gazing out on the assembly of legislators, cabinet officials, and top state jurists on the night of January 8, 2020, Ralph Northam had reason to be cheered. Never mind the ongoing, daily assaults on right-wing radio and blog posts. Not only was the reception for his annual State of the Commonwealth speech as raucous and friendly as any sitting governor might wish, but the optics—at least on the Democratic side—were something to behold.

Twisting at the podium to salute the president pro tempore of the senate and the Speaker of the House of Delegates, seated behind him, Northam uttered words never spoken by any of his predecessors. "And good evening to Madam Speaker and Madam President," he said with a nod to House Speaker Eileen Filler-Corn and Senator Louise Lucas, two Democrats who had just become the first women elected to either leadership post. "The Chamber looks pretty good from up here, doesn't it?" he quipped.

Turning back to the assembly, Northam applauded the diverse congregation facing him. The body had long been the exclusive domain of White males. No longer. "It's a proud moment to look out and see a General Assembly that reflects, more than ever, the Virginia we see every day. This is truly an historic night," he said.

Indeed. An observer would have needed to dial back 139 years to find a Virginia governor and a biracial majority in the General Assembly so united in determination to advance the fortunes of minorities and the working class. During a narrow, two-year window from 1881 to 1883, the White Readjuster Party joined forces with Black Republicans to command the leadership in both chambers, as well as the governorship. Their handiwork reflected a flowering of concern for the common man and woman. They refinanced Civil War debt to allow more spending on schools and other public services; appointed a state school superintendent sympathetic to Black education; abolished the poll tax for voting; established the Virginia Normal & College Institute (later Virginia State

University), the nation's first state-financed, four-year college for Black citizens, as well as the first black mental hospital for Black Virginians; and abolished the whipping post as an instrument of public punishment, among other acts.[1]

That brief stretch represented the pinnacle of Black political influence in post–Civil War Virginia. Between 1867 and 1899, nearly one hundred Black men served in the General Assembly.[2] But their influence steadily waned after conservative Democrats bent on reasserting White rule gained control of the legislature in 1883. By 1902, when a new state constitution severely restricted Black voting through the poll tax, literacy tests, and other measures, the rout was complete. Not until 1968 did another African American—Richmond physician and civil rights activist William F. "Fergie" Reid—take a seat in the Virginia Assembly.

The legislature that convened in January 2020 offered the brightest hope for Black progress through biracial power since the Reconstruction era. African Americans held almost two dozen of 140 legislative seats, as well as an assortment of leadership posts, including eight committee chairs and the jobs of majority leader in the House and president pro tempore of the Senate.

The principal question as Northam prepared to unveil his aggressive agenda was whether the allies faced a fleeting, two-year opportunity, akin to that in the 1880s, or whether demographic changes in Virginia foretold a more extended grip on power. After years of pent-up demand under Republican legislative control, Democrats were raring for change on everything from early voting to environmental justice to parole reform to marijuana decriminalization.

"There were so many things that when I was in the Senate and then as lieutenant governor that we had been fighting for that we'd never been able to get accomplished," said Northam, describing a moment almost giddy with anticipation. Coming out of the 2019 election, "I had a lot of discussion with the leadership, a lot of communication with them, with the Black caucus. We had a well-orchestrated plan to get done what we wanted to get done. We thought that the majority of that we could get accomplished."

The situation looked different through a Republican lens. Predicting a "jewelry store smash and grab," GOP senator Bill Stanley held out hope that the revolution would be brief. "They're going to grab everything they possibly can while they can get it before the lights go on and the siren goes off. And I think when Virginia wakes up and sees what they've just done, potentially in one session, I think you may see a sea change occur in this body two years from now."[3]

Dramatic change already was underway as Northam faced the assembly that night, and not in a positive way. "Our country is divided," he lamented. "People are angry—left, right, center, urban, rural, men, women. Politics has grown too much about tearing each other down and too little about public service. And eight days into 2020, we know we have a long and painful election year ahead."

Northam was more aware than most of the impending danger. His calls for legislation surrounding gun purchases and usage had spawned a surge of hate mail. He might appear to the assembled crowd to be his normal self that night. He was not. As he spoke, underneath his shirt, coat, and tie, he was wearing a bulletproof vest. For the rest of his time in office, he would keep two sets of clothing in his office—one in his normal size, the other large enough to accommodate the vest.

Secretly, for the next two years, until he left office, he would rarely appear in public without that protection.

INTEL REPORTS REACHING THE FUSION CENTER at state police headquarters in Richmond in early January 2020 prompted chilling memories of the 2017 debacle in Charlottesville.

Part of a little-known network created in the wake of the 9/11 terrorist attacks, the central Virginia center functioned through a collaboration of federal and state agencies, working with local law enforcement to detect and disrupt terrorist activity. In the years since 2001, domestic extremism had become as potent a concern as external threats.

Across the state gun rights activists were arming for the annual Lobby Day at the capitol on Monday, January 20. The Virginia Citizens Defense League and the National Rifle Association, longtime staples of state politics, were rallying members for a show of force against a package of eight gun-control measures introduced by Northam and his allies. This time, it appeared, new faces would join the homegrown crowd. Anti-government and White supremacist factions such as the Proud Boys, the Three Percenters, and the Boogaloo Boys had entered the mix. If scuttlebutt flying across the internet and various back channels was correct, some of the newcomers—possibly some old-timers also—had more than peaceful protest in mind.

Law enforcement had picked up talk about individuals planning to storm the state capitol. The insurgents would be armed with powerful weapons. Some chatter welcomed the event as an opportunity to accelerate the start of a long-anticipated race war. No one knew then, of course, that the precise scenario feared for Virginia's government complex in January 2020 would play out at the US Capitol a year later. Based on the 2017 events in Charlottesville, law enforcement and political leaders did know to take nothing for granted.

"I was worried. These are troubled people," said Northam.

The governor was not alone in his concern. The First Lady had noticed the thick, white shell hanging in her husband's closet a few days earlier. He had not mentioned the vest to her, but she knew immediately what it was. During a postelection Women's Summit at the University of Virginia in November 2017, Pam had first seen one when Hillary Clinton observed that her Nehru jacket fit well over her bulletproof vest. "My heart was broken for her," she said. "It's so unfair that people who chose to serve the public have to worry about their lives."

Now, Pam's husband was wearing one as well. "When I saw that the first time, that was tough," she said. "You know that [danger] in your head, but to feel it in your heart is a whole other thing."

Planning for Lobby Day had gotten underway immediately after the December holidays as attendance forecasts swelled into the thousands. Convoluted lines of authority complicated the preparations. Capitol police held authority within the capitol building. State police oversaw the capitol grounds. And Richmond city police were responsible for surrounding sidewalks and streets. "If twenty thousand people are coming, regardless of what they're coming for, this is a logistical big affair to work out," said Grant Neely, the governor's communications chief. "But when they're coming to protest and they're angry, and there's this whole jurisdictional issue," then the potential for calamity mounts.

Critical questions needed deciding: Would the capitol building and the grounds be opened or closed to protesters? Would a curfew be set or not? And in light of Virginia laws allowing open carry of firearms, would there be any constraint on weapons, especially assault rifles? The latter question especially riled Northam. Few topics animated him more.

"What bothers me when they have protests up here, and they have these folks walking around with assault weapons, it's nothing more than to intimidate people. And in Virginia, we don't need the intimidation," he said. "If someone wants to carry an assault weapon, go join the military or a police force, which is probably something they couldn't do anyway, so now there's a bunch of wannabes out there."

Meeting with representatives of the various law enforcement groups in his cabinet conference room, Northam heard their advice that the protesters be allowed to bring weapons onto the capitol grounds. The concern was that "if we didn't let them, it would upset them, and then it would spill into the city of Richmond," Northam recalled. The image incensed him. "I just sat there and said, 'Nope. We're not going to let people come on these capitol grounds with assault weapons.'"

His clarity on a deeply held conviction prevailed. "They didn't like it, but they said, 'Okay, we'll make arrangements.'" To Northam's mind the decision sent a necessary message. "We are not going to sit here and be intimidated with people walking around with assault weapons, especially when you're threatening to storm the capitol," he said.

Five days before the scheduled protests, surrounded by law enforcement leaders and other top officials, Northam informed Virginians of the ground rules. An emergency declaration, extending from Friday to Tuesday, banned all weapons from the capitol grounds. The list included sticks, bats, chains, projectiles, and, yes, guns of any type. Metal fencing would soon surround Capitol Square, offering access at a single point equipped with multiple metal detectors. This was not an assault on the First or Second Amendments, he insisted. It was a prudent, necessary step in response to clear danger. Police were even picking up talk of weaponized drones. They had evidence that individuals had been conducting hostile surveillance operations within the capitol, monitoring exits and entrances.

"These are considered credible and serious threats," Northam continued. "This intel comes from mainstream channels both offline and online such as alternative dark web channels used by white nationalists outside of Virginia. These are fueled by misinformation and conspiracy theories. No one wants another incident like the one we saw in Charlottesville in 2017. We will not allow that mayhem and violence."

Anxious to reduce partisan blowback, the administration urged Republican and Democratic legislative leaders to meet at the Fusion Center at state police headquarters for an intelligence briefing in an ultra-secure setting with no electronics or weapons allowed. About a dozen showed up. "Everyone came away convinced that we needed to take it seriously," said Secretary of Public Safety Brian Moran.

Any remaining doubts were erased on Thursday when the FBI announced the arrests in Maryland of three suspected members of the Base, a violent, paramilitary group dedicated to creation of a White ethnostate, a political jurisdiction excluding people of color. The armed trio, including a former Canadian Army reservist trained in explosives, were reported to have been on their way to Richmond for the gun protest.[4] The next day three more members of the Base were arrested in Georgia. Almost two years later, in presentencing court filings, federal prosecutors revealed that two of the men arrested in route to Richmond had discussed assassinating Speaker Filler-Corn, who is Jewish.[5] Eventually two of the men received nine-year prison sentences; the third, five years.

Moran and other Virginia officials were alarmed at having not been notified in advance of the pending arrests, given the potential for violence had the men eluded authorities. But they were grateful to leading state Republicans who rose above partisanship to reject extremism outright. "So there's no mistake, this is my message to any group that would subvert this event: you are not welcome here," Delegate Todd Gilbert of Shenandoah, the burly, newly elected House Republican leader, said in a statement. "While we and our Democratic colleagues may have differences, we are all Virginians and we will stand united in opposition to any threats of violence or civil unrest from any quarter."

Northam was relieved, as well, when the Virginia Supreme Court upheld the Capitol Square weapons ban, just hours before it was to take effect.

AS JANUARY 20 DAWNED, masses of gun aficionados began pouring into downtown streets, a human throng unprecedented in memory. By midday officials estimated that six thousand weaponless protesters had passed through metal detectors onto Capitol Square. Guesstimates of those packing streets and sidewalks outside, weapons attached, were twice that number—or more.

Bent on making their voices heard, out-of-town militia groups, some reportedly from as far as California, marched in formation until the growing throngs blocked movement. Pistols bulged from holsters. AR-15 and .338 Lapua rifles swung from shoulders. Camouflage and tactical gear outpaced jeans and ski jackets as the outfit du jour. Flags, banners, and handheld placards announced opposition to anything other than an unfettered, unregulated right to bear arms. "Come and take it," challenged a white flag emblazoned with a picture of a semiautomatic gun. Celebrity conspiracy theorist Alex Jones drove by in a Humvee, exhorting listeners to stand against "tyranny." Delighted protestors equated the impassioned but peaceful carnival atmosphere to a Second Amendment Super Bowl or a gun-friendly Woodstock.[6]

From afar President Trump tweeted out support and a call to arms: "The Democrat Party in the Great Commonwealth of Virginia are working hard to take away your 2nd Amendment rights. This is just the beginning. Don't let it happen, VOTE REPUBLICAN in 2020."

Battalions of local and state police watched the scene impassively from rooftops and street corners, patrol cars and bicycles, stepping forward at the least hint of provocation. When a homemade guillotine appeared with a sign taunting, "The only penalty for treason is death," the officers quickly removed it. Gun-control advocates lessened the potential for violence by urging their supporters to stay away.

The undisputed villain of the crowd was monitoring events from a secure location outside Richmond. He was not personally frightened, Northam said, but his protective unit had decreed that he must not put himself near harm's way. Given the online vitriol aimed at the governor, that advice seemed sound. Protesters amplified the disdain. One poster pictured Northam with a Hitler mustache and a Nazi armband. A man circulated a petition demanding the recall of the man he labeled "Radical Ralph." Another teased, "Governor Northam, I think I found the white supremacist. Unfortunately, it's you!"

As the crowd began to disperse in early afternoon, Northam and others in the administration breathed a collective sigh of relief. There had been only a single arrest, that of a young woman who had refused to remove a face covering in defiance of state law. Even that charge was dismissed some weeks later. "We are all thankful that today passed without incident," Northam responded in a statement. The weeks of planning had paid off.

Some gun activists gloated that the huge police presence had been unnecessary for a group of largely patriotic citizens. On the surface the argument held merit. Events a year later exposed the limitations of that narrative. The question bore asking: If the same level of preparation and resolve to prevent violence had greeted protesters in Washington, DC, on January 6, 2021, might one of the most horrific episodes in the nation's history have been defused?

Despite the size of the January 20 demonstration, polls showed that a large majority of Virginians wanted constraints on easy access to guns. Legislators elected on the promise of action were not about to be intimidated. Over the next weeks, seven of the eight bills endorsed by Northam flew to passage. The measures established universal background checks for all firearm purchases; limited handgun purchases in Virginia to one a month; created an "Extreme Risk Protective Order," also known as a red flag law, allowing firearms to be temporarily seized from a dangerous person; mandated reporting of lost and stolen firearms within forty-eight hours; increased penalties for recklessly exposing children to firearms; ordered individuals subject to protective orders to turn over their firearms to authorities; and clarified the right of localities to regulate firearms in public buildings and spaces.

All told, the package was among the strongest passed in any American state in recent decades. It did not, however, include a final, eighth measure, the one dearest to Northam's heart: a ban on assault weapons.

"VICTORY!!!!!!!!!!!!!!!!!!!!!," tweeted Philip Van Cleave, president of the Virginia Citizens Defense League and the organizer of the January gun rights rally, after the ban failed. "Bunch of wimps," groused senate President Pro Tempore Lucas of the four Democrats in her caucus who had joined with Republicans to defeat the bill. "We will be back next year," gamely promised Alena Yarmosky, Northam's press secretary.[7]

A year later that promise had evaporated. An assault weapons ban did not make Northam's list of 2021 legislative priorities. The omission affirmed a deeply disappointing reality. He and his team could not put together the votes. "It's not going to happen while I'm governor, but I hope it will in time," he sighed. "We just don't need those."

CHAPTER 14

Democrats Rising

Like water bursting through a breached dam, progressive legislation pent up for years gushed through the General Assembly, setting Virginia government on a new course. With dizzying speed, Democratic lawmakers, Black and White, steered their way past Republican barriers decades in the making. In committee hearings and floor debates, the new majority set out to strike down restrictive voting laws, a stagnant minimum wage, protections for Confederate monuments, a carbon-dependent electric grid, abortion constraints, gender discrimination, hefty penalties for marijuana possession, and years of opposition to an Equal Rights Amendment to the US Constitution.

Throughout early January Northam's days were steeped in announcements of proposals for momentous change. He stood side by side with Democratic legislative leaders, many of them Black, announcing a thirteen-point "Historic Justice and Equity Plan" here, an eleven-point "Common-Sense Virginia 2020 Plan" there, a fifteen-point criminal justice reform agenda on yet another day.

As newly installed leaders scrambled to gain a footing and legislators raced to meet the deadlines of a two-month session, the busy schedule at home left little time for noticing events abroad. Three days after Northam addressed the opening of the 2020 session, Chinese state media reported the first death from a mysterious pneumonia that had sickened dozens. As the weaponized throngs from Lobby Day headed home just under two weeks later, the United States confirmed its first case of what had been identified as a novel coronavirus. The patient, a Washington state resident in his thirties, had recently traveled to Wuhan, China, the epicenter of the outbreak.

In Richmond such startling news did not compete with the challenges of a political revolution—not yet.

For the Virginia Legislative Black Caucus, the 2020 session was a celebration of years of work in the political trenches and an opportunity to press for long-denied goals. Emboldened by its newly acquired clout, the twenty-three-member Black caucus pressed both publicly and privately for a public policy reboot.

Press releases applauded Northam's actions while observing that success would be measured by more than words. The caucus's 2020 legislative agenda, released on January 8, stressed equal access to the ballot box, freeing communities from mass incarceration, empowering workers through an increased minimum wage and employee protections, providing housing stability as a human right, expanding access to quality health care, disrupting the school-to-prison pipeline, recognizing the devastating impact of climate change on communities of color, and embracing the gun-control agenda. "We accomplish equity of opportunity by breaking down barriers to education, economic security, justice, and democracy," the caucus stressed.

That agenda, combined with the sharpened determination of his boss to advance racial equity, fit the long-held priorities of Northam chief of staff Clark Mercer. "Housing has always been my issue—where people can live and their access to capital, and their ability to pass wealth on to the next generation is 'the' equity issue," he said. "For me, getting into some of the structural racism issues, I was very excited."

Mercer's job demanded coordinating the executive branch with legislative leaders to turn aspirations into reality. His office whiteboard was jammed with objectives for the new session. "I asked the governor when he became governor, in your wildest dreams what would be your top list of things you'd like to get done? It was Medicaid expansion. It was getting Amazon here. [The groundwork for snaring the corporate behemoth's second headquarters in Arlington had been laid by the McAuliffe administration.] It was becoming the best state in the country for business. It was increasing the minimum wage, increasing the felony larceny threshold. It was becoming a leader in the country in clean energy, broadband."

The term "racial equity" did not make the list, although several of the ideas circulating under that banner in the 2020 session did. The blackface scandal had caused the administration to push reset. Initiatives on the old list aimed at erasing barriers to equal opportunity had been elevated to the forefront. New ones had been added.

Given Mercer's life experiences—attending a majority Black high school, cross-racial dating, having a Black family member, writing a senior thesis at Yale on Baltimore's urban renewal, working for several years at the Urban Land Institute—the chief reflected a new generation of White leaders at the capitol. He and his wife, Kelly Thomasson, serving in Northam's cabinet as secretary of the commonwealth, had come of age as racial taboos were toppling. Friendships with several members of the Black caucus had increased his pain during the blackface scandal. As the governor reemerged, those connections also contributed to an opportunity for shared progress. "You kind of have to build those relationships, and some folks don't have 'em. We do," he said matter-of-factly.

Mercer recognized what many in the lobbyist, press, and governmental circles did not: the old days were behind them. "There are members of the Black caucus who folks don't reach out to, and they're the ones running the capitol now. There's a cultural and generational shift going on," he said.

Sitting in an office decorated with colorful one-gallon oyster tins, a reflection of his paternal ancestors' livelihood on eastern Virginia's watery Northern Neck, Mercer mused over both his and Northam's evolving understandings on race. "My cup runneth over with White privilege. I recognize that. I have a lot left to learn," he said. Still, he argued, among both Black and White people, "probably this generation is in a little bit better spot" than many preceding ones to recognize racial injustice and effect change.

A year after it struck, the blackface scandal had receded somewhat into the background, but it remained permanently fixed in his mind. "It's not anything that we'll ever, quote-unquote, 'put behind us.' I use it every day as motivation to do good work," he said. In Mercer's view White critics might deride Northam's lapses, but they would be better served to mirror his example. "I think to be a middle-aged man that grew up in rural Virginia and to be willing to listen and learn and admit that he didn't know everything," that offered a potent model. "It's important for this country that more White guys, like myself, be willing to question our preconceived views."

Northam's low-key style meshed with the emerging Black assertiveness in legislative power circles. "When we need to, he'll step out and he'll say something, but we haven't needed to have a lot of bravado. We're not going to go out there and take all the credit for things happening. We're not spike-the-football type folks," Mercer said.

Northam's showing himself to be a share-the-glory partner was another step toward reconciliation. "As time went along, we built that trust back up," said Delegate Bagby. What caused the rebound? "The commitment to the agenda of the caucus, the budget, a whole lot of things."

A FEBRUARY 12 HEADLINE in the *Virginia Mercury* documented the earthquake: "In Five Weeks, Virginia Democrats Reshape Decades of State Policy."

"At the halfway point of a hectic, 60-day legislative session, Virginia's new Democratic majorities are dismantling decades of Republican-approved policy and advancing a broad progressive agenda," the online news outlet reported. Voters in the November election "wanted change. They wanted action," House

Speaker Filler-Corn told reporter Graham Moomaw. "And we are doing exactly that."

The changes were both substantive and symbolic.

In a state so steeped in Confederate iconography and deference to Lost Cause symbols that even many progressives had become blind to them, the eye of government had refocused. Why was Robert E. Lee, a US Army colonel who had committed treason against the United States, one of two native sons representing Virginia in Statuary Hall at the US Capitol? Why, especially, when Lee had been the only one of eight West Point graduates from Virginia holding the rank of colonel at the beginning of the Civil War to renounce his oath?[1] Why for 131 years had Virginians celebrated Lee's birth with a state holiday, adding the name of a second West Point graduate and defector—Gen. Stonewall Jackson—to Lee-Jackson Day in 1904? Why if a city or county, even a majority-Black one, wanted to banish a Confederate statue from a place of public honor, say, a courthouse lawn, did state law block it from doing so?

None of those actions seemed justifiable to Northam and his allies in 2020. Each would be swept into history's dustbin before the year passed. Black caucus members took center stage in their demise. Legislation sponsored by Senator Lucas of Portsmouth and Delegate Jeion Ward of Hampton called for Lee's removal from Statuary Hall and created a commission to name a replacement. Within months Barbara Rose Johns (Powell) had been chosen to replace him. As a sixteen-year-old Johns had led a student walkout in Prince Edward County in 1951 that would result in one of the five legal cases later combined into *Brown v. Board of Education of Topeka, Kansas*, desegregating the nation's public schools.

Bills sponsored by Delegate McQuinn of Richmond and Senator Mamie Locke of Hampton overturned Virginia's prohibition against removing public war memorials, a restriction aimed primarily at shielding the scores of Confederate monuments saturating the Virginia landscape. In creating a public process for dismantling such iconography, the legislation opened a legal path for removal of the Lee statue in Charlottesville, which had ignited the fatal Unite the Right rally in August 2017. Efforts to topple the statue had been snared in a legal web ever since.

Lee-Jackson Day also was put to rest. Launched in 1889 in tribute to Lee, the holiday had included a bizarre, sixteen-year run in the 1980s and '90s as Lee-Jackson-King Day. Admirers of Dr. Martin Luther King Jr. had recognized the combination as the only way to get a Virginia holiday honoring the slain civil rights icon. Legislation sponsored by Senator Lucas and Delegate Joe Lindsey of Norfolk ended the anachronistic practice of deifying the Confederate generals. The assembly designated Election Day as a state holiday instead.

"Racial discrimination is rooted in many of the choices we have made about who and what to honor, and in many of the laws that have historically governed this commonwealth," Northam said in signing the bills. A version of history "that doesn't include everyone . . . has been given promise and authority for far too long." Regrettably the reforms passed each chamber essentially on party-line votes, without Republican support.

By the time the General Assembly adjourned, the tumbling cascade had become a torrent. Once the new laws took effect on July 1, the revisions would impact almost every corner of Virginia government.

Citizens no longer would have to justify voting absentee by choosing from an approved list of excuses. They could do so for any reason whatsoever up to forty-five days before an election. The penalty for possessing small amounts of marijuana had been slashed from jail time and a five-hundred-dollar fine to a twenty-five-dollar civil penalty. A study group had been set up to work toward legalization. The felony larceny threshold, the point at which penalties for theft soar, had been hiked to one thousand dollars, up from just two hundred dollars two years earlier. The Virginia Values Act, first of its kind in the South, prohibited discrimination against the LGBTQ community in housing, employment, lending, and other venues. A mandatory ultrasound and a twenty-four-hour waiting period before obtaining an abortion had been overturned. Abortion clinics no longer would be regulated by the same restrictive rules as hospitals. After four decades of refusal, Virginia had become the thirty-eighth state to ratify the Equal Rights Amendment to the US Constitution. The minimum wage would go from $7.50 to $12.00 over a three-year period. An estimated three hundred thousand undocumented immigrants could obtain driver-privilege cards. Local governments were empowered to engage in collective bargaining with employee groups, and five cities were authorized to hold referenda on adopting casino gambling. The state's dominant energy company had been directed to generate all electricity from 100 percent renewable sources by 2045.

Not every priority of the Virginia Legislative Black Caucus had been achieved. Disputes between a more liberal House and a more moderate Senate had stopped some measures. "We walked out with the understanding that we had unfinished business, especially in the area of justice reform," said Delegate Bagby.

Still, progressive goals unrealized through legislative generations had been achieved. To those who said lawmakers had gone too far, Mercer had a ready rebuttal: "That's not their job to stay in the majority for fifty years. Their job is to put good policies on the books and improve the lives of Virginians." He insisted that in most cases lawmakers had done nothing more than what a majority of state residents wanted. "The state has changed. Not everyone in Richmond catches up with that."

THE ELATION WAS SHORT-LIVED. A new villain soon quieted the celebration.

The same day lawmakers ended the 2020 legislative session, March 12, Northam switched hats, turning his focus from politics to medicine. Alarmed by evidence that the virus now known as COVID-19 was spreading rapidly, he declared a statewide emergency. A day later President Trump issued a national-emergency order. Simultaneously Northam took the dramatic step of closing Virginia public schools for a minimum of two weeks. During the stretch he would assess whether they could reopen safely, he said.

The next day, March 14, Virginia reported its first COVID-19 fatality, that of a seventy-year-old man in the southeastern Peninsula Health District. The man, who had contacted the virus from an unknown source, died of respiratory failure.

For the next fifteen months, the governor's office would operate by split screen, one eye focused on the regular workings of government, the other on the most perilous public health crisis to hit the world in a century. Three months later a third screen—social justice—would join the mix.

For the time being, two challenges proved arduous enough.

CHAPTER 15

A Viral Disruption

The nation's only physician-governor recognized early on the signs flaring around COVID-19. They spelled danger.

"The first case in Virginia was up in Fort Belvoir," he said. "But the first wave of individuals was in James City County [near Williamsburg]. Some folks that had traveled, come back, gone to a party. A number of them were sick, but one or two of them died, and that's what really got my attention. There were a lot of unknowns, but I saw how it was spreading and I saw that people were dying from it, so I knew that we had a problem on our hands."

Northam understood how deadly viruses, unimpeded, hopscotching from city to city, then nation to nation, can explode exponentially over weeks and months into a full-bore global pandemic. As an army doctor, trained in chemical and biological warfare, he knew the importance of rapid testing, isolating infected individuals, and protecting caregivers. He recognized the potential for normal health-care systems to be overwhelmed. Knowing all that, he was on edge. Even with training, "I'd never lived through one. It was learning as you go." Much later he would be able to say, "I think things happen for a reason. I've been able to wrap my arms around it." At the beginning there could be no such confidence.

Northam's communications office issued its first COVID-related press release on March 4. There were no reported cases in the state—yet. State health officials had created an incident management team shortly after the virus was identified in Asia. The group was "continuously monitoring" the coronavirus's progress worldwide.

Less than two weeks later, the quiet evaporated. Northam's March 12 emergency order activated services across the commonwealth. Already, to the governor's mind, there were signs of dysfunction in the national response. "It has become increasingly clear that states must take a primary leadership role in the national response to COVID-19," he noted in the announcement. A spate of orders and directives over the next several days drew an ever-tighter dragnet around the lives of ordinary Virginians. On March 17 the governor ordered restaurants, theaters, and fitness centers to reduce capacity to ten patrons or close. A week later he banned gatherings of more than ten people and shut schools for the remainder of the year, becoming the nation's second governor—six days behind Kansas governor Laura Kelly—to take that radical but soon-to-be-common step. Directives postponing elective surgeries, ordering Virginians to stay at home for nonessential outings, and narrowing occupancy in retail establishments followed in rapid succession.

Always an early riser, Northam took to arriving at the office between 7 and 7:15 AM for a daily meeting with Mercer, Secretary of Public Safety Moran, Secretary of Health and Human Resources Carey, state health commissioner Norman Oliver, and communications chief Neely. Frequently Secretary of Defense and Veteran Affairs Carlos Hopkins joined the group. The team reviewed data on rising caseloads and honed short- and long-term strategy. That pattern continued for months. Daily Press briefings became a three-times-a-week staple. A goal was to project calm, but the sea of unknowns and the mounting consternation over a lack of national direction were alarming. "We were in the dark about so much of this," recalled Moran. No one knew the impact of the virus on children, for instance. The gap especially troubled a pediatric neurologist such as Northam.

One rapid decision called for consultant Mark Bergman to be near the governor's side. As Northam faced the second full-blown crisis of his term—the blackface scandal was the first—he wanted instant access to Bergman's expertise on messaging and political fallout. Both Ralph and Pam Northam appealed to Bergman to consider moving from Connecticut to Richmond. Easy airline commutes likely would soon be shutting down. Bergman's wife, Rachel Goldstein, was seven months pregnant with their second child. The couple was worried about the rapidly escalating COVID caseloads in the Northeast and the possible dangers of delivering a baby in the altered climate.

By March 17, just two days after the Northams made their request, Bergman, his wife, and young son were en route to Richmond. They moved in temporarily with his parents and brought down the rest of their household goods a month later. Their uprooting reflected the sense of crisis and upended normalcy for many as the nation entered a stretch unlike anything most living Americans had experienced.

As Northam worked to craft a state response to COVID-19, his astonishment and outright disgust at some of what was happening—or not happening—in Washington, DC, grew. "We were asked as governors to fight a biological war with no direction from Washington and pretty much zero supplies," he said.

The army training he'd received on chemical and biological warfare was predicated on rapidly mustering resources and establishing sharp lines of command. Instead states were being forced to compete for essential equipment, and to his mind much of what was emanating from the White House was gibberish.

"The testing we had initially was being sent to the CDC [Centers for Disease Control and Prevention] in Atlanta with a turnaround time of ten to fourteen days, and that helped nobody. We had no PPE [personal protective equipment, such as gloves, gowns, and face masks]. PPE wasn't being manufactured in this country. A lot of it was coming especially from Asia, and everybody was jockeying around. There was no coordination coming from Washington. Each day the numbers kept creeping up, creeping up. It was difficult, and what was really difficult was Mr. Trump and his attitude," the governor recalled.

Among the claims triggering Northam's disdain was Trump's assertion in early March that "anybody that wants a test can get a test. That's what the bottom line is . . . and the tests are all perfect." That was far from the truth. Repeatedly the president made far-fetched comments similar to one on February 27: "It's going to disappear. One day—it's like a miracle—it will disappear," he said of the virus. That too was a lie. "And one of my favorite days," said Northam, "was the press conference when he talked about using disinfectants, putting them in the body. And light." Trump later walked back the statements, but at an April 23 press conference he had speculated about the prospects for attacking the coronavirus with a disinfectant "by injection inside or almost a cleaning" of the human body. He also wondered that day what might happen if "we hit the body with a tremendous, whether it's ultraviolet or just very powerful, light."[1]

Regular briefings for the nation's governors heightened Northam's scorn. In one, attended by Trump himself, Northam said he was so dismayed by the obsequiousness of Republican governors that he left the phone call. "I have never been in a situation where just one after the other, these Republican governors would just tell President Trump how wonderful he was and all the good work he was doing, and it was literally nauseating to me. I said [to staff], 'You all can keep listening, but I can't take it anymore. I'm out of here.'"

He was equally rattled by a conference call with Dr. Deborah Birx, the White House coronavirus response coordinator. "I was down in the situation room, and I asked her a question: 'If we don't get this under control from the leadership perspective, what do you see as the worst-case scenario?' And she totally danced around it. And I didn't say anything out of respect, but it's like, dammit, you're in a position where you've got the president's ear, and either he cooperates with the science and with Dr. Fauci and what you all are recommending, or call him out on it. And she never would and never did. That was very frustrating to me."

As least so far as Trump was concerned, the contempt appeared mutual. In mid-April, just after releasing an "Opening Up America Again" plan that assigned ultimate responsibility to governors, Trump issued back-to-back tweets deriding three blue-state chief executives, including Northam. "LIBERATE MINNESOTA," he began, followed by "LIBERATE MICHIGAN," then "LIBERATE VIRGINIA, and save your great 2nd Amendment. It is under siege!"

At the time Northam's COVID stay-at-home order extended into June, one of the longest such periods nationally. Meanwhile Michigan governor Gretchen Whitmer was under mounting attack at home for her shutdown and masking protocols. As armed activists swarmed the Michigan capitol by the hundreds over the next weeks, the danger posed by presidential flame-throwing grew more apparent. The general public was not fully aware of how perilous the situation had become until the following October. Then thirteen individuals attached to a far-right group known as the Wolverine Watchmen were charged with a combination of federal and state crimes for allegedly plotting to kidnap Whitmer and overthrow the state government. Once again, what seemed outlandish at the time appeared less so after January 6, 2021, when an insurrection played out in Washington, DC.[2]

During a hearing in federal district court in Grand Rapids, Michigan, in mid-October, the FBI said the scheme extended to the Old Dominion. Citing Northam by name, Special Agent Richard Trask II said anti-government instigators meeting in Dublin, Ohio, had listed the Virginia governor as a possible target along with Whitmer.[3]

Unaware that he had been in such danger, Northam said he did not dwell on the report. A far greater sense of intimidation had come during the summer between Trump's "LIBERATE VIRGINIA" tweet and the federal court hearing in Michigan. Speaking at an outdoor parking lot in Rocky Mount about plans for broadband expansion in southern Virginia, Northam was confronted by an assault-weapon-toting member of the Boogaloo Boys. The man, who wore an ammunition vest and wielded a laser pointer, stood just a few feet from Northam, mouthing derogatory retorts as the governor spoke. Northam's armed protective unit took up positions on both sides of the man as the talk continued.

"There were eight or ten other Caucasian individuals that were waving Trump flags. I think two different groups," he described the scene. "That was really unnerving, to be standing there, this guy the distance from me to you." Despite heightened adrenalin, Northam did not retreat. "I never want to give in to let them feel like they're winning," he said.

At the time the incident went unreported. For Northam, in retrospect, the moment offered a personal taste of hazards to come.

AS SPRING ADVANCED COVID-19 perils extended beyond public health. The state budget also faced jeopardy. With state revenues sinking and businesses struggling to avoid collapse, expensive progressive priorities, tantalizingly within reach, suddenly began to recede. Hoping to prevent backpedaling, the Virginia Legislative Black Caucus urged Northam not to abandon hard-won causes. "The VLBC strongly urges you to sign into law, as is, the various worker protections and worker support measures, especially raising Virginia's minimum wage," the Black lawmakers pressed. It would be "inhumane," at a time when the federal government was offering businesses loans and grants, to leaving essential workers struggling "under less than a livable wage," they wrote on April 8.

As for "the most progressive budget in Virginia history," the VLBC urged Northam not to cancel funding for historically Black colleges and other equity-based initiatives.

To no avail. Much as he shared the VLBC's goals, Northam felt global insecurity trumped, at least temporarily. Disappointing liberal allies, on April 12 he froze all new discretionary spending, including the hundreds of millions of dollars intended to address longstanding inequities in K–12 school funding, expansion of the Virginia Preschool Initiative, and support for historically Black colleges and cultural and heritage sites. Based on raw revenue numbers, Northam saw no choice. "We hit the pause button on a lot of the investments we'd made," he said. "It was just what we had to do."

Nor, with the economy reeling, did the time seem right to him to saddle employers with new financial obligations. He resisted Republican calls to abandon worker advances altogether, but he postponed the effective dates of several historic pieces of legislation: an increase in the state's minimum wage, a requirement that some government contractors pay "prevailing wages," and provisions allowing public workers to unionize.

A second letter from the Black caucus a few weeks later tested its members' alliance with Northam. The VLBC warned in graphic terms that a first-phase reopening of a shuttered state, planned for mid-May, could perpetuate a history of neglect and outright abuse for domestic, factory, and other low-income workers. "Under the current plan, and with the already existent racial disparities that this pandemic and economic crisis are perpetuating, we will be creating a situation where Black and Brown Virginians . . . will become guinea pigs for our economy," the caucus warned. "Black and Brown people have been experimented on and used as unwilling test subjects before—we cannot allow that to be repeated here."

The suggestion that the administration might intentionally conduct experiments on people of color went too far for Northam and Mercer. "We all took serious issue" with the language, despite understanding the overall sentiment, the chief of staff bristled. Even so, there was no dispute that, as with so much else, the pandemic had a disproportionately cruel impact on people of color. The tragic fact would become undeniable as the year progressed. Nationwide the CDC reported in November 2020 that residents of Black communities were being hospitalized at 3.7 times the rate in White communities. In Richmond at a similar point, the hospitalization rate for Black city residents was more than five times that for White residents, even though the two groups accounted for roughly equal shares of the city's population. Latino deaths and hospitalizations were starkly disproportionate as well.

As the months passed, the delivery disparities would remain a point of contention between administration officials struggling to keep pace with a widening pandemic and community activists wanting them to do more to curb historic patterns of disadvantage for low-income workers and people of color. Senator McClellan observed one such gap. Traditionally, she knew as a parent, health departments communicated about free clinics or Medicaid enrollment by sending flyers home with schoolchildren. With schools shut down, that avenue of communication about masks and other safety protocols evaporated. When it came to COVID and working or low-income parents, "they're not watching the press conference. They're not getting the governor's email. They're not getting the press release, so what is the plan to intentionally share that information with them?" she asked.

McClellan's efforts to urge the administration and local health officials to create an alternate method of flyer distribution failed. Frustrated, she observed, "There are blind spots because of who is or isn't in the room and whose perspective is or isn't there" when decisions are made. A verbal commitment to end disparity went only so far. In the midst of a crisis, the gap between White leadership and on-the-ground realities in marginalized communities remained.

MAY PROVED A TESTY MONTH FOR NORTHAM as citizens struggled with isolation, financial insecurity, and uncertain futures. The national focus at that moment was on testing, and Virginia was not stacking up well against its peers. For a brief time, the state was at or near the bottom in tests per capita. Scrambling to unravel and correct the problem, officials combined the numbers of viral tests and antibody tests, in effect, mixing apples and oranges. When scientists called them out in the *Atlantic* magazine, Mercer and Northam were left trying to explain away the decision. Over time the problem was corrected.[4]

Once again a public opinion poll gave Northam greater confidence than the daily news digest. A Roanoke College poll, conducted between May 3 and May 17, showed that his job approval rating had soared during the pandemic, improving by nineteen percentage points since February. The rebound from 40 percent approval to 59 percent suggested that Virginians were rallying around their leader in a time of crisis. Northam's steady, comprehensible updates in his regular COVID-19 briefings appeared to resonate.

Still, amid frightening uncertainty and a volatile political climate, any misstep was bait for critics. Back home in Virginia Beach over Memorial Day weekend, Northam mingled maskless with oceanside visitors. Poised to impose a mandatory mask requirement the following week, the governor appeared to be violating his own standards. He had not yet specified whether the mask mandate would apply outdoors. It turned out to be indoors only. Even so, critics charged hypocrisy in his wandering the boardwalk without a mask and posing elbow-to-elbow for photographs.

"Physician, heal thyself," chided Gilbert, the House Republican leader.[5]

On Sunday, May 24, Northam acknowledged that he had erred the previous day in leaving his face covering in the car. "We are all learning how to operate in this new normal, and it's important to be prepared," his office said in a statement.

Within twenty-four hours, a killing by police twelve-hundred miles away in Minneapolis, Minnesota, set off yet another national upheaval, prompting emergency orders of a different sort. As racial norms shattered, one truth seemed indisputable. There would be no going back to the old ways.

PART IV

INTO THE BREACH

The tipping point for Barbara Rose Johns came on a morning in 1950 when she was so busy rushing her younger brothers and sisters to the school bus that she forgot her own lunch. By the time she'd retrieved it, the vehicle carting Black children to Robert Russa Moton High School in the county seat town of Farmville had come and gone. Barbara was left standing by the country roadside, hoping to thumb a ride into town.

An hour later, the fifteen-year-old was still standing when a school bus half-filled with White children motored by on its way to the all-White Farmville High School. The bus, she knew, would go right by her school. There was no good reason in her mind for the driver to ignore her, but he did. "Right then and there, I decided indeed something had to be done about this inequality—but I still didn't know what," she wrote later in a personal account.[1]

The idea that she and other Black students in Prince Edward County were receiving a second-class education was not new to Barbara. The bright, introspective student had traveled to various competitions and meetings across Virginia, and the gap in White school facilities and her own was plain to see. "I spent many days in my favorite hangout in the woods on my favorite stump contemplating it all," she wrote.

"My imagination would run rampant—and I would dream that some mighty man of great wealth through God built us a new school building or that our parents got together and surprised us with this grand new building and we had a big celebration—and I even imagined that a great storm came through and blew down the main building and splattered the shacks to splinters—and out of this wreckage rose this magnificent building and all the students were joyous and even the teachers cried.

"But then reality would set in and I would be forced to acknowledge that nothing magical was going to produce a new school." Other times she prayed, "God, please help us. We are your children, too."

The thinking went on for months, "sometimes as I chopped the wood, sometimes as I fed the pigs—as I did my work, as I sat quietly it would crop up in my mind—because I felt we were not treated like any other students.

Their classes were not held in the auditorium, they were not cold, they didn't have to leave one building and transfer to another, their buses weren't overcrowded. Their teacher/bus driver didn't have to make the fire before he could start classes."

The school bus snub brought matters to a head. "That night, whether in a dream or whether I was awake, . . . a plan began to formulate in my mind." She would convene trusted students. They would organize a student strike. "We would march out the school and people would hear us and see us and understand our difficulty."

After months of preparation, the strike unfolded according to plan on April 23, 1951. What came next exceeded even the far reaches of Barbara's fertile imagination. A month later three prominent civil rights attorneys from Richmond filed *Davis v. County School Board of Prince Edward County, Virginia* in federal court, challenging the constitutionality of segregated education in the county. The case later combined with four others in *Brown v. Board of Education of Topeka, Kansas* the US Supreme Court ruling on May 17, 1954, striking down segregated education in America's public schools.

Sixty-six years later, on December 16, 2020, the Virginia Commission for Historical Statues in the United States Capitol selected Barbara Johns Powell, who had gone on to a quiet life as a school librarian, mother, and minister's wife, to replace Confederate general Robert E. Lee in the capitol's National Statuary Hall Collection.

"It had been given to me," said Barbara, who died in 1991, of the weeks when she courageously defied school officials and even some reluctant Black elders to demand fairness. Following what she believed to be divine instruction, "all I had to do was do it."

CHAPTER 16

A Reckoning

Pent-up rage exploded in the former capital of the Confederacy beneath a mask of darkness.

Richmonders awoke Sunday morning, May 31, 2020, to the shock of a night of vandalism and arson. The chaos followed by two days the city's first massive protest set off by the murder of George Floyd, a Black man pinned at the neck by the knee of a White Minneapolis police officer for eight minutes and forty-six seconds. The initial, biracial Friday march had been intense but peaceful. It mirrored similar demonstrations sprouting nationwide. That night officers and protesters clashed outside police headquarters in the city center. By Saturday morning the detritus included two burned-out vehicles—a police cruiser and a city bus.

Throughout Saturday the passion and the troubles escalated. A pattern that would become familiar over the next weeks emerged. Daytimes pulsated with civic activism, with protests uniting young and old, families and individuals in a demand for racial justice. A palette of skin shades, Black to White, defined the marchers as they chanted: "I can't breathe." "No justice, No peace." "Say his name—George Floyd." "Black Lives Matter." When evening stretched toward midnight, families went home. Anger and ugliness spiraled. Demons unleashed by powerlessness and injustice smashed through laws and convention. Windows shattered. Storefronts buckled. Many of the instigators were Black, some were White. No one quite knew who was who, where they all had come from, or what motives lay at their core.

There was no disputing the results. The downtown scene that Sunday morning elicited shock. Smoke stains from a fire started by dissidents streaked the imposing marble facade of the national headquarters of the United Daughters of the Confederacy, the womb of Lost Cause myth-making. Inside the flames had done untold damage. "FUCK 12," "Police are creepy," "One Love," and "Abolition" shrieked the message board that the UDC walls had become. Down Broad Street, store owners and citizen volunteers, Black and White, swept up debris and nailed plywood over damaged storefronts. Passersby gawked at ransacked businesses—a thriving bicycle shop stripped bare, a state liquor store emptied of bottles. A hint of ash from smoldering trash can and dumpster fires lingered in the air. Reports circulated of tear gas dispersing an angry throng as it had faced off against police in riot gear in the early morning hours.

Along Monument Avenue, the storied home to the nation's largest collection of bronzed Confederates, the "context" recently recommended by a city commission had been stamped more plainly than any panel of historians had imagined. A noose dangled from the neck of Jefferson Davis, the president of the Confederacy. The giant base of the statue of General Lee, the grandest monument of them all, had been festooned with the first markings of what, over the next few weeks, would become a full-body-suit tattoo: "No More White Supremacy." "AmeriKKKa." "A.C.A.B [All Cops Are Bastards]." "BLM." "One Love." A sidewalk message adorned with a pink heart demanded "Stop killing Black people."

Approaching yet another major crisis, his third, Northam sensed that the pain and hard work of the previous year had prepared him for this pivotal moment. He was horrified by the killing of George Floyd, but he was far less surprised than he would have been had he not heard so many Black citizens describe perilous encounters with police. Once he had thought that abuse of Black people by law enforcement was an anomaly. No longer. He still believed most officers conducted themselves professionally, but there was simply too much evidence to dismiss claims of mistreatment as an aberration.

As the drama around George Floyd's death unfolded and White Americans confronted a reality and a history many preferred to ignore, Northam felt both clarity and urgency about sharing what he had learned.

"I'm sixteen months ahead of the general population on being open-minded and listening and trying to understand the history and why a lot of these things are offensive," Northam said. The marchers pouring into the nation's streets were recognizing, as he had, that "this isn't fair, and we need to make some changes." He believed the lessons he had learned needed to be taught—importantly, not just by Black people, as had long been the norm, but by White people like himself. "That's where I can kind of help people understand," he told himself. "The burden of talking about these things and educating people has always been in the laps of African Americans, and I think it's important that people who look like me, that have listened and learned, can help others."

First, he would have to penetrate the din. The idea of how to jump-start that conversation did not come to him instantly. When it did, a week later, propelled by various voices within the administration, Northam did not hesitate. In a split second, he crossed yet another threshold into a higher level of racial engagement. He would not look back.

THE NORTHAMS HAD ANTICIPATED a much-welcome weekend over Memorial Day at Camp Pendleton in Virginia Beach, named for Robert E. Lee's chief of artillery during the Civil War. A classic white-frame, screen-porched cottage at the military installation had served for years as a secure getaway for Virginia's chief executives. George Floyd's death did not immediately penetrate the salt air.

When Northam returned to Richmond for press conferences on Tuesday and Thursday after Floyd's Monday death, not a single question focused on events in Minneapolis. COVID-19 mask requirements and the rules for business openings dominated the news. Aides were sufficiently aware of the mounting bedlam across the nation, however, to urge Northam to remain in Virginia Beach temporarily for safety's sake. The January gun rally had alerted them to how rapidly danger could escalate in times of turmoil.

Although Virginians were unaware, as chaos mounted in capitals and major cities around the nation, the governor did not spend another night in Richmond until June 14. For biweekly press conferences, he left Virginia Beach around 7 AM, arrived to prep for the upcoming event, confer with aides, and conduct any business requiring his presence. He usually left Richmond in late afternoon. Meanwhile, from a distance, he conducted a normal workload by Zoom and telephone, venues that masked his location and already typified his schedule because of COVID.

Northam's first official recognition of the national crisis came on Friday. He issued a six-paragraph statement lamenting the mayhem of the past few days and decrying the violent deaths of Floyd; Breonna Taylor in Louisville, Kentucky; and Ahmaud Arbery in Glynn County, Georgia. All three were Black. Taylor, twenty-six, had been shot and killed in March by police officers acting under a no-knock warrant aimed at a boyfriend with whom she no longer lived. Arbery, twenty-five, had been pursued and killed while jogging the previous February by three White residents. No one had yet been held accountable for either killing.

"People are crying out for justice and healing. But those aren't feelings—they're actions, and we have a lot of work to do in this country and in our Commonwealth," Northam said. "I make the commitment to ensure that we continue to address these issues head on, even when it is uncomfortable and difficult, because I believe our diversity is our greatest strength."

That same day in Washington, President Trump took a markedly different tone, issuing what amounted to an incendiary threat in the face of unrest.

"When the looting starts, the shooting starts," he promised. That night the violence that already had descended on Minneapolis, Memphis, Los Angeles, Saint Louis, and Chicago flared in Atlanta, New York—and Richmond. Reacting Sunday to the overnight looting and police face-offs in Richmond and elsewhere, Northam declared a state of emergency. The order allowed for mobilizing the Virginia National Guard, among other actions. He imposed an 8 PM to 6 AM curfew in the state capital.

Tensions mounted on Monday as the president challenged and bullied the nation's governors to meet fire with fire. "You have to dominate. If you don't dominate, you're wasting your time. They're going to run all over you, you'll look like a bunch of jerks," Trump inveighed in a video teleconference with Northam among those on the line. "It's a movement that if you don't put it down, it will get worse and worse. . . . The only time it's successful is when you're weak, and most of you are weak."[1]

Such insults did nothing to stir sympathy in Northam when Secretary of Defense Mark Esper called that day requesting that up to five thousand Virginia National Guard troops be sent to Washington by evening to help quell violence. Despite misgivings, Northam figured a request from so high an official could not be ignored. Bergman remembered a frantic call from Mercer, urging him to convince the governor of the potential political dangers. The chief of staff had spent part of the day conferring with his counterparts in the District of Columbia and nearby states. Not only was DC mayor Muriel Bowser unaware of Esper's request, but if all the troops the administration was requesting turned up, Trump would have command of a sizeable army. "This could have catastrophic consequences," Mercer worried. Bergman agreed.

The consultant rarely crossed Northam's thinking. That day proved an exception. "He was inches away. He thought it was his duty," Bergman said. If any of the Virginia guard troops wound up in a fatal encounter with protesters, the burden would be on Northam, Bergman warned. "You do this, it will undo all the work we've done on racial equity. All of it." The governor recognized the peril. Trump understood that he could not bring in military forces, Northam reckoned. "That's what dictators do." But a large enough guard force could substitute. "When they're in Virginia, I'm in command of them," Northam said of the Virginia guard. "If they'd gone to D.C., he'd have been in command."

Unwilling to fuel Trump's authoritarian tendencies in defiance of the city's mayor, Northam called Esper back to decline. "I said, 'Sir, we've got protests going on in Virginia.'" The Virginia guard needed to be on standby at home.

Unspoken was that the governor was not about to turn over command of the Virginia forces to a man in whom he had so little trust.

Regardless, the situation on the ground in Richmond and many other cities was becoming increasingly dangerous. Outrage deepened in the Virginia capital when city police released tear gas into an essentially peaceful crowd at the Lee monument twenty minutes before the 8 PM curfew went into effect Monday evening. The police department initially defended the action, which affected children as well as adults, before reversing course. Later that evening, Police Chief William Smith—whose days in office were numbered—apologized for the "unwarranted action" and promised to discipline violating officers.

WIELDING A BULLHORN, LEVAR STONEY tried to shout over the crowd. To no avail. A throng of furious protesters, many of them young, crammed to within an arm's length of Richmond's mayor, yelling their disgust over the previous night's tear-gassing. "Where were you? Where were you?" screamed members of the swarm outside Richmond's city hall. "Let him speak," demanded a voice through the din. "Why should we let him speak?" echoed the response. Stoney's black skin was no protection against the rage. The noise escalated. For well over an hour, Stoney struggled to mouth his apologies. "It was wrong what happened yesterday. It should have never happened. . . . Disciplinary actions will be taken," he called out through the speaking device. Unsatisfied, a voice in the crowd roared back: "Fire every last one of their asses." Cheers drowned out the mayor's response. The chaos dragged on.

A block to the east, Northam walked to the podium in the large, wood-paneled chamber in the Patrick Henry Building where he regularly conducted press conferences. Pastor Kelvin Jones had driven from the Eastern Shore to stand with him. Janice Underwood and Delegate McQuinn flanked the governor as well. Stoney had been slated to join the speakers. He was occupied down the street.

"Our country is in a moment of turmoil, and we have to talk about it," Northam began, hoping to showcase his deepened understanding. "We often fail to draw connections between our past and our present, but what we're seeing today didn't spring out of thin air. Racism and discrimination aren't locked in our past. They weren't solved with the Civil Rights Act. They didn't disappear. They evolved." He ticked off a list of racial disparities in school suspension rates, incarceration rates, COVID-19 infections and deaths, unemployment statistics, and so on. "I cannot know how it feels to be an African American person right now or what you are going through. I cannot know the depth of your pain, but what I can do is stand with you and I can support you. And together we are going to turn this pain into action."

As the session moved to a Q&A period, street noise began to penetrate the building's thick walls. Outside, part of the crowd had moved on from city hall. Scores of people were banging on the glass doors of the state office building, demanding entrance. Glass cracked in one of the doors. In normal times the protesters could have gained easy access. COVID-19 had put the building under lockdown.

"We're sitting there. We start hearing noise," Secretary of Public Safety Moran recalled the scene. "The chief of staff and I, we walked out into the hall. We looked to the left, out toward Broad Street, with all the glass windows, and it was full of people. They were banging and screaming. It was dramatic for us because we didn't know what they were up to."

Around the country public buildings were under siege. Was the Patrick Henry Building, home to the governor's office and the cabinet, next? Moran had no way to know. High office—governor, mayor—no longer functioned as insulation.

A former Alexandria delegate who had held the same cabinet position when the Charlottesville debacle occurred in 2017, Moran was taking no chances. He telephoned the superintendent of the Virginia State Police. Meanwhile the capitol police who were on the scene had called for backup, which arrived quickly. "They were in full gear," as was a member of Northam's protective unit, said Moran. Northam ended the press conference, and "they whisked him away."

Shaken, Moran texted Mercer at 3:08 PM with a thought that had been on his mind as he watched protesters trying to topple Confederate statues in Richmond and elsewhere. "Take it down," he said.

Mercer knew what Moran was referring to—the Lee statue on Monument Avenue. He texted back, "You should talk to him."

"Agree," chimed in Grant Neely, who was on the thread. Later Neely added, "Brian—you should find a few minutes to talk w the Gov one on one."

Staff sometimes joked that Moran was the office conservative. While that designation would likely surprise Republicans who had served with him in the legislature, it was true that he was older and more cautious than many in the younger crowd. The combination made Moran something of a kindred spirit for a governor who shared the characteristics.

The idea of dismantling the Lee statue, the only one of Richmond's Confederate monuments under state control, had long appealed to many on the staff. Having Moran broach the subject with Northam seemed prudent. If the public safety secretary approved, that might allay any fears about stirring up a White supremacist mob.

Neely happened to be in the governor's office when Moran's call came through. The communications chief had expected possible questions, maybe even minor resistance from Northam. There was none. "I think you're right," he replied. As much as anyone else in the office, Northam had been waiting for the right moment to take a step he had settled on three years earlier.

He wanted a way to salve the pain spilling out across the state and nation. As symbolic actions went, dethroning Lee was as powerful a one as he could muster.

RITA DAVIS ALSO HAD BEEN PREPARING for Lee's demise. Soon after accepting Northam's offer to become his chief counsel in 2018, she led her team to start talking about the possibility of stripping Lee from Monument Avenue. Her primary question: Did Northam have the legal authority to order such a step? Popular wisdom said that he did not. The widespread assumption was that only the legislature could authorize taking down the venerated relic.

As a Washington & Lee undergraduate and a descendent of enslaved people, Davis had had plenty of opportunity to think about the role of the Confederate general in southern history. For her, his exalted image in the seat of state government served as a bitter reminder of ancestral suffering and ongoing disparities. Speaking in a slow, distinct cadence that added weight to her words, she explained: "It symbolizes this glorification of a way of life, a society, a culture that I can't help but think, if it had prevailed, would have had no place for me, and certainly wouldn't have allowed me the opportunities and experiences that I've had, for no other reason than that I'm Black."

Like Northam and Mercer, she assumed that, even if legal hurdles could be overcome, so bold and controversial a step as removal would have to wait until just before the governor left office. "There was this perception that it was going to be a very difficult thing to do," she said. Acting prematurely might distract from other important parts of the governor's agenda.

With the blackface scandal, the discussion inside Davis's office became less theoretical. The pen-to-paper phase began that summer when she assigned a legal intern, Samantha Galina, to research the statue's history and possible legal avenues for its removal. "We had weekly meetings. She would present a draft. We'd go over the draft, work the questions, work in new angles, work the legal analysis," Davis recalled. Given the project's sensitivity, the team assigned it a code name, "Project Traveller," and told no one except Mercer about their work. Traveller, a gray American saddlebred, was Lee's renowned Civil War mount.

The Lee statue's presence in Richmond dated to May 1890, when four huge boxes containing horse and rider arrived by flatcar from New York. They had been shipped there by the French sculptor Antonin Mercié. "The Statue Is

Here," a headline in the *Richmond Dispatch* rejoiced in welcome. There was no need to say what statue. Everyone knew. The report raved: "The head is the size of a half-barrel. The bronze is as dark as that of Washington on the Capitol Square. . . . The face will be about sixty feet above the level of the ground in Lee Circle. At that distance from you[,] you will see in Mercié's work the dignified, calm, and courageous commander of the Army of Northern Virginia . . . a hero whose fame will forever gild our history's pages."[2]

"Marse Robert" was to be moved to his new home in a former wheat field west of the capitol promptly at 5 PM on May 7. A band would lead the procession, trailed by various infantries, guards, and associations. Businesses were urged to close at 4:30 PM so that employees could join the caravan. When the time came, ten thousand people—*ten thousand*—were said to have pulled the ropes attached to the four wagons bearing Lee and Traveller. Thousands more waited at the monument grounds, where a band played "Dixie," a song composed for White minstrel-show actors in blackface, and "the Confederate colors were omni-present." Pieces of the ropes were distributed as souvenirs. Except for a brief aside, any Black presence went unmentioned: "Very few colored persons took hold of the ropes, and most of those who did were nurses attending children."[3]

Finally a storm cloud and "copious showers" disrupted "the beautiful evening," and the crowd went home.

The celebrating was not finished. Later that month a throng of Confederate veterans descended on the city for the official unveiling. The *Dispatch* headlines told the tale: "UnVeiled!" "A Great Holiday." "Business Suspended—The Population in the Streets." "Myriads of Visitors." "Cheers of Joy." "Beautiful Parade." "The Battle-Flags." "Generous Applause for the Gallant Old Confederate Leaders." "Rebel Yells of Delight."[4]

It took John Mitchell Jr., the crusading Black editor of the *Richmond Planet*, to point out that "nowhere in all this procession was there a United States flag. The emblem of the union had been left behind." The rebel yells and such trappings as a gigantic Confederate flag draping city hall "told in no uncertain tones that they still clung to theories which were presumed to be buried for all eternity." The South "takes the wrong steps in so doing and forges heavier chains with which to be bound," the editor warned.[5]

The irony would not have been lost on Mitchell more than a century later when some White southerners, without any apparent sense of contradiction, could both rebuke former football quarterback Colin Kaepernick for kneeling during the national anthem and lament the dismantling of iconography glorifying men who were—*how else to put it?*—traitors to the union. Mitchell would no doubt have recognized the common thread: the Blackness of the targets.

In his June 7 issue, Mitchell wrote his epitaph for the Lee celebration. Referring to those who helped put the base in place, he said, "He [the Black man] put up the Lee Monument, and should the time come, he'll be there to take it down."

The prophesy contained only one misstep. It was a she, not a he, who answered the call when Clark Mercer stuck his head into Rita Davis's door on the afternoon of June 2, 2020, and asked, "Can we do it?"

Months of scouring the Virginia code had convinced Davis that Northam had absolute authority to remove the statue without the legislature's or anyone else's approval. She replied to Mercer with full confidence, "Yes."

A mere two days later, on June 4, Northam returned to the press conference room for a stunning announcement. His standard time slot for press updates had been changed to avoid conflict with George Floyd's memorial service later that afternoon. As usual the governor greeted reporters without fanfare. Typically he conveyed even breaking news calmly, matter-of-factly, and with a slight smile. He began with a history lesson. "When Americans first dreamed of life, liberty, and the pursuit of happiness, they dreamed here in our Commonwealth," he said, citing the 1776 Virginia Declaration of Rights, which became the basis for the US Bill of Rights.

"In a church on a hill just fifteen blocks from here, Virginia's first elected governor helped launch the American Revolution when he cried, 'Give me liberty or give me death,'" Northam continued. Patrick Henry's ultimatum is among the "inspiring words and high ideals" that form America's greatest legacy, he said, "but there is a whole lot more to the story," because "at the bottom of that very same hill, one of the country's largest slave trading markets was coming to life."

The time had come to start telling a complete history, not just the glossy parts. Contributing to a false narrative, he said, was the state's decision generations earlier "not to celebrate unity but to honor the cause of division" by erecting scores of monuments to defeated troops. Lee himself had argued against such iconography. He was ignored. No longer.

Verging arguably into wishful thinking himself, Northam turned to the underpinnings of what he was about to announce. "In Virginia we no longer preach a false version of history—one that pretends the Civil War was about states' rights and not the evils of slavery. No one believes that any longer, and in

2020 we can no longer honor a system that was based on the buying and selling of enslaved people."

Yes, he concluded, the Lee statue on Monument Avenue had been in place for a long time. "But it was wrong then and it is wrong now. So we're taking it down."

That night a pulsating mass of honking cars and jubilant celebrants wound through the city for hours, late into the night, exulting in an action few could have imagined even weeks before. After 130 years and one month, as in *The Shawshank Redemption*, time and pressure had converged.

CHAPTER 17

A Summer of Rage

Janice Underwood was seething.

It was the Monday morning after George Floyd's death, and Clark Mercer had called the Northam cabinet together for a virtual meeting. The capitol was shut down. The governor was sequestered in Hampton Roads. Folks had been told to stay at home because of the rioting. Everyone was reeling. They needed to chart a way forward together.

Settling in for the online conference, the state's chief diversity officer was startled to hear her name announced first. "Today we're going to start with Dr. Underwood," began the chief of staff. "We want to hear from Dr. Underwood." Her reaction was a stunned inner gasp. "Because he's so supportive he wanted to start with me. And he wanted me to set the tone and tell everyone what we were going to do."

"Jesus Christ," she muttered under her breath, recalling the incident a year later. "It's like, 'Could you have given me a heads-up, sir?' I remember thinking, 'Could you have called me right before then, and just say, 'Hey, I'm going to start with you?' I myself was still hyperventilating from an awful weekend. The city is charred. There wasn't like a 'How are you doing?' I just had no idea he was going to start with me."

Asked to speak off the cuff to some of the most emotional days of her life, Underwood did her best to spontaneously construct a plan. But when the call ended, "I went into my closet and I cried. I sat on the floor, and I cried because it was like all the anxiety, all the pain and anguish I felt, not only from all my ancestors and what I was watching on television, it just all culminated in this moment where I had to demonstrate exemplary leadership and, like, try to channel it all and be a voice for the voiceless."

To Underwood the moment was a very "delicate, complicated example" of how well-intentioned White people can unthinkingly create barriers to the success of people of color. Sometimes people accused her of hogging the microphone, even upstaging the governor. That was not her intent. In her own mind, she had to be poised, prepared, at every moment an example of excellence, because she carried so conscientiously the crush of both history and opportunity.

Of Mercer and the incident, she said, "It would never occur to him that that impacted me so much." Violating her own rule about open communication, she never spoke to the chief of staff about the episode. It cut too deeply, and too much else demanded attention at the time.

That poignant, personal moment offered a tiny glimpse into the emotional wringer that exhausted policy makers and citizens alike in the weeks following George Floyd's murder. As protests stretched on, filling nights with the whirr of helicopters and the shriek of sirens, as cellists and ballet dancers melded with assault rifles and police lines at the Lee circle, as demands soared for both justice and a clamp on violence, and as COVID-19 continued its grim march, weighing heaviest in already marginalized communities, the challenges to Northam outstripped even those of February 2019.

Given his years of military and medical training, he felt better equipped to navigate the emotional fault lines than when he himself had been the target. Containing the toxic swirl spun far beyond the abilities of one man, and it was impossible to predict outcomes. He knew only that he felt great sympathy for those marching in the streets and that, no matter the peripheral costs—the violence at the extremes and the sometime-vicious scrawls ("Save a Life. Kill a Cop" read one foul message on a downtown Richmond wall), he believed the bulk of the marchers properly were calling the nation to account for centuries of disregard, sometimes benign, more often deliberate. History, he felt, would vindicate their actions and demands.

"For African Americans to watch a person of color being held down and basically killed by a White police officer, that just causes these types of responses. People were hurting. They were saying, 'Enough is enough,'" Northam said. He acknowledged "the bad actors—throwing things at police, balloons filled with urine. . . . It puts well-intended law enforcement in a difficult position." He believed some of that violence stemmed from infiltrators. Even if much did not, a four-hundred-year history of oppression, replete with poverty, mass incarceration, curtailed job opportunities, and second-class education, had culminated in a predicable explosion.

"There was a tremendous amount of pain," he said. "It's a reality out there, and when you see protesters, especially as a doctor, I can recognize the pain that's out there."

IT TOOK ONLY FOUR DAYS for blowback over the Lee statue to rear up.

A descendant of one of the original donors of the land at the Lee circle filed a civil suit on Monday, June 8, alleging that Northam had failed to uphold the terms of the 1890 agreement between the state and the donors. That document had called for the state to "faithfully guard" and "affectionately protect" the Lee statue for posterity. A local state judge imposed an injunction, temporarily halting the statue's removal. Earlier that morning the Virginia Department of General Services, charged with overseeing state property, had brought in inspection crews to assess how the statue could safely be removed. Mercer and others had hoped briefly for quick removal. That clearly was not to be.

Soon a group of five property holders, most of them living on or in the vicinity of Monument Avenue, bought a second claim, arguing that removal would lead to lost tax credits and declining property values. The group's claims would evolve over upcoming weeks.

When Northam called on Rita Davis to comment on the state's legal position at a June 9 press conference, her voice unexpectedly broke. "Let's be clear about one major thing here," began Davis, stern and unsmiling, her lawyerly navy suit brightened by her distinctive "Boss" necklace (a gift from her younger sister) and her halo of black curls. "Though this monument was cast in the image of General Robert E. Lee, the purpose of this monument was to recast Virginia's history, to recast it to fit a narrative that minimized a devasting evil perpetrated on African Americans—"

She stopped, sighed deeply, composed herself, and finished the sentence. "—during the darkest part of our past." Even reading a prepared text, Davis had been briefly overwhelmed by the intensity and the struggle behind her words. The state looked forward to the upcoming litigation and expected to win, she concluded briskly.

When it came to the various Confederate statues dotting Richmond's landscape, angry protesters had no intention of demurring to legal niceties. A century-old chit had come due. Late Saturday night, June 6, Gen. Williams Carter Wickham had become the first to topple. The lawyer and plantation owner, who had voted against secession but went on to leadership in the Confederate army, was splashed by demonstrators with red paint and pulled from the pedestal in Richmond's downtown Monroe Park, where he had stood since 1891.

Four days later Confederate president Jefferson Davis, subject of the most ornate of the structures on Monument Avenue, met an inglorious fate as well. The monument's fluted columns and scrolled messages suggested a grandeur worthy of ancient Rome. Already festooned with Pepto Bismol–pink paint, the alabaster-white likeness was found lying on the street, dethroned by a crowd from its lofty perch. A tow truck carted Davis away.

Further to the southeast in Portsmouth, that same night, a man helping dismantle a Confederate statue was left in a coma after being struck by a piece of the heavy structure. Earlier Christopher Columbus had been torn down in Richmond's Byrd Park, dragged to the nearby Byrd Lake, and bestowed a watery benediction. "Columbus represents genocide" read a message spray-painted on the still-standing pedestal.

Confronted with mounting anarchy, Northam pleaded for calm at his biweekly press conference. The previous winter, he reminded Virginians, lawmakers had created a process for removing Confederate monuments. The law would take effect July 1. Already Mayor Stoney and the city council had announced that they intended to act as soon as the statute took effect. "I know these statues are causing a lot of pain, but pulling them down is not worth risking someone's life," the governor urged. "Let's do this the right way and keep all Virginians safe."

Safety was becoming a paramount concern in yet another way. Nighttime confrontations between police and demonstrators risked tragedy. In one episode a group estimated at two to three hundred surrounded Stoney's apartment building, shouting slogans and writing graffiti. A couple dozen protesters penetrated the front lobby before being escorted out. Stoney's office called the incident "irresponsible and uncalled for," a hinderance to the Black Lives Matter movement. Undeterred, demonstrators continued the face-offs with police and public officials.

In another scary moment, a Richmond police officer drove his SUV over a curb and through a crowd during a protest at the Lee monument. Several pedestrians wound up on the ground. Luck held: none was seriously injured. When hundreds marched in protest of that event, however, police responded with tear gas and pepper spray, deepening the divide. Accounts of what had occurred in the original incident differed. The officer maintained that he had been trying to escape a threatening crowd. Marchers saw the incident as unprovoked violence. Either way, the city was slip-sliding on ice.

As they jointly confronted the mounting perils, Stoney and Northam cautiously reforged the relationship severed during the blackface scandal. "We did not talk for months," Stoney recalled. "And then, there was just a coming around. Before the pandemic, I would see him at an event. He would see me at an event. 'Hi' and a hello would turn into more of a conversation." With the arrival of COVID-19, the need for communication between the two offices grew.

With George Floyd's death, the tentative reunion became imperative. In an early night of rioting, Stoney recalled, "I'm getting some serious reports about fires here and windows being smashed in." Unable to reach anyone on Northam's leadership team, Stoney decided, "What the hell? I'm going to call the governor." It was after 11:30 PM, but Northam answered. By the next morning, he had acquiesced to Stoney's request for a curfew in the city, and the Virginia National Guard had been put on standby for action in Richmond. "Those events right there actually brought us closer," Stoney said.

THE BULLSEYE OF THE BLACK LIVES MATTER protest movement in Virginia lay at the Lee traffic circle on Monument Avenue.

The city's signature address mirrored an Old South postcard—a grassy, tree-lined median, a border of elegant mansions, and, of course, the statues. By midsummer only Lee remained of the five Confederates once distinguishing the wide boulevard. A sixth statue, erected in 1996 to honor tennis legend Arthur Ashe, still stood. As a young boy, Ashe had been barred from playing on the city's premier public courts, solely because of his race.

Davis had been the first of the avenue's statuary to go. Gen. Thomas J. "Stonewall" Jackson came next.

Since Northam's June 4 decision to remove Lee, both Mercer and the state department of general services had been on a mission to find a construction company capable of—and, equally critical, willing to—perform the work. They contacted dozens of offices that either did not have the equipment or were skittish about tackling so controversial a project. "We moved quickly to try to secure a contractor," Mercer said. "It didn't work. The crane companies in Virginia are pretty close-knit. All of them said no to us."

Mercer remembered having met a young, African American entrepreneur with a construction company during an event at Norfolk State University. Unbeknownst to Mercer, Devon Henry, who sat on the board of visitors of the historically Black institution, had served as general contractor on a new memorial to enslaved laborers at the University of Virginia. He also had handled more than $100 million in federal projects during the previous decade.[1] "I texted him out of the blue, and said, 'Hey, can we talk? I'm having real trouble locating anybody, our team is, that will do this work. Are you interested?'" Mercer recalled. "He said, 'Yeah, let me make some calls.'"

Northam and Mercer's initial hope of quickly dismantling Lee had been put on pause by the courts. Even as various rulings upheld the state's legal position, temporary injunctions barred the statue's removal from Monument Avenue. As the summer wore on, everyone agreed that a decision likely would wind up with the Virginia Supreme Court, if not the US Supreme Court. That could take months, even years.

The four city-owned Confederate monuments were another matter. The new state law allowing localities to remove war memorials came with a detailed process, including public hearings and possible local referenda. Secretly Stoney was devising a plan to short-circuit those restraints. The city had already devoted years to arguing the statues' merits. A commission had recommended removing Davis and contextualizing the rest. Stoney had dragged his heels on making those changes, angering some on the commission, but the political landscape had altered. The nation was undergoing a racial reckoning, and the monuments were serving as a flash point for violence. Stoney wanted them down. Word reached the mayor that Henry might be willing to help.

On July 1, the effective date of the new law, a crane moved alongside the Jackson monument, several blocks down from Lee, and began dismantling it on orders from Stoney. As word spread and an astonished crowd grew, hundreds descended on the intersection of Monument Avenue and the recently renamed Arthur Ashe Boulevard, where Jackson reigned. Hours of tedium followed. The crew manipulated straps and calculated angles. Few observers budged. Then, just before Jackson swung free from his base, thunder boomed, and a drenching rain washed the crowd. As Jackson separated, first by inches, then feet and yards, the deafening shouts, the applause, and the tears matched the elements. "You did it, man," exclaimed Rodney Henry, Devon's brother.[2]

From across the way at Richmond's historic First Baptist Church, witness to and participant in many of the city's best and worst moments over more than two centuries, the Reverend Jim Somerville authorized the ringing of church bells.

The rewards for Henry, psychic as much as monetary, came with a price. Trying to line up subcontractors, he had encountered resistance. One Hampton Roads man reneged on taking the job after his father threatened to disown him. Another shot back that the contractor should take down a statue of Martin Luther King Jr. instead. Giving up on Virginians, Henry hired crews from Wisconsin and Connecticut. He tried to mask his own participation by forming a shell company, NAH LLC, to process the $1.8 million contract for removing Jackson and several other statues. Public disclosure requirements quickly exposed that ruse. As Henry had feared, ugly, threatening phone calls followed, as well as a special prosecutor to investigate his political ties to Stoney. The contractor installed extra security cameras at his home and business. He began routinely carrying a weapon and wearing a bulletproof vest.[3]

A year later the investigation concluded that no skullduggery had occurred. Henry's contract had nothing to do with political favors. He simply was the only contractor willing to take on so risky and potentially explosive a job.

Watching from the governor's office and preparing for the state to take down the Lee statue with Henry's help, if and when the courts allowed, Mercer concluded: "Devon is the hero of this story. He's the absolute hero."

AS THE SUMMER PROGRESSED, nighttime protests including small clashes with police continued. By daytime the Lee traffic circle transformed into an almost magical destination point. Where once drivers had hurried by on their way to or from downtown and Black people rarely had set foot, thousands gawked in amazement and joy at a transformation that seemed to have sprung organically from the soil. The statue's massive base and a concrete barrier surrounding the circle became revolving billboards, revealing the depth of anger buried beneath a centuries-deep veneer of disempowerment. A rainbow palette screamed out messages: "People Over Profit." "Fuck Cops." "We're not Leaving." "Northam did blackface." "Defund Police." "Love is Law." "Breathe." To the east side of the pedestal, for a time, an artist's portrait pictured Ahmaud Arbery, Breonna Taylor, and George Floyd enthroned with gold halos amid a field of sunflowers.

Surrounding the base, several dozen markers identified Black and Brown men and women killed by police in recent decades. Eric Garner, New York City, 2014. Ezell Ford, Los Angeles, 2014. Keith Lamont Scott, Charlotte, North Carolina, 2016. Marcus-David Peters, Richmond, 2018. A twenty-four-year-old biology teacher, Peters was shot and killed during a mental health crisis, as he ran, naked, after being tased, toward a police officer along I-95 in downtown Richmond. A loose confederacy of protesters had renamed the circle in his honor. "Welcome to beautiful Marcus-David Peters Circle, Liberated by the People MMXX," an eight-foot banner proclaimed. Princess Blanding, an impassioned defender of her brother's memory, was greeted as royalty whenever she appeared at the circle.

Some of the bystanders watching from the perimeter registered disgust. More often, broad grins widened the faces of those wandering the circle. Visitors snapped selfies and children scrambled up the base to pose for family photographs. With the improbable enchantment of a Wes Anderson movie, portable basketball hoops appeared. Raised beds blossomed with marigolds, basil, tomatoes, and melons. Cookouts and concerts comingled with voter registration sign-ups, public health brochures, and clothes collections for the homeless. The stunning image of George Floyd's face superimposed on the statue's base with the letters BLM emblazoned in white on Traveller's chest adorned the cover of *National Geographic*'s "Best Photos of 2020" special edition. The *New York Times* proclaimed the vibrant, redecorated statue to be the most influential piece of American protest art since World War II.

"That was the happiest and proudest day I've had in Richmond," said Don Baker, a retired newspaperman who had lived on Monument Avenue a block down from the Lee statue for more than three decades. He recalled one of the early marches: "Thousands of people, all colors, all ages, holding little kids by the hand, going up to the circle. What a wonderful, united moment that was. I tear up thinking about it."

Some neighbors had a different emotional response. "Well, it's dreadful," said E. Morgan Massey, in his nineties at the time. Outfitted in jeans, crewneck sweater, and loafers on a Saturday morning, Massey spoke in a halting, gravelly voice as he described the actions that had led him to join one of the lawsuits stalling the demise of the Lee statue. "We have a corrupt mayor. The governor is just about as bad, having allowed, encouraged the same thing."[4]

Massey's family footprint ran deep in the city and state. His great-grandfather, who fought for the Confederacy, had hailed from Stuart, Virginia, a town renamed after the Civil War in honor of J. E. B. Stuart, a Confederate hero. When Massey's grandfather moved to Richmond to sell coal, he located near the Stuart statue out of admiration for the man. The energy company bearing the family name had since passed into other hands, but its legacy left Massey as a wealthy man, capable of endowing a foundation with beneficiaries including the renowned Massey Cancer Center.[5]

Still active as an entrepreneur, Massey held a bleak view of the Black Lives Matter movement. He termed it a "terrorist organization supported by the Democratic Party." Based on a report from Helen Marie Taylor, a Monument Avenue neighbor and fellow plaintiff in the lawsuit, he claimed the most violent of the protesters had been paid two hundred dollars a day by billionaire investor George Soros. Asked for proof, Massey said both he and Taylor had been told that by some of the protesters themselves. No news accounts documented, or even suggested, such a link.

"There are Blacks that are absolutely as good or better as any Whites," Massey explained his philosophy on race. "But the majority, the average is not there because there's still a large percentage of the Black generation that have no families. They never learned anything from their families. They didn't go to the best schools. They didn't have the money to be educated as well as the Whites."

And is American society in any way at fault in that equation? "Yeah, it's difficult," he said, "but that's still no reason to go out and tear down statues."

Massey was not alone in his distaste for the encampment that had sprung up near his doorstep. Where many saw a beautiful awakening, others lamented an underbelly of disorder. One couple living a few houses down from the circle, declining to be named, spoke of their car being vandalized, of loud music playing late into the night, and of yards desecrated with urine, feces, and trash. "So many tents were being set up, it started to look like Portland," the wife lamented.

Walking home from dinner one night, she and her husband were surrounded by a taunting group, one man displaying a gun. "I was terrified," she said. "I don't think the bad characters were called out enough by the good characters."

Northam saw the conflicting forces. Speaking out against violence, he urged restraint from both police and those demonstrating for change. What he did not do was back away from his fundamental commitment to removing Confederate symbols from public spaces. Even his own father lamented the disappearance of Lost Cause figures, an indication of how deep White affinity went. "I don't like to see all the monuments torn down," acknowledged Wescott Northam. He did not convey the sentiment to his son, he added. "When we talk, we talk boats and fishing and things we're both interested in. I'm not trying to influence his thinking."

The governor had no such doubts. What defenders of the statues failed to confront was their inextricable link to a slave society, he believed. Deification of those who fought to disband the union represented the ultimate form of cancel culture. The apologists had replaced the truth of history with a fabricated version, one that erased the reality of the suffering and degradation of millions of Black lives.

"It's a learning curve, an arc or learning curve. If you asked me what I knew about African American history prior to February 1, 2019, and what I know now, it's like a book and maybe a couple of volumes to it. So sitting here now and knowing when these statues were put up, what era in our history or time frame and why they were put up, they just all need to come down in my opinion.

"And I know a lot of people aren't comfortable with that, but I'm very comfortable with it."

Any number of prior Virginia governors—certainly a Tim Kaine or a Terry McAuliffe—might have acted similarly. It was Ralph Northam, however, who was sitting in Virginia's top executive post when the streets exploded. The protests could not have found a more sympathetic ear.

CHAPTER 18

Black Voices Leading

Northam had long planned to bring lawmakers back to Richmond in late summer to review the state budget. With luck, revenues would have rebounded enough to restore some of the painful COVID-related cuts. Without it, more slicing might be needed.

A new mission emerged with demands for police accountability after George Floyd's death. In midsummer the governor announced a special session focused on criminal and social justice reform, as well as the budget, beginning August 18. Bracing for a once-in-a-lifetime opportunity, Black lawmakers already were honing strategy.

Over the next months, White officials, including Northam and House Speaker Filler-Corn, largely deferred to Black leadership, elevating the guidance of those who bore most intimately the toll of harsh policing and over-imprisonment. The weight of responsibility rested heavily on the shoulders of the members of the Virginia Legislative Black Caucus.

"I felt, for the first time in a really long time, hope," said Senator McClellan, channeling the biracial protests following Floyd's death. Along with exhilaration came a solemn duty: "We've got to deliver." After the 2017 Unite the Right tragedy in Charlottesville, McClellan had thought there might be a broad accounting. To her mind, there had not been. "Then I thought blackface would be it, and it wasn't."

In the wake of the madness of the deaths of Floyd, Taylor, and Arbery, she reasoned, "if we don't do it, we'll never have a reckoning."

Delegate Jeff Bourne, one of the caucus's rising leaders, echoed her determination. "We were cautiously optimistic that maybe this was the time that many of our White colleagues actually got it, or at least got it better than they had in the past, and we could make progress," said the bearded, almond-eyed Richmond lawyer. Prudence and history bred caution. "We'd seen this movie before," he added. "Hopefully, we'd have a director's cut with a different ending."

What was not in question was resolve. "We were completely unified and energized that win, lose, or draw, we were going to leave it all on the field during the special session," said Bourne. "History would not be able to say that the Black caucus did not push for everything it wanted and felt it was due."

The pressure to perform was not just political. For most it also was deeply personal. Almost every Black legislator's journey around equity had a private story that touched on criminal justice. Bourne knew the chill of seeing the lights of a police car in his rearview mirror. "Many of my [White] colleagues in the General Assembly, many of my friends, they see blue lights come on behind them, and they don't worry. They pull over. They start to reach for their registration and their license. Whereas, I pull over. I have to keep my hands on the wheel. I have to go through all of this self-protection."

Bourne was intimately familiar, as well, with the racism that penetrated some law enforcement agencies. In the mid-1980s, when his family moved from Connecticut to Wytheville to give him and his brother a small-town childhood, his father—with twenty-five years of experience in law enforcement—could not get hired in the field. His marriage to a White woman, Bourne's mother, proved taboo. The elder Bourne eventually took over a trash-hauling business and worked as a maintenance supervisor. Bourne's mother, a teacher for more than two decades, also tasted discrimination. Turned down by local school districts, she found employment waitressing at a truck stop, where she eventually rose to general manager.

Lamont Bagby, the VLBC chair, carried the images of numerous childhood friends, including his brother, who wound up on the wrong side of law enforcement. He figured that, save for sports, he easily could have been among them. His childhood in a Richmond housing project might have come straight from a Notorious B.I.G. lyric: "Because the streets is a short stop / Either you're slinging crack rock or you got a wicked jump shot." Bagby had the shot.

He felt certain that many of his contemporaries who got into trouble could have thrived in a more prosperous, forgiving setting. Sometimes the biggest troublemakers were the smartest kids. "I truly believe that given an opportunity those same individuals that were incarcerated or murdered in my neighborhood would flourish. A lot of times, they are natural leaders."

Countering Morgan Massey's narrative of deficient Black families, Bagby was saved in part by a grandfather who taught him to fish, wash cars, and garden. "He showed me how to do everything from nurturing pear and apple trees to taking care of grapevines to planting tomatoes, to making sure I cut the grass to the right lines, fertilize everything properly, and water everything properly."

With his booming voice and imposing size, Bagby tried to pay that debt forward by mentoring young boys and girls in his job at the Peter Paul Development Center in Richmond's East End.

He saw the upcoming legislative session as a once-in-a-lifetime opportunity to carve a less dangerous future for those Black youth and for adults deserving of a second chance.

Senator Mamie Locke, a history and political science professor at Hampton University, a former city mayor, and the chair of the Senate Democratic caucus, brought her own generational memories of Black suffering at the hands of the law. Behind her sometimes stern, no-nonsense countenance lay myriad tough experiences, including the one she credits with launching her civil rights journey.

Locke was a high school sophomore in Jackson, Mississippi, in May 1970 when two young men died and twelve people were wounded after state and local police opened fire on a girls' dormitory at Jackson State University. The action, just past midnight, followed an evening of fiery protests, spurred in part by false rumors of the killing of a civil rights leader and his wife. Police claimed to have seen a sniper in the building, which they splattered with hundreds of bullets. No evidence of a sniper was found. One of the dead was James Earl Green, just two weeks from his high school graduation, who had taken a shortcut through campus on his way home from his job at a grocery store. He had been uninvolved in the protests.[1]

"For those of us who were in high school, okay, here's a seventeen-year-old, high school kid like us, in his own business who just happened to get in the way," Locke remembered the shock. "And so we organized, and we were essentially told by our high school principal, 'You'd better not walk out, better not participate in any protests.' But we did anyway. That was kind of like my political awakening."

It had not escaped notice by Locke that the Jackson State killings, if remembered at all, usually serve as a footnote to events that occurred eleven days earlier at Kent State University in Ohio. There four students were killed and nine wounded by National Guardsmen during Vietnam War protests. The similar time and circumstances bred a reasonable conclusion: the nation's collective memory puts more value on White deaths than Black.

Such stories were multiplied many times over in the life experiences of members of the Virginia Legislative Black Caucus as they approached the August special session.

Both House and Senate Democratic caucuses prepared for the upcoming event by holding community listening circles around the state. "What are the chief things that need to be done in light of the protests, the marches, the deaths?" they asked. "We kept hearing over and over the same things," said Locke. "Get rid of no-knock warrants. Get rid of chokeholds. Police need more training. People are getting arrested for minor things, like something hanging out of their window or their trunk. Why do our law enforcement agencies have to look like the military?"

Simultaneously the leaders asked members to list pieces of justice legislation that they'd promoted but failed to get out of committee. The response was a flood. Locke, for instance, had tried to curtail the movement from one locality to another of police officers who had been disciplined or were under review for using excessive force. Marcia Price had promoted something similar in the House. Neither had gotten traction.

Others had sought community review boards with the authority to investigate complaints of police misconduct or a mandate that mental health professionals, not police, respond to calls involving an emotional breakdown. For years defense attorneys had complained about Virginia's status as one of only two states in which juries, not judges, set penalties after a jury trial. Juries often hand down tougher penalties, creating a huge disincentive to go to trial. The result was an overwhelming reliance in Virginia courts on plea bargains, giving prosecutors powerful leverage and exacerbating mass incarceration.

The list went on.

Often, on such bills, "we never got any kind of hearing because we were being told that we were anti–law enforcement," Locke said. Black members and their White allies braced for similar attacks as they planned an aggressive agenda. Statistics strengthened them against the anticipated assault. It was pro-justice, not anti-police, to know that something was awry when Black people were 20 percent of the population, 42 percent of 2019 arrests in the state, and 55 percent of the prison population.[2]

Approaching the session, the members asked themselves: What might be done to ensure that racial variations in incarceration reflected true differences in crime, not just an imbalance in policing? How might lawmakers minimize police abuse and hold rogue cops accountable? How could they prevent youthful transgressions from ruining a life? How could the return to society of previously incarcerated individuals be changed to make release more than a revolving door?

The tragedy in the death of George Floyd "encompassed all of what we'd been dealing with, probably our entire lives," Bourne said. "To know that we had the ability to get into that 'Good Trouble' that John Lewis talks about, to be able to press the green button to know that you're changing the law, one, but more important that you're changing lives," that awareness corralled the focus and determination of Black legislators, he said.

THE SPECIAL SESSION THAT OPENED IN MID-AUGUST was arguably the most consequential and certainly the most unusual in Virginia legislative history. Operating under the threat of COVID-19, the House of Delegates met virtually, while the Senate relocated to the Science Museum of Virginia to allow social distancing. The reality of the medical danger was driven home when both the governor and First Lady announced in late September that they had tested positive for the virus. A mansion staff member appeared to be the source of the infection.

Entering quarantine for two weeks, Northam reported only a loss of taste and smell. Pam was described as having "mild symptoms." Her own account, many months later, made that assessment sound overly cavalier. "It's more than people realize," she said the following summer. The first night "I had such a crushing pain in my chest. It was like an elephant sitting on my chest." Over the next weeks, she would "force myself to get up and go a little further every day."

A year later Northam still had not regained full taste and smell.

AT THE LEGISLATURE, WEEKS OF WRANGLING resolved gradually. Sometimes the fights were against Republicans charging that Democrats were out to hamstring police; sometimes progressives and moderates tangled within the Democratic fold. Northam proved a steady ally for the Virginia Legislative Black Caucus. "There's credit to go around, but you don't get this stuff done without the governor's support," said Bourne. By the time most of the session's work was complete in mid-October, dozens of pieces of legislation were ready for Northam's signature. The lot held potential for cosmic change.

Among the bills most celebrated by the Legislative Black Caucus:

Police had been banned from executing no-knock search warrants. Virginia became the third state nationwide, and the first since the death of Breonna Taylor, to impose a ban.

The so-called jury penalty, which had resulted in an overabundance of plea bargains and contributed to a soaring incarceration rate, was gone.

Citizen panels had been empowered to investigate citizen complaints of police misconduct and issue binding disciplinary rulings. The approved bill did not mandate such panels, as some had hoped, but it created the potential for more extensive citizen influence than the mere advisory role such panels previously were allowed.

Police chokeholds, while not banned, had been contained. Violators of the new rules were subject to administrative decertification.

Officers who failed to intervene when a colleague used excessive force would be subject to disciplinary action themselves.

An assortment of traffic offenses that had been used as pretexts for stopping motorists—disproportionately African Americans, it was believed—had been downgraded. In the future drivers could not be pulled over for such infractions as a broken taillight, loud exhaust pipes, tinted windows, or objects dangling from a rearview mirror unless the problem was coupled with a more serious offense.

Vehicle searches could no longer be triggered by the smell of marijuana alone.

The Criminal Justice Services Board had been directed to adopt the state's first statewide code of conduct for police officers, including instruction against racial profiling.

New hiring requirements would make it harder for officers under investigation for misconduct to resign from one locality and move to another without detection.

A network of "community care teams," composed of mental health professionals, would join police in responding to events such as the 2018 episode that resulted in the death of Marcus-David Peters in Richmond. The first five such teams were to be in place by December 2021.

The state attorney general had been empowered to investigate patterns or practices of discrimination within local police departments.

Not everything turned out as Bagby and the VLBC leadership hoped. Failure to make progress on expunging certain criminal records, a step expected to ease the path for ex-offenders to get jobs, topped disappointments. Hopes of stripping away police immunity from civil suits alleging violations of constitutional rights were dashed by opposition from the Virginia Association of Chiefs of Police and its allies, including several Democrats. That change would open a Pandora's box of lawsuits, crippling police recruitment and retention, critics warned. For still other Black members, McClellan and Locke among them, the lack of bipartisan action in the session formed their deepest regret. "I wasn't surprised, but I was very disappointed," said McClellan, who had hoped that broad support for the initial summer protests might translate into a less partisan mood.

Yet the list of accomplishments far outweighed the setbacks to most minds. The victories extended beyond criminal justice to creation of a Juneteenth state holiday, formalizing a step Northam had taken in the wake of the Floyd protests. The celebration commemorates the day in 1865 when enslaved Black people in Texas learned of their emancipation. Rebounding budget numbers also allowed Northam to restore significant portions of the earlier cuts to progressive priorities.

The most sobering part of the equation, as Black lawmakers hailed their successes, was the understanding that Black advancement depended on far more than improved policing. The mass incarceration of Black bodies, criminal in itself, served as the canary in the coal mine. Without dramatic changes in education, housing, and job opportunity, advances in criminal justice could not balance broken scales.

If conservative lawmakers thought Democrats had gone too far, some of those on the far left politically believed the opposite.

Princess Blanding was among them. A middle-school science teacher, devastated by the police killing of a brother she described as "a bubbly, silly kid who loved his family," Blanding had spent the intervening two and a half years trying to make sense of Marcus-David Peters's death. Clearly he had been experiencing a mental breakdown—his first, so far as the family knew, she said—when he rammed several cars on a downtown interstate highway and emerged naked and unarmed from the vehicle. By Blanding's telling her brother ran toward the highway, was swiped by a car, and began doing snow angels in the road. A recreational vehicle was protecting him from being hit as an officer rushed to the scene.

Her words tumbling out, her brown eyes brimming with tears, she described a scene in which the officer, who was also Black, should have waited for state police backup before acting. Instead he deployed a Taser, to no avail. With Peters charging at him threateningly, the officer shot twice. The bullets hit Peters in the abdomen. He died the next day. Reviews by two commonwealth's attorneys, both Black, concluded that the officer had followed protocols and done nothing wrong.[3] If that was so, Blanding insisted, then the standards of right and wrong were a joke. "At the end of the day, he was unarmed, undressed, clearly not in the right frame of mind. You cannot kill an undressed and unarmed man."

Her fury spilled over when Northam and key lawmakers assembled outside the governor's mansion in mid-December for a ceremonial signing of the bill creating a series of mental health teams to assist police in cases involving emotional breakdowns. Sponsors saw the final product as an important step toward transferring, or at least sharing, authority. Blanding saw it as a weak substitute for the statewide mandate she believed was needed.

Offered the microphone, she launched into castigating the legislation and the company. "Please take a moment to pat yourselves on the back for doing exactly what this racist, corrupt, and broken . . . system expected you all to do: make the Marcus Alert bill a watered down, ineffective bill that will continue to ensure that having a mental health crisis results in a death sentence."[4]

The assembled crowd, including Northam, had hoped to silence her, she charged later. "I can smell the bs a mile away."

Senator McClellan, Delegate Bourne, and others attending the event absorbed the criticism and pledged to keep working for a stronger measure. For the governor's part, "I just try to understand where they're coming from," Northam said of such critics. "Obviously, she'd lost a family member. What she's trying to advocate for, I just try to be understanding of it."

Blanding wanted action, not understanding. Two weeks later she announced her bid for governor in 2021 on the newly formed Liberation Party ticket.

CHAPTER 19

Virginia Military Institute under Assault

The dust barely had settled on the special session when James Henry Binford "Binnie" Peay III, four-star army general, retired, tendered his resignation as the fourteenth superintendent of the Virginia Military Institute (VMI). The departure had been both a long and a short time coming. Ever since the first five Black cadets entered the institute in 1968, making VMI the last public college in Virginia to racially integrate, there had been an inevitable march toward the moment when traditions steeped in Confederate history and nostalgia would no longer stand. Still, the final collapse came with bullet speed.

A mere nine days separated the October 17 publication of a *Washington Post* exposé describing "relentless racism" at the nation's oldest state-supported military college and Peay's stepping down. Advocates for the eighty-year-old leader made a bold defense, insisting that "systemic racism does not exist here." But the school's virtually all-White leadership, its continued reverence for Stonewall Jackson, its ongoing glorification of VMI's role in helping defeat the Union at the 1864 Battle of New Market, its relatively mild disciplining of a professor who reminisced in class about her father's exploits in the Ku Klux Klan, and the racially disparaging remarks of students on an anonymous chat app spoke for themselves. "I wake up every day wondering, 'Why am I still here?'" William Bunton, a Black senior from Portsmouth, told the newspaper.[1]

Such traditions and attitudes had not escaped Northam's gaze. He had felt for some time that the culture at his alma mater trailed current sensibilities, and he had tried to address the problem by diversifying appointments to the school's governing board. Change had proven to be a slog. As calls for racial reckoning intensified in the wake of Floyd's death and as Northam's commitment to removing symbols of Confederate nostalgia solidified, he recognized that VMI could no longer operate in a silo.

In early June, just as the governor announced his planned removal of the Lee statue in Richmond, a recent Black VMI graduate launched a petition urging the school to "acknowledge the racism and black prejudice that still occurs." Central to the overhaul should be removal of the campus's most prominent relic, its statue of Stonewall Jackson, the petition urged. For years hero worship for Jackson, an enslaver who taught at VMI prior to emerging as a Civil War officer and Confederate icon, had extended to requiring students to salute his statue every time they exited the barracks through an arch that bore his name.

That custom had disappeared a few years earlier, but the statue, the arch, and a good bit of the hero worship remained. Within twenty-four hours the petition had gained more than five hundred signatures, although a counterpetition defending the school would soon swamp the showing. "I don't consider the administration or anything like that racist, but the school is built upon being racist, which gives an opportunity for the people that are racist at VMI to slip between the cracks and kind of hide," explained Tyriuq Trotman, a recent graduate and one of those urging action by the school.[2]

Back in Richmond, Northam already had VMI in his sights. He welcomed Superintendent Peay's public response to the petition. VMI "must and will self-reflect and be open to growth," Peay told the *Roanoke Times* in mid-June.[3] Still, Northam wanted to see deeds, not just words, and soon. He told his inner circle, "If VMI doesn't have the vision to make changes and to get the Confederate history off the front page, get the monuments out of there, the buildings that are named after Confederate generals, get rid of the Battle of New Market ceremony where they literally make everybody including African Americans go relive that history, if they don't, then they're going to have problems."

The ongoing celebration of VMI's role in the Confederate defeat of Union forces in the New Market battle, near Staunton, in May 1864 remained its most astonishing enduring ritual. A battalion of 257 cadets, ranging in age from fifteen to twenty-five, had marched north eighty-five miles from the campus to help a stumbling Confederate force prevail against the odds. A century and a half later, the annual Cadet Oath ceremony, administered to first-year students, still took place at the site, with young men and women expected to reenact the cadet charge across the battlefield. The memory was held so dear that cadets at one point were required to memorize the names of the ten students who died there defending the Confederacy.

How in the twenty-first century could such traditions endure?

VMI was, after all, a public institution, not a private fiefdom. And in the governor's view, there was simply no way that African American students in a publicly financed and approved Virginia school should be expected to revere men or a cause that took up arms against the US government in defense of slavery.

THE LEXINGTON-BASED INSTITUTE, Virginia's smallest public college, had long held an outsized claim on the state's imagination and its political elite. With its stark, mustard-colored buildings and carefully tended parade ground, the seventeen-hundred-student school elevated creeds of honor and service as guiding principles. Less admirably the brutal rigors of the Rat Line and the machismo of a male-dominated society also encouraged an exclusionary mindset that rejected both outsiders and outside interference. In 1996, three decades after the arrival of the school's first Black males, state lawyers battled all the way to the US Supreme Court to protect the ranks from female admissions. When the High Court decreed that a publicly funded school could not bar women, alumni worked furiously to raise funds to turn VMI into a private college. As that effort stalled, even in the face of the Supreme Court's ultimatum, the board vote in September 1996 to admit women was a wisp-thin 9–8.

The political clout wielded by the institution was laid bare in early 2020 when the legislature finally approved allowing localities to determine the fate of Confederate statues within their jurisdictions. The Lee sculpture on Monument Avenue had been outside the purview of the new law since it was state-owned. Only one other location escaped the legislation's reach. As the assembly debated, Senate Minority Leader Tommy Norment, Northam's wily, whip-smart nemesis, slipped into the bill a provision protecting the institute that both men had attended. The amendment specified that nothing in the new law "shall apply to a monument or memorial located on the property of a public institution of higher education within the city of Lexington."[4]

Just one school fit that description: VMI.

As Northam awaited an evaluation of racial practices at VMI, promised by General Peay in the wake of national unrest and the Black-student petition, the governor's doubts about VMI's intentions intensified. He heard scuttlebutt that Peay had told a gathering of alumni that the Jackson statue would not come down on his watch. A telephone mix-up did nothing to dampen skepticism. "On July 4, my phone rang, and I couldn't pick it up, but I saw that it was General Peay," Northam recalled. "I listened to the message. He thought he was talking to Tommy Norment, because I guess Northam and Norment are close on his phonebook."

The message: "Hey, Tommy, Binnie Peay calling. I want to wish you a happy Fourth and talk to you a little bit about statues and what I'm thinking.

Obviously, been a couple of things there as a result of your legislation, and I hope we just hang tough."

Northam paused. "And it was like, well, I see where you are on this."

A few days later, Peay called again, this time intending to reach the governor. When Northam returned the call, he was blunt: "'You called me three days ago, or you called who you thought was Tommy Norment. But it actually was me.' And there was silence. And I said, 'General Peay, the direction that you're taking VMI in right now is not in your best interests and it's not in the best interests of VMI.' And he said, 'Thank you.' Pretty much the end of the conversation."

On July 29, in a seven-page document, Peay laid out his plan for moving VMI forward. He acknowledged the need to recruit more "marginalized youth" and a more diverse faculty and staff. He spoke of hoping to better integrate cadet athletes, a large segment of the Black population at VMI, into the broader school experience. And he described plans for improving the curriculum to provide a more nuanced understanding of history. The massive flagpoles currently next to the Jackson statue would be moved, shifting the "symbolic focus" of the school. And in the future the Cadet Oath ceremony would not take place at the site of the Battle of New Market.

Peay's document made clear, however, that he did not intend to remove the statue of Jackson, whom the superintendent lauded as a "military genius, a staunch Christian." Nor did he plan to rename any buildings. And while the location of administering the Cadet Oath would be moved from New Market, first-year cadets—known as Rats—would still be transported annually to the battlefield to learn "the character of these young cadets in a war long ago, just as we introduce them to World War II battles and Normandy and service, leadership, pride in country."[5]

Back in Richmond, Northam stewed. He had fondness for VMI, although it was lessening, but the school appeared determined to limp forward with one foot firmly planted in the past. When the *Washington Post* article outlining ongoing racism within the VMI family appeared on October 17, time ran out. Two days later Northam led Virginia's top elected state officials and the entire Democratic leadership of the General Assembly in penning a stern rebuke. They would no longer tolerate "outdated traditions that glamorize a history rooted in rebellion against the United States," the eleven wrote. The group was ordering an independent third-party review of racism at VMI with preliminary results due by year's end.[6]

The next day, John Boland, VMI Class of '73, president of the Board of Visitors, fired back on behalf of a sea of VMI loyalists. The incidents cited by the

Post had more to do with individual lapses of judgment than with institutional culture, he said. "Systemic racism does not exist here and a fair and independent review will find that to be true."[7]

The response reminded Northam of the die-hard opposition when women had pushed to end the school's all-male status. Agreeing, furious assembly leaders gathered in the governor's conference room on October 23 in person and by phone. Senator Janet Howell of Fairfax County, chairman of the Senate Finance Committee, questioned why the institute even should exist as a state school with a $19 million state appropriation. The group voiced overwhelming support for a change in leadership. Some urged an immediate legislative vote of no confidence in General Peay. Northam did not agree to the harsh sanction, but he listened.

Back in his office, Northam turned to Clark Mercer. "There's a storm on the horizon" for VMI and for General Peay, he said. The general deserved notice. He instructed Mercer to contact Richmond attorney Richard Cullen, who was close to Peay. If the general wanted to avoid an ugly scene, he had options. He could revise the recently issued report, taking firmer stands to erase a White-male-dominated culture. Or if he was unwilling to adjust, he could announce his own departure, perhaps over the upcoming Thanksgiving break. That would be one face-saving way to avoid an almost-certain legislative censure.

The precise words exchanged between Mercer and Cullen cannot be reconstructed, but the result can. The following Monday, the retired general ended his seventeen-year service at VMI with a terse letter: "The Governor's Chief of Staff conveyed that the Governor and certain legislative leaders had lost confidence in my leadership as Superintendent of the Virginia Military Institute and desired my resignation. Therefore, effective today, 26 October 2020, I hereby resign."[8]

In Northam's mind, he had attempted to avoid a blow-up, not create one. Given his recent blackface experience, "if I was going to ask General Peay to resign, I would have had the courtesy to call him," he said. Any such subtlety was drowned out in the uproar. Regardless of how Northam's message had been conveyed, Peay had been correct about one thing: key state officials had lost trust in his leadership. However, many VMI stalwarts had not. Outraged alumni posted multiple tributes to Peay in newspapers around the state. "The discourteous dismissal of the VMI superintendent and the slanderous assault on VMI is only the latest example of politically correct carnage," fumed former state delegate L. Scott Lingamfelter, Class of '73, in one of many such letters.[9]

Hospital administrator and former VMI board member Carter Melton took out a full-page ad in the *Richmond Times-Dispatch* to record his disgust. Any fair review would recognize that "sometimes college students (even at VMI) do stupid and wrong things regardless of prevailing norms and standards." He sardonically needled the governor, "You, of course, are familiar with this last point."

Others, less vocal, welcomed the change. In a handwritten note that Northam kept within reach in his desk, US District Court Judge Steven J. McAuliffe of the District of New Hampshire, Class of '70, praised the governor's tenacity: "I felt compelled to drop a quick note to let you know that there are many of us who think you are on the right course and admire your resolve under difficult circumstances. The very qualities VMI instills in its alumni will prove to be the source of its survival and continued success—time to evolve!"[10]

Northam regretted the uproar, but he did not doubt his and the state's course. He saw in the VMI story a parallel to his own trials. It vexed and offended him that Peay and his top aides had been so unwilling to do the work that he had done—put down their defenses, make themselves vulnerable, and listen, truly listen, with empathy to the experiences of young Black men and women who felt wounded by their time at the institute.

"I was in the same situation back in February of '19. People were on me and telling me to resign. My response, and it wasn't a smooth one, was to take responsibility. That's the way I was raised, and that's what they taught me at VMI. No excuses. And that's why I did what I did. Then I said, 'I'm going to listen and learn and improve myself and improve Virginia as a result.' That was very hard work. And I put a lot of time into that. Their decision was not to take responsibility and not to do what needed to be done."

The times demanded soul-searching, not reflexive denials, Northam believed. "We were willing to make changes. And they weren't willing to do that."

On October 29, three days after Peay resigned, the VMI Board of Visitors—minus two members who had walked out before the tally—voted 15–0 to remove the Stonewall Jackson statue from its central location on campus. Several weeks later workmen began unceremoniously preparing it for transfer to the New Market Battlefield State Historical Park. Meanwhile plans advanced for the $1 million outside review ordered by Northam and assembly leaders. The results would be revealed seven months later, shortly after VMI announced the hiring of Maj. Gen. Cedric T. Wins, US Army, retired, as its first Black superintendent.

Change had arrived in Lexington.

CHAPTER 20

The Guardrails Collapse

The third most memorable week of Northam's term, following the blackface scandal and George Floyd's death, began with a whispered message.

COVID-19 vaccines were newly available, and Virginians were clamoring to know when they could get a shot. At 2 PM on January 6, 2021, the governor opened the press conference at which he planned to tell them. He sported an easy, conversational manner and a message filled with information about doses per day and categories of recipients. "Your turn is coming," he consoled impatient constituents. "But for now, unless you work in health care or live or work in a nursing home, you don't do anything. It's not yet your turn."

Then, with almost the exact look of guileless glee that had marked his moon-walking fiasco awhile back, he announced that a surprise guest would be coming in a few days. "You want to hear from the most trusted man in the country. Who would that be?" he teased, grinning like a kid watching the elephant walk at the circus. "That's Dr. Anthony Fauci." With a satisfied pause, he urged listeners to stay tuned for Fauci's online visit in two days.

Thirty-six minutes into the press conference, Northam handed the microphone to Dr. Norman Oliver, Virginia's health commissioner, pulled up the mask draped around his neck, and walked over to confer with his press secretary, Alena Yarmosky. She whispered into his ear. Returning, Northam's focus had shifted. "I regret," he began his next response. "It's very disappointing what's going on right now in our nation's capital."

Moments later, as the state's chief workforce adviser took the microphone, Northam ducked aside again. Another whisper from Yarmosky, and he was back at the podium. "I'm going to take one more question and then we'll wrap that up," he said. "There's a lot of news going on in our country today."

What viewers at home could not see was a flurry of activity at the back of the room. Aides all seemed to be scanning their cellphones. Mercer and Moran had disappeared into the hallway. Members of the state police unit who protected the governor appeared distracted as well. Later the governor would learn that the chief of staff and secretary of public safely had been huddling over a request from Washington mayor Muriel Bowser to send state police to the city, as quickly as possible. Chaos had broken loose at the Capitol, and security forces there were severely outnumbered by an angry, violent mob.

Moran had the authority to dispatch state police if the governor was unavailable. Even before the press conference ended, the secretary had done so. About two hundred state troopers already were on their way to Washington. Members of the Virginia congressional delegation, hiding with colleagues behind locked doors, reported cheers from lawmakers as television footage showed the Virginia troopers rolling into town about 3:15 PM.

When Yarmosky first pulled Northam aside, she had told him the mob appeared to have breached the Capitol. By the second time, the situation had become dire. Communications director Grant Neely texted her: "It's gotten bad fast in DC—they need to talk to you now. Let's wrap this up and get back upstairs." In Northam's years in office, staff had pulled him aside perhaps five times during a press conference. Now they had done so twice in less than an hour.

Back in the governor's offices, both Mercer and Neely were hearing from aides to Senators Warner and Kaine that various top officials, including New York senator Chuck Schumer, soon to become Senate majority leader, needed the governor's cell phone number pronto. Shortly Northam's phone rang. He had talked to House Speaker Nancy Pelosi a few times previously. Those calls had been arranged by staff. This time her frantic message contained no preliminaries. "She said that glass was being broken all around her and that there had been gunfire. She said, 'Please, do whatever you can to send help.' I assured her that help was on the way," Northam said. "She was very concerned. You could tell it in her voice."

As he watched what was unfolding on the television screen, Northam was stunned. "It was like, how can this be happening in our country? Just the people running in there and busting up, breaking glass and knocking down doors. And the one image of the police officers that had their weapons drawn that were pointing at the door" of the House chamber, while protestors banged on the other side. It all seemed unfathomable. Northam would spend the next hours executing paperwork and arranging to deploy more than two thousand members of the Virginia National Guard to Washington. Announcing the step, he castigated President Trump for refusing to accept the 2020 election results and for fanning the flames of insurrection. "Let me be clear," he said. "Virginia will be there for as long as it takes to protect our nation's capital and ensure the peaceful transfer of power."

Over the next few days, as he traveled to Washington to thank Virginia guard members for their sacrifice and as he reflected on what had occurred, his dismay deepened. During his visit, "I was actually standing on the porch of the Library of Congress, but you could see right over to the U.S. Capitol building, and to think, one, of the security that was there and to think that that particular building which is kind of the temple of our democracy had been invaded and breached, it was kind of a surreal experience," he said.

What Northam also saw as he pondered a historic milestone were its racial implications. He thought he might have missed that part, or at least seen it less clearly, had he not spent significant time over the previous two years contemplating racial inequity. When Black Lives Matter protests had swept America the previous June, the Trump administration had ordered a "show of force" mission by military helicopters, which flew over a crowd of demonstrators near the White House. Tear gas and pepper spray had been used by law enforcement to push hundreds of protesters from Lafayette Square shortly before President Trump appeared there to threaten mobilization of "thousands and thousands of heavily armed soldiers."[1] An Interior Department inspector general's report later concluded that the police did not clear the park to allow Trump's speech, as was initially assumed by many. However, the report did not explain the use of excessive force or address the nature of Trump's verbal threats.[2]

"So to see how they were treated," Northam said, "then you fast forward to when people were literally going through the barricades, scaling the walls of the national Capitol. Can you imagine what would have happened if they had been African Americans or Muslims?

"I can't articulate it, because that's not my talent," he continued. "But it's really become more apparent. When you look at the population that breached the security, and they were mostly forty-, fifty-, sixty-year-old White men, a few White women, that was the population. To see the guy who was sitting in Nancy Pelosi's office, the gentleman—I use the term lightly—who sat in the president of the Senate's chair, it was a show of force of White supremacists. And just the contrast of how White people were treated by police officers, versus how it happened back in June, that was just a glaring example of the disparity or inequity" that is described in the term "White privilege," he said.

A second recognition by Northam was more deeply personal. Touching on his origins and his continuing affection for the rural community of his birth, the message conveyed perhaps more clearly than any previous words or action how he had changed. Two busloads of Eastern Shore residents had gone to Washington on January 6 to participate in the "Stop the Steal" rally called by Trump.

"I've tried to wrestle with this, because I grew up with a lot of these people," he said. "I've tried to think through this, what is their objective? What are they trying to prove?" He paused, his voice hardening. "It's not, and I know them well enough, about conservative values of the Republican Party, such as fiscal responsibility and less government. That's not why they got on the bus. They got on the bus because they're White supremacists. And I think that has to be clear, and I don't think for any other reason.

"Why'd they get on the bus? Because they're very insecure. I've used the term, worried about losing their parking spot. You look at the flags they were flying, 'Don't Tread on Me,' the Confederate flags that just go back to that premise that they've never been able to let go."

Did he think participants felt a conscious attachment to racial superiority?

"I don't know. I wish I could figure out the psychology. . . . It's just, I guess, I don't think that their eyes have been opened to White privilege, to Black oppression, to racism, to the systemic racism that exists. I'd like to say that I knew a lot of that. But, certainly, after the yearbook incident, my eyes have been opening up. I have learned a whole lot.

"There are so many good people, and that's what keeps me going," he continued. "But there are also people that don't want to change. A lot of the people, I suspect, that ride around here honking their horns and the ones that were up on the Capitol, they're White supremacists. They might not know they are White supremacists. They might not know or realize they're racist, but they are. I don't think they're willing to open their eyes. Some of that may be from a lack of empathy; it may be from a lack of education. I think they're very insecure about their place in society."

Those were not words the Ralph Northam of January 2019 ever would have spoken or even thought.

IN A WEEK UNLIKE ANY OTHER, Northam prepared to deliver his annual State of the Commonwealth address. That, too, would be unique. Due to COVID-19 protocols, the usual capitol crowd would be watching along with the rest of Virginia, at home. The assault on the Capitol, costing lives and untold damage to both property and the national psyche, had laid bare in the governor's mind the racial schisms rending America. The nighttime speech on January 13 would allow him to showcase some of what he had done and hoped to do to tackle those rifts. The final year of his four-year term would not be a quiet fade into the sunset. It had been twenty-three months since the governor came close to leaving Richmond in shame. He intended to use all the time available to him to ensure a different legacy.

Entering the stately House chamber, Northam walked the center aisle alone. Elbow bumps with a couple of officials waiting for him at the dais substituted for the standard raucous welcome from assembled lawmakers. Removing his mask, Northam greeted the television audience with a smile. The nearly empty chamber held one advantage for Northam. Unlike the previous year, when his push for gun controls had prompted threats, his protective unit saw no need for him to be wearing a bulletproof vest under his suit.

Only slightly rattled by a malfunctioning teleprompter, Northam began by reminding Virginians of the major achievements of 2020: passage of stringent gun-control laws, over the objections of an estimated twenty-two thousand gun-rights protesters who had swarmed Richmond the previous January; landmark clean-energy legislation, making Virginia the first southern state to commit to zero-carbon generation by 2045; the repeal of nearly one hundred instances of racist and discriminatory language in the state legal code; and budget and other changes benefitting hundreds of thousands of poorer Virginians. All this, and much else, had come with Northam's leadership or backing.

Responding to George Floyd's murder, the special fall legislative session had approved a host of measures aimed at curtailing police abuse. In the upcoming legislative term, he and his allies would press for even more change aimed at racial justice. That night he was unveiling proposals for two historic firsts—eliminating the death penalty and legalizing marijuana. In each case, if it happened, Virginia would be the first state in the South to take such action.

His plans did not end there. A host of budget amendments impacting housing, health, education, and commerce would make Virginia a more equitable place. Meanwhile he awaited the report of a commission he had appointed to unearth ways in which current laws impact White people and minorities differently. He looked forward to taking down the Lee statue in Richmond once the courts approved. Additionally he proposed removing from Virginia's capitol square a likeness of former governor and senator Harry F. Byrd, the regional leader in opposition to school desegregation in the 1950s. "It's time we stop this celebration too," Northam said.

He could not close without addressing the carnage at the Capitol. As he did the usually placid governor came as close as could be remembered to an emotional outburst. Seven days earlier a mob of domestic terrorists had stormed the Capitol. "They were egged on by conspiracy theories and lies from a president who could not accept losing," he said. Their goal had been to overturn a legal and fair election. "So tonight I say to every elected official in Virginia. You can be part of our democratic institutions, or you can use falsehoods to try to destroy them, but you can't do both. Words have consequences. Inflammatory rhetoric is dangerous. This is not a game."

Northam began the next sentence calmly enough. "When elected leaders purposely reject facts and truth—" he started. Midway his face contorted in an angry grimace, and his choked voice rose almost to a shout. "—and fan the flames of conspiracy, all in pursuit of power, they are taking dangerous steps." Recognizing his anger, Northam dialed back. Later he said that he had been thinking at that moment of the danger implicit in the next sentence in his speech: "God forbid we see anything worse." Joe Biden's inauguration was still a week away, and no one knew whether it would proceed without violence. The FBI was warning of protests and possible attacks at statehouses nationwide during the upcoming weekend. Plywood covers had been added to some windows at the Virginia capitol, and temporary fencing surrounded the complex. He and Pam were about to be whisked out of town to a secure location. The situation was infuriating.

"What really maddens me, and it might have come out a little last night," he said the next day, "I served in the Iraq conflict, and it was clear who our enemy was, and it was the Iraqis. I felt good about what I was doing for the country. Well, now, we're using all the resources, the state police, the national guard to defend against Americans who have become domestic terrorists. And that does make me mad. We're in the middle of this pandemic. We're using the National Guard to do testing, and we want them to do vaccinations. So now, instead of them being here helping with that, there's 2,229 of them who are parked out at the US Capitol to defend democracy from Americans. It's maddening."

As Northam entered the final year of his term, no one, admirer or critic, could dispute the conclusion of a *Roanoke Times* editorial that had appeared on the morning of his annual speech. In the many alterations he had made in both himself and the state, the headline read, the governor "has been dizzingly [*sic*] transformational."[3]

IN THIS RAREST OF WEEKS, Northam performed one more task that likely had never made the schedule of a sitting Virginia governor.

For all the change he was bringing to the state and to himself, he remained in many ways the person he had always been, unpretentious, a man of simple pleasures, rarely happier than with a fishing rod or a car wrench in his hand. Few enjoyments ranked higher than tinkering with the 1953 Oldsmobile he had lovingly rebuilt. He had turned the car into a beauty with fire-engine-red sides and hood, a creamy white roof, polished chrome trim, and plaid upholstery. He had brought the car to Richmond, housing it in the mansion garage. Something had gone wrong with the transmission, and a tow truck was scheduled to take it back to the Eastern Shore. First, the drive shaft needed removing.

Heading into the darkness with a screwdriver, a hammer, a half-inch wrench, and a flashlight, he squiggled his way underneath the car, which sat close to the ground. He offered a primer on his next steps. The drive shaft, he explained, "connects from the transmission, so it's like a gear that slides in over teeth, into the transmission. Then on the rear where the back wheels are, it's called the universal or the rear end, and so the drive shaft connects to that, and when the engine turns the transmission, it makes the wheels turn, because there're gears inside the rear end."

To dismantle the draft shaft, Northam first removed four bolts, each covered by a protective clip. After getting the flashlight set, with his arms forced tight against his sides and chest by the narrow space, he maneuvered the screwdriver and hammer to create a wedge between each bolt and clip, then forced the clips off. Next he loosened the bolts, which were frozen with age. Finally he used the hammer to knock the drive shaft toward the transmission, which was locked, to pull it away from the rear end. The job took about twenty minutes.

When the tow truck arrived the next day, the driver asked, "Who took this drive shaft out?" When the mansion staff replied, "The governor," the driver was in disbelief. For Northam the episode provided a brief smile in a week that had contained precious few. Not everything about him had changed.

Dr. Cassandra Newby-Alexander listens as Northam and members of the VLBC outline priorities involving equity and justice for the 2020 legislative session. Office of Governor Ralph Northam, photographer Jack Mayer.

Governor Northam addresses a pro–gun control rally on the steps of the Virginia capitol on July 9, 2019, the day of a special legislative session on gun controls. Office of Governor Ralph Northam, photographer Jack Mayer.

Left: In the wake of George Floyd's death, massive crowds of protesters march through Richmond streets. *Richmond Free Press*, photographer Sandra Sellars. *Right:* Peaceful demonstrators are hit with tear gas and pepper spray by Richmond police on June 1, 2020, thirty minutes before a city curfew is due to take effect. *Richmond Free Press*, photographer Sandra Sellars.

Despite "Black Lives Matter" signage, a window on Main Street in Richmond is shattered as nighttime protests in the city grow more violent. *Richmond Free Press*, photographer Regina H. Boone.

The Robert E. Lee Monument in downtown Richmond is transformed into a protest signboard in the months after George Floyd's death. *Richmond Free Press*, photographer Sandra Sellars.

The Lee circle on Richmond's Monument Avenue is unofficially renamed by protestors the Marcus-Davis Peters Circle, honoring a Black man killed by police during a mental-health breakdown. Courtesy of Stephen Retherford.

Northam visits with Virginia National Guard troops in Washington, DC, following the January 6, 2021, insurrection. Office of Governor Ralph Northam, photographer Jack Mayer.

Descendants of the Martinsville Seven respond to the surprise announcement that Governor Northam is pardoning their ancestors. Office of Governor Ralph Northam, photographer Jack Mayer.

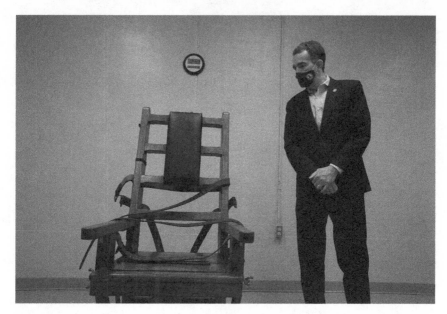

Governor Northam eyes the electric chair used to execute scores of Virginians at the Greensville Correctional Center on the day he signs legislation eliminating the death penalty in Virginia. Office of Governor Ralph Northam, photographer Jack Mayer.

Workers prepare the Lee statue on Richmond's Monument Avenue for removal on September 8, 2021. *Richmond Free Press*, photographer Sandra Sellars.

Delegate Delores McQuinn wipes away tears as she watches the Lee monument come down. Senators Mamie Locke and Louise Lucas, along with Pam Northam, savor the moment. Courtesy of David Cary.

Senator Jennifer McClellan and Governor Northam embrace at the September 2021 unveiling and dedication of an Emancipation and Freedom Monument in downtown Richmond. Office of Governor Ralph Northam, photographer Jack Mayer.

The Northams attend the August 2019 Day of Remembrance, recognizing the four hundredth anniversary of the arrival of the first captive Africans in Virginia. Office of Governor Ralph Northam, photographer Jack Mayer.

PART V

LEGACY

Carpenter, stonemason, laundress, cook.

Mother, brother, grandmother, son.

George, Agnes, Zebray, John.

——, ——, ——, ——.

Occupations. Relationships. Names. More than faceless figures born to enrich White masters. Alongside the labels, blank dashes representing lives recorded only by number and dollar value. Unknown spirits adrift in time.

In the spring of 2021, the University of Virginia atoned in part for its buried history by dedicating a memorial to the roughly four thousand enslaved laborers who built and serviced Thomas Jefferson's "academical village" from 1817 to 1865. The observance came some two centuries after the nation's third president, accompanied by an overseer and ten enslaved workers, first visited the abandoned farm where he envisioned planting his university.[1]

The event followed by less than four years the lurid scene on the evening of August 11, 2017, when hundreds of torch-carrying White nationalists marched through the center of the university, shouting racist tropes, "Jews will not replace us" and the Nazi-associated "blood and soil."

Two concentric rings, broken at the entrance to resemble shackles, anchor the memorial's design. Along an outer wall, the names of 577 workers whom researchers have been able to identify, however sketchily, are imprinted in the granite. Just over 300 more are identified by occupation or kinship. Thousands of empty slashes signify the rest.

A timeline inscribes the lower, inner wall. It documents a complex, often disturbing history. A sampling of the listings:

1825—"UVA opens for its first session with 123 white male students. 90–150 enslaved people also live on the grounds." 1825—"In October, rioting students beat a professor's enslaved servant." 1826–27—"Nelson cares for horses at a stable, works as a gardener, chops wood, and makes bricks." 1832—"Three professors purchase Lewis Commodore at public auction for the school's use." 1838—"Two students savagely beat an enslaved man named Fleming."

1843—"Abraham, Shelton, and Kenny lay bricks at the university." 1849—"Falling ill during her pregnancy, Flora suffers a stillbirth and does not recover for months." 1856—"An enslaved eleven-year-old girl is beaten unconscious by a UVA student. Claiming his right to discipline any slave, he suffers no consequences." 1863-65—"More than 250 African American men, born in Albemarle County but dispersed by sale, flight, and migration across the South, enlist in the Union army." 1864—"Aaron chops wood at the university."

Some two hundred yards away, atop a grassy knoll, sits the Rotunda, the architectural crown jewel of Jefferson's campus. Within its graceful, curved, brick walls, sculpture and memorabilia pay homage to the founder. "This institution will be based on the illimitable freedom of the human mind," Jefferson promises in a highlighted quotation. "For here we are not afraid to follow truth wherever it may lead, nor to tolerate any error so long as reason is left free to combat it."

Truth and reason have led to the story of Isabella Gibbons, enslaved as a cook at the university until Emancipation. Having taught herself to read and write while in servitude, she became a teacher as a free woman. Words written by her in 1867 cement the memorial: "Can we forget the crack of the whip, cowhide, whipping-post, the auction-block, the hand-cuffs, the spaniels, the iron collar, the negro-trader tearing the young child from its mother's breast as a whelp from the lioness? Have we forgotten that by those horrible cruelties, hundreds of our race have been killed? No, we have not, nor ever will."

This is what history looks like when it elevates truth-telling. Messy. Triumphant. Mundane. Cruel.

Thomas Jefferson, Martha Jefferson, Sally Hemings.

Sukey, Primas, Isham, Lucinda.

——, ——, ——, ——.

CHAPTER 21

Balancing Justice

For three decades the clay-colored walls of the Greensville Correctional Center in rural Southside Virginia housed a grim cavity, the state's death chamber. On March 24, 2021, Ralph Northam joined a handful of officials and members of the news media destined to be the final group to tour the unit before it became a historical artifact.

"I had never had a feeling quite like that," the governor said, describing the moments spent in the place where some one hundred men and one woman were executed by the state. A sense of gravity and gloom pierced the air. "The thing that really struck me—just the coldness of being inside the building, nothing but concrete blocks and steel gates and doors. And then, when I walked in, the first thing I saw was a gurney or stretcher, looked almost just like what I would use in a hospital. And I thought about how many times I've been up to a stretcher like that to start IVs and give fluids and medicines to save someone's life. And here, in this building, it was a stretcher to put an IV in and give an injection that would kill somebody. And that was powerful."

He continued: "And then three to four yards over was the electric chair. And just to see that and how it was bolted into the floor, the electric line coming into the back of it. And then, right in front of the gurney and the electric chair, it looked like a little home theater. It was a window with chairs, kind of an incline, twenty to twenty-five chairs for people to view an execution."

For someone who had stood at the precipice of life and death many times, the thought of deliberately pushing someone over the edge defied training and principle. The notion of viewers gaping at the killing added a gruesome image, evoking old postcards depicting crowds gawking at southern lynchings. As governor Northam had been spared having to approve an execution, which—he figured—was a good thing. Law and politics aside, he did not think he could have done it. His disdain for capital punishment had grown to that degree. "I just don't think I could," he said.

IN LATE 2020, AS THE ADMINISTRATION APPROACHED Northam's last year in office, the governor and his aides scrutinized the political landscape. They were searching for bold initiatives, capable of leaving a lasting imprint. Who knew when the legislature and the governor might again be so aligned in their determination to right the scales of justice? Such rare opportunity demanded audacity.

"We don't want to spend the last year of our term going around the state and telling people all the great things we did," Northam said in early winter. "We really do want to sprint to the finish line."

The governor and his aides did not consciously focus their attention on criminal justice, but the centerpieces of their 2021 legislative agenda—elimination of the death penalty and the legalization of marijuana—fell within that sphere. A decade or so earlier, Northam might not have attached his name to either cause. His thinking had evolved. The transition was based in no small measure on data showing the disproportionate impact of each on people of color.

Since the death of Capt. George Kendall by firing squad at Jamestown in 1608, Virginia had executed more individuals than any other state. It ranked second, behind Texas, in executions since 1976, when the death penalty was reinstated nationally after a four-year pause. For centuries stark double standards separated Black and White jurisprudence in Virginia. In the years leading up to the Civil War, Black men could be executed for any crime that netted a free man a sentence of three or more years in prison—a long list.[1]

In the twentieth century, 296—or 79 percent—of the 377 defendants executed by Virginia were Black, while the state's population was about one-fifth Black. Every one of the 68 individuals executed for rape or attempted rape was Black.[2] In fact, there is no record of a White man having been executed anywhere in the nation for the rape of a Black woman who was not killed.[3] Seven Black Virginians, the Martinsville group, were executed in February 1951 for the rape of a White woman who survived.

By the twenty-first century, despite efforts to purge racial disparities, subtle evidence of injustice remained. A 2020 Death Penalty Information Center analysis found that since 1977, in cases with victims of a single race, 295 African Americans had been executed for the murder of a White victim. In contrast only 21 White convicts had been executed for the murder of a Black victim. The center cited multiple studies concluding that the discrepancies could not be explained away by such possible variables as a greater number of Black offenders or the comparative gruesomeness of crimes.[4]

A *Washington & Lee Law Review* report published in the spring of 2021 summed up the information that had reached Northam's desk earlier. Three categories of people are executed in Virginia and much of the nation, concluded University of Richmond law professor Corrina Barrett Lain: the severely mentally ill, defendants who have themselves experienced severe trauma, and those with the "bad luck" of getting substandard legal representation, being charged with a crime in a county with a "capital-punishment-happy" prosecutor, or being Black and killing a White person.

Contrary to the belief that capital punishment is reserved for the "worst of the worst," Lain concluded, take away those categories and "there simply aren't enough offenders left to keep the system going."[5]

POWERFUL AS SUCH FINDINGS WERE, they were not the sole cause of Northam's evolution. As a doctor he had long felt skittish about the notion of the state extinguishing a human life. Even so, back in 2009, in the aftermath of a series of horrific, random killings by John Allen Muhammad and his seventeen-year-old accomplice, who became known as the DC snipers, Northam had voted to overturn the state's triggerman law, potentially opening the door to more executions.

The rule dictated that only the perpetrator of a killing could be sentenced to death. The requirement had initially confounded prosecutors in the sniper case, since it was unclear who had fired the assault rifle used in the shootings. When the legislature approved overturning the exemption, then-governor Kaine vetoed the bill. Supporters, including Northam, fell three votes shy of a veto override.

In the intervening decade, Northam's awareness of the downsides of capital punishment had grown. His father and brother had spoken to him about the shockingly inferior legal representation received by poor defendants throughout the court system. To Virginia's credit, that gap had been addressed in capital cases through creation of a special legal unit assisting indigent capital defendants. Revealingly, death sentences had virtually disappeared since formation of the office. Northam saw that fact as evidence of how flawed previous representation had been and might someday be again.

Along with much of the rest of the nation, he had become aware also of how frequently errors occur in the criminal justice system, even in capital cases. In Virginia, Earl Washington Jr. had spent eighteen years in prison—nine and a half of them on death row—for a 1985 rape and murder of which he was later proved innocent. At one point he came within nine days of execution. It was hard to know whether other innocent men had been less fortunate, because Virginia for many years had so restricted the appeals process that reversal was almost impossible.[6] While the situation had improved in recent decades, the possibility of getting an execution wrong weighed heavily on Northam. "The worst case would be someone being put to death that didn't commit the crime," he said. "That would just be the worst thing that could happen in my mind."

WHEN SENATOR SCOTT SUROVELL RAISED ELIMINATING the death penalty as a possible priority for the Democratic caucus in the wake of the 2019 elections, "I want to say five to seven hands went up" in support, the Fairfax County lawyer told the *Washington Post*.[7] A year later Surovell and Delegate Mike Mullin, a prosecutor in Hampton, saw their cause catapult to the head of the party agenda thanks to an invaluable new team captain: the governor. The lawmakers, both White, would lead the legislative fight.

In Northam's office Mercer and Neely, among others, favored abolition. As the administration hammered out its 2021 priority list, their boss needed no encouragement. The Virginia Legislative Black Caucus, many of whose members had long favored halting executions, fell quickly in line. "The death penalty is lynching's stepchild," argued a solemn Senator Locke, quoting activist Bryan Stevenson of the Alabama-based Equal Justice Initiative, when the proposal reached the Senate floor. It is no accident, she said, that states with the highest concentration of lynching now lead the nation in executions and no surprise that a lopsided number of those executed are Black.

Senator McClellan echoed the outrage. Capital punishment, she said, is a "barbaric system that disproportionately harmed Black and Brown people."

For years Senate Majority Leader Richard "Dick" Saslaw had stood firm against eliminating the penalty in Virginia. Abolitionists had been lobbying the Northern Virginia gasoline retailer, however, and he was paying attention to evolving public attitudes. George Floyd's death added to the deepening pressure for change.

As key votes approached, Northam, Mercer, and others pressed Saslaw for support. In conversations "I just told him that I'd thought about it for a long time. I've listened to a lot of people, and I really think this is the time to do this," Northam described his argument. More pointedly he and others cautioned Saslaw against being out of step with his caucus on so grave a matter.

When the critical committee vote came, both the majority leader and another former Democratic opponent, Senator Chap Petersen of Fairfax, joined the abolitionists. "That's when you knew you could get it done," said an elated Mercer.

Hopes for a broadly bipartisan coalition evaporated as several Republican senators declined to vote for the bill unless it also imposed mandatory life in prison without parole for each of the dozen or so capital crimes for which punishment was being reduced to a life sentence. "We weren't asking too much," said a disappointed Senator Stanley, who voted no despite originally serving as a bill patron.

Democrats had come to view mandatory sentences as more punitive than productive, however. They had seen too many individuals, too many of them Black, shackled for too many years by prescribed sentences. With Democrats coalescing behind the abolition bill, they did not need Republicans for passage. Stripping judges of discretion as Republicans were asking was, indeed, asking more than they were willing to give. In the end one Republican senator and two delegates voted for abolition. One House Democrat voted no.

On a misty day in early spring, flanked by key legislative leaders—Black and White—under a tent outside the Greensville prison, Northam used four pens to sign legislation few had expected to see in their lifetimes. Virginia formally became the first state in the South, the twenty-third nationwide, to abandon a 413-year-old practice.

In what he later described as perhaps his proudest moment as governor, Northam asserted: "We can't give out the ultimate punishment without being one hundred percent sure that we're right, and we can't sentence people to that ultimate punishment knowing that the system doesn't work the same for everyone." Chance and human imperfection could never be entirely eliminated, he believed. It was time for capital punishment to end.

NORTHAM PLAYED A PIVOTAL ROLE in marijuana legalization as well.

Once again his thinking had evolved, due largely to clear evidence that Black citizens suffered more than White from similar violations of the laws. A study by Virginia's legislative watchdog agency had laid out the case. Between 2010 and 2019, the average annual arrest rate for marijuana possession in Virginia was 3.5 times higher for Black citizens than for White, although national studies show that the two groups use the drug at approximately equal rates. The conviction rate was 3.9 times higher for Black citizens, the report said.[8]

"Before all this happened, as a pediatrician, as a father, I would say, 'Well, I'm not sure I can really condone the use of marijuana.' I could talk both sides of that topic," Northam said. After the blackface scandal led him to focus on equity, he became alarmed by the lopsided arrest rates. The conversations with his father and brother about indigent representation resurfaced also. "These people would come to court, my father was witness to it, and they would never even talk to their [court-appointed] attorney before they walked into the courts. Boom, next thing you know, they're in jail. Whereas the person of means has got their lawyer and has worked out a situation with the commonwealth's attorney."

Once a person has a criminal record, the negative consequences involving housing, employment, and the legal system spiral, sometimes becoming an almost insurmountable weight.

Data on marijuana arrests between July and December 2020 further angered Northam. Earlier that year the General Assembly had decriminalized possession of one ounce or less of marijuana, setting a twenty-five-dollar civil fine and eliminating jail time. Previously conviction for possession of half an ounce or less could net a five-hundred-dollar fine and thirty days in jail. Northam and other advocates had expected that the change would nearly erase the human cost for minor marijuana violations while the state set up a legal market over the next several years.

But when a coalition of advocacy groups obtained data from the state supreme court on how the first six months of the new law played out, the same old racial double-standard surfaced. Of the 4,500 people charged with simple possession in general district courts across Virginia during the period, 52 percent were Black and 45 percent White. By comparison the state's population is about 20 percent Black and 70 percent White, meaning that Black Virginians were roughly four times more likely than White to be cited. In some localities the disparity cut deeper. In Hanover County north of Richmond, for instance, Black people represented 10 percent of the population and 60 percent of the 240 summonses written for minor marijuana possession.[9]

In practice the rules still were crippling one set of people far more than another.

The marijuana legislation Northam had introduced in January contained a complex array of ideas. It called for legalization by 2023, design of a regulatory system, a tax structure expected to generate hundreds of millions in revenue, various educational and health initiatives, and a licensing program encouraging business participation by individuals who had suffered from the war on drugs. "The communities that have been among the most impacted—namely the Black community—will reap significant benefits," the VLBC's Bagby said in praise of the plan.[10]

While Republicans were opposed from the start, disagreements between House and Senate Democrats almost sank the legislation. As the session wound down in late February, House Democratic floor leader Charniele Herring, herself Black, urged adoption of a House-Senate conference report that had coated over differences and would allow legalization beginning in 2024. "Legalizing cannabis does not end systemic racism, but it does remove one of the tools used in advancing systematic racism," she urged.

Marcia Price and a group of her Black caucus colleagues were unimpressed. The idea of continuing to punish constituents while the business components of legalization were hammered out appalled them. Price outlined her concerns in a House speech conducted by Zoom. "I was so excited when the governor announced that this was a huge priority of his," she said, widening her eyes and stretching out the word *s-o-o-o* in emphasis. With her brow creased, Price pleaded for quicker relief. "Some of my constituents are in jail right now and more may be sent to jail while we are establishing a regulatory authority for the business piece," she said. Incarcerating someone for a practice that was about to become legal was indefensible.

Behind the scenes Northam and Mercer were lobbying hard to keep the bill alive. Pass it now, they urged, and the governor would work with the critics over the next thirty days, prior to a reconvened veto session, to find a better solution. Taking a leap of faith in Northam, Price and six colleagues "took a walk" when the tally came, voting neither yes or no. The final count for passage was 48–43 with two abstentions. Republican floor leader Gilbert quickly challenged the propriety of the delegates' being present and not voting. The seven nonvoters should be counted with the nays, he argued. Speaker Filler-Corn ruled Gilbert out of order. The session moved on.

Price's trust proved merited. When the assembly reconvened in April, Northam proposed amending the bill to legalize—not just reduce criminal penalties for—possession of up to one ounce of marijuana, beginning July 1. His amendments also would allow individuals to cultivate up to four cannabis plants and would speed the process for expungement of the criminal records of anyone whose prior actions would soon be legal.

With victory at stake, the governor traveled across town to the Science Museum of Virginia, where the senators were meeting because of COVID-19. There, in a side room off the main meeting hall, he lobbied a last Democratic holdout—Senator Joe Morrissey of Richmond, who had hoped to barter for support of a bill eliminating most minimum mandatory sentences. "I just told him how important this was. He said he'd think about it. He didn't commit to me at that time, but he went back and voted the correct way," Northam said.

With Morrisey's backing, the final Senate tally making Virginia the first state in the South and sixteenth in the nation to legalize marijuana was a 20–20 tie, broken by Democratic lieutenant governor Fairfax. The House vote was 53–44 with two abstentions.

In that result the faith that Marcia Price had lost in Northam in February 2019 was largely restored. "The evolution of my feelings was slow because I wanted to make sure that this was not transactional, that it was not performative," she said. "I knew that was going to take time for me to see." When she and fellow rebels in the Black caucus refused to vote for the marijuana conference report and spoke out against the absence of justice in an African American community devastated by mass incarceration and the war on drugs, "the governor heard us," she said.

"I think he could have just stuck with the business part, because those are the easy parts, right?" That he did not "showed me that he is listening to the most impacted communities," she said. The realization did not erase her disappointment that Northam had not taken ownership, one way or the other, of the blackface photograph. "I think a person would know if it were them or not in the picture. So the flip-flop was super disappointing," she said. "And if not sure, take ownership of the situation or environment that your life was such that you can't remember whether or not you posed for such a crazy picture."

Still, the marijuana legislation had told Price what she needed to know about Northam's commitment coming out of the scandal. In that very critical moment, he was putting the experience of Black people, not himself and not White business leaders and power brokers, at the center of his decision-making.

REPUBLICAN DISMAY OVER SO MANY CHANGES in so short a time coalesced in outrage at the release from prison by the Virginia Parole Board of Vincent Martin, a Black man who had served forty years of a life sentence for the 1979 killing of an on-duty Richmond police officer. Community protests from law enforcement officers, the victim's family, and others helped spur an investigation by the Office of the State Inspector General (OSIG). As hotline tips about parole board actions escalated, the investigations expanded into the release of more than a half dozen other convicted killers.

By the spring of 2021, the matter had devolved into a first-class scandal, including leaked documents, the firing of the woman who wrote the original OSIG report, allegations of intimidation by Mercer and Secretary Moran against OSIG staff, and verbal fisticuffs between GOP legislative leaders and Northam's office. What seemed most clear was that the five-person, Democrat-appointed parole board had sometimes violated prescribed procedure for notifying victims' families and prosecutors in affected areas as they considered parole. Also evident was the unambiguous philosophical chasm between those believing that the perpetrators of certain crimes, including the murder of a police officer, should never merit release from prison and those advocating for second chances in a flawed criminal justice system.

During the April 2021 reconvened session, Northam tried to quiet the furor by securing a $250,000 appropriation for a third-party review of the inspector general's investigation into the parole board's handling of the Martin case. That review—in effect an investigation of an investigation—fell far short of what Republicans felt was needed: a full probe of recent parole board releases as well as claims of intimidation by Democratic officials.

The report commissioned by Democratic leaders concluded that OSIG's lead investigator had "a high likelihood of bias" against Martin, who had been described by others as a model prisoner, and that the office should have been more thorough in its investigation. To no surprise, given its genesis, the study also absolved Northam and other administration officials of exerting improper influence. It did not take sides on whether Martin should have been released.[11]

Disgusted Republicans rebuked the results. "Today's report is merely a campaign document," Minority Leader Gilbert said in a statement. He called the conclusions "entirely predictable." They largely were. Other party leaders echoed his dismay. With elections for top state offices and the entire House of Delegates approaching in the fall, voters soon would get a say in whether Democrats had gone too far in their approach to criminal justice. Republicans for many years had found accusations that Democrats are "soft on crime" to be a dependable voter-turnout tool. In an era when calls to defund the police escalated that alarm, Northam and his administration had just handed the Virginia GOP a powerful cudgel.

As the debate roiled, the hamlet of Windsor in southeastern Virginia provided startling new evidence of the risks to Black men in police encounters. A federal lawsuit, filed in April in the Eastern District of Virginia, recounted the experience of Caron Nazario, a twenty-seven-year-old college graduate and army second lieutenant who was driving home on the evening of December 5, 2020, in his new Chevrolet Tahoe. Nazario, who is Black and Latino, had not yet received license plates from the Department of Motor Vehicles. Temporary plates were taped to a back window.

Apparently failing to see those plates and alarmed that Nazario had continued driving to a well-lit gas station rather than pull over immediately at their command, two town officers drew weapons as they approached the car and ordered Nazario out. Setting his phone on the car dashboard, he recorded what came next. "What's going on?" he asked. "What's going on is you're fixin' to ride the lightning, son," replied Officer Joe Gutierrez, identified in press reports as Hispanic.[12]

Nazario, dressed in army fatigues, was then pepper-sprayed multiple times. "You made this way more difficult than it had to be if you had just complied," Gutierrez scolded on the video.

Blinded and struggling to exit the car, Nazario asked for the officers' supervisor. Out of sight of the video, but according to the lawsuit, Nazario was struck in the knees and knocked to the ground. He was hit several more times before being handcuffed. Gutierrez later was fired.

Meeting with Nazario in the governor's office, Northam learned that the young man had been among those he had deployed to the Capitol with the Virginia National Guard after the January 6 insurrection. That a loyal citizen had been handled so outrageously appalled the governor. "To be in his car, in uniform, and treated the way he was treated, pepper-sprayed, it kind of reaffirms why what we've done with police reform is so important.

"I always thought from a position of being naive that this didn't happen very often," he said. "Now, seems like every time I turn around there's abuse from a police force, especially toward people of color."

His eyes were seeing what his mind had come to know.

THAT KNOWLEDGE BOLSTERED Northam in exercising a constitutional prerogative: the gubernatorial power of the pardon. By the end of August, he had issued 604 pardons. Before he left office in January 2022, the number had grown to 1,100, more than all previous governors combined. Northam did not regard those actions as leniency or coddling criminals but as recognition that the justice system had failed in some instances and that, in others, individuals had proved themselves worthy of a second chance.

Early in his political career, "if somebody did something, lock 'em up," he said. "Now, I've realized a number of individuals have been wrongly convicted. And a lot of these folks when they were younger, their judgment wasn't as good as it should have been. The person you're dealing with at fifty is not the person at eighteen." There are some convicts, he said, whose brains are wired in such a way that they are a permanent danger to society. "But there are a lot of people in our penitentiaries, especially there for drug-related issues, who just had bad luck and poor representation."

An opportunity to right one of the most dramatic examples of misplaced justice in Virginia history came courtesy of a petition from relatives of the Martinsville Seven. The group urged Northam to issue a posthumous pardon for their kin. All seven of the men convicted of the rape of Ruby Stroud Floyd, a White woman who was brutally attacked as she walked through a Black neighborhood after collecting money that was owed her, had signed confessions. At trial, however, several insisted that they had been bystanders and that the statements had been coerced.[13] A logical conclusion from the evidence is that, while all seven may have been present, their degree of involvement in the crime varied greatly.

All-White juries sentenced each of the seven to death. Appeals courts dismissed data showing that only Black men had been executed that century for rape in Virginia. Amid national protests the men were electrocuted in February 1951. In 1977, a quarter century later, the US Supreme Court banned executions for the rape of an adult woman as disproportionate and excessive punishment.

"This is about righting wrongs," said Northam. A group of descendants was meeting with him in a large conference room on the last day of August. Northam's announcement that he was granting posthumous pardons for the seven had taken them by surprise. Shouts, applause, and tears followed a moment of stunned silence.

"They did not receive due process. Their punishment did not fit the crime," the governor explained his decision. His simple pardons did not address guilt or innocence, only process.

Long memories attach to such crimes for the families of perpetrators and, undoubtedly, for the families of victims also. James Grayson had been a toddler when his father, Francis DeSales Grayson, was executed. The white-haired son sheltered his weeping eyes with his hands as Northam announced the father's pardon. "All this has affected me my whole life," he said.[14]

Northam said later that he was not dismissing the seriousness of rape. Rather, looking at the details of the case from a twenty-first-century perspective, seeing the racial overtones, recognizing the gaps in evidence, and knowing how frequently error occurs, "it's like this is terrible, unacceptable."

Once again, he did not know if the old Ralph Northam would have recognized the injustice. "That's the world they lived in—maybe still are living in," he said. "I don't think people that look like us appreciate that until they really start listening and knowing our history better."

CHAPTER 22

Lee Surrenders

Long-awaited calls began pouring into the governor's office on Thursday morning, September 2, 2021.

Joe Damico, director of the Department of General Services for the commonwealth, and Attorney General Herring were among the first to report the news. The Virginia Supreme Court had just ruled—unanimously. The Monument Avenue statue of Gen. Robert E. Lee could come down. One-hundred-and-thirty-one years after Lee and Traveller took up residence in downtown Richmond, they were about to need a new home.

Three long months earlier, Virginia solicitor general Toby J. Heytens had argued before the court that a handful of private individuals could not force "the Commonwealth of today and tomorrow" to ignore political and community will. During pleadings he noted that a year already had elapsed since Northam announced plans to remove the general. He urged speedy action.

The court's summer recess had delayed a decision. As weeks passed some wondered whether Northam would leave office the following January with Lee upright. Now, speaking in a single voice, Virginia's highest court had decreed that "the Lee Monument has been, and continues to be, an act of government speech." Deeds drawn up in 1887 and 1890 could not compel the state "to express, in perpetuity, a message with which it now disagrees."[1] The ruling had been written by Justice S. Bernard Goodwyn, one of the few Black men to sit on the court in its history. Goodwyn's parents had not finished high school, but they had loftier dreams for their son.

Hoping to head off a federal appeal, Mercer and Damico quickly scanned the calendar for the first available date for dismantling the statue. The upcoming Monday was Labor Day, too quick a turnaround. The following weekend included both the anniversary of the September 11 terrorist attacks and a Richmond NASCAR race. Planners preferred not to overlap with either. They settled on a weekday, Wednesday, September 8.

NO MYSTERY LAY BEHIND THE ADULATION heaped on Lee by legions of White southerners, many of whom disagreed with the step Northam was about to take. Douglas Southall Freeman's four-volume, Pulitzer Prize–winning 1935 biography of the general had for decades stood as the definitive portrait: a Christ figure, humble, self-sacrificing, kind, uncomplicated, spiritual. He was "calm when others were frenzied, loving when they hated, and silent when they spoke with a bitter tongue," Freeman wrote.[2] The incident that best typified Lee's life, the author concluded, came when a young mother brought her baby to be blessed. Taking the child in his arms, Lee "slowly said, 'Teach him he must deny himself.'"[3]

Many White northerners, not just southerners, viewed Lee as an exemplary figure, in part perhaps because admiring him presented an opportunity to bridge lingering regional political and social rifts. Addressing the 1960 Republican national convention, President Dwight Eisenhower observed that he kept pictures of four great Americans in his office. Lee was one. Later, in correspondence, he defended that decision, describing the Virginian as "one of the supremely gifted men produced by our Nation."[4]

Beginning in the late 1960s, scholars led by former University of South Carolina historian Thomas L. Connelly began to take a more nuanced view of Lee's character and military prowess.[5] As interpretations rumbled back and forth, Lee's attitudes toward and treatment of Black people took greater prominence in the texts. Freeman had written that Lee "met with every visitor, every fellow worker, with a smile and a bow, no matter what the other's station in life."[6] Not quite.

Collegiality had not extended to the enslaved people under his care. Historian Elizabeth Brown Pryor, tapping a trove of Lee letters, was among those illuminating his description of slavery as "a painful discipline" but nonetheless part of God's design. In 1865, as the war ended, Lee described "the relation of master and slave, controlled by human laws, and influenced by Christianity and enlightened public sentiment, as the best that can exist between the white & black races."[7] At another point he termed slavery "a greater evil to the white man than to the black race."[8]

Pryor described, as have others, the most shameful episode attributed to Lee. Designated as the executor of his father-in-law's will in 1857, he elevated payment of debts and substantial legacies to his daughters above emancipation of George Washington Parke Custis's enslaved workers, many of whom believed they had been promised freedom. When three of the enslaved bolted, almost making it to Pennsylvania before being captured, Lee ordered fifty lashes each to the two men and twenty lashes to the woman. After Lee's overseer refused to administer the punishment, he enlisted the constable, instructing him to "lay it on well." Afterward Lee ordered the three washed down with brine.[9]

The primary source about the episode is an interview given by one of the whipped men to an antislavery newspaper in 1866. "We might be tempted to dismiss it as the exaggerated ranting of a bitter ex-slave," Pryor wrote. "Except for one thing: all of its facts are verifiable." She found less believable other accounts that Lee had administered some of the lashes himself.[10]

As the Lee statue was about to be dismantled in Richmond, yet another biography appeared. In it Allen C. Guelzo, an acclaimed Civil War historian, acknowledged Lee's virtues. "His dignity, his manners, his composure, all seemed to create a particular sense of awe in the minds of observers," Guelzo wrote. On race he found Lee better than many of his contemporaries while acknowledging the assessment as faint praise. All else aside, Guelzo settled on a fatal flaw: treason. "What often seems to disappear from view in modern condemnations of Lee was a defect that unsympathetic contemporaries complained was a far worse offense, and that was treason. . . . No one seems to conform more plainly to the constitutional definition of treason against the United States."[11]

That flaw had not gone unrecognized. A year earlier retired brigadier general and West Point historian Ty Seidule had elevated the indictment, pairing treason with its ugly counterpart: slavery. "Lee's decision to fight against the United States was not just wrong; it was treasonous. Even worse, he committed treason to perpetuate slavery," Seidule wrote. "To those who say I am trying to change history, they should realize that the history of Confederate monuments represents a racist legacy all people should abhor."[12]

Ralph Northam understood the fact as he prepared to remove the Lee statue. No matter how noble, how diligent, how self-effacing Lee was—or wasn't— as a man, as a public figure he is inseparable from leadership of a traitorous cause that, if victorious, would have left millions of humans subjugated and brutalized.

The statement is not corrupted history; it is true history. And, to Northam's mind, it was why Lee could no longer be celebrated in a public space on public land. The only way to conclude otherwise was to write the historical experience of Black people out of the narrative.

WEDNESDAY DAWNED MOSTLY OVERCAST with a hint of mottled clouds.

Streets surrounding the Lee statue had been closed to traffic since the previous day. Police officers were stationed at every entry point, blocking even pedestrians. Tight security was a given in so volatile a political era. Aware of the dangers and the international spotlight, Clark Mercer had barely slept the night before. He arrived at the site about 6 AM, determined to see that all went as planned.

Ralph and Pam often shared a dark humor about the gauntlet of political life. "We just want to leave alive," they quipped. It was not entirely a joke. The grassy median on Monument Avenue that would serve as a viewing ground for a group of officials, special guests, and media personnel was surrounded by rooftops and second- and third-story windows. The man who had ordered Lee's removal might present an easy target. His security detail had warned the governor. They could not guarantee that no one would be sitting there with a gun. A hidden sniper could pick him off. They might not be able to prevent it. The image made Northam uneasy about attending.

The Northams often sought Mark Bergman's advice on dicey matters, and they had phoned the consultant the night before. Should he go? Pam tilted toward a yes; Ralph was hesitant. "This is a moment for the history books, the picture that will live on for decades. You ordered this down. You should be part of the picture," Bergman told the governor.

The conversation ended without a decision. "I didn't know what he was going to do," Bergman remembered. "Then I got a text from him in the morning, saying, 'Okay, we're going to do it.'"

For about an hour, work crews prepared methodically for the liftoff. Red ropes dropped from a crane and looped under Lee's arms formed a sort of carnival headdress. Blue ropes circling Traveller's legs and haunches moored the horse to the apparatus. At about 8:54 AM, a man in an orange vest signaled go, and the twelve-ton statue slowly inched up from its base. A group of onlookers who had skirted through back alleys to gain a viewing spot close to the Lee circle broke into song: "Na na na na, na na na na, hey hey, goodbye." Little by little, Lee swung outward then settled gently onto the ground.

Over the next hour, the giant torso would be sawed in half and loaded onto a flatbed truck for transport to storage while officials settled on a final destination. Months later, the statue was placed under the control of the Black History Museum & Cultural Center of Virginia.

"It's just a proud day for Virginia and our administration," said a smiling Northam as state legislators and elected officials milled about him. "It was a long time coming. It started with Charlottesville in August '17 with that terrible tragedy. I knew the statues were divisive and needed to come down. You can see the emotions of how people are responding. It was the right thing to do."

Tears and hugs flowed through the crowd. "It's been such a reflective moment for me," said Delegate Delores McQuinn, who regarded the event in part as reward for her faith in Northam. "'Great day' is an understatement of the perseverance and tenacity" that had been required for so momentous a step. "I hope in some way the ancestors feel vindicated."

Rita Davis marched across the median in sparkly stilettos to join her former coworker Mercer at the statue's base. With the administration winding down, she had resigned a few weeks earlier to take a high-level job in the defense department. She had come back to celebrate and to collect on a promise.

The new job required that her cell phone be secured during the day, so she had not learned of the Supreme Court decision until hours after it was announced. Her response when she opened her phone, she recalled with a grin, had been a scream—"a little out of character." She was proud to have played a role, with many others, in the day, she said. "We can't erase the atrocities that have happened, but we can eliminate the public celebration."

At Davis's farewell Mercer had given her a bottle of tequila and exacted a pledge that "when the statue comes down, you'll be there and you'll smoke a cigar." Standing in Lee's shadow, he produced two Ashton cigars, and the pair lit up.

Surveying the scene, Senator McClellan wiped a damp eye. "It feels like a weight has been lifted off my shoulders. The healing can begin," she said. "Now we have to continue the work of dismantling systemic monuments. As hard as this was and as long as it took, that's harder."

CHAPTER 23

Prescriptions for Racial Progress

Where even to begin on demolishing systemic monuments?

As Northam had learned, America's Black citizens trail Whites in every indicator of social well-being, from life expectancy to home ownership to annual income to years of education. A comparison between Richmond's heavily White Windsor Farms and heavily Black Gilpin Court captured the gulf, one that could be duplicated in virtually any American city. A baby born in Windsor Farms, where median income exceeds two hundred thousand dollars annually, could expect to live to age eighty in 2015. In Gilpin Court, some five miles away, where median income is closer to ten thousand dollars annually, that same baby would likely live to just sixty-three, on a par with babies born in Haiti.[1]

What accounts for such divides? Black inferiority? Insufficient striving? White racism? Deliberate obstructionism? Or is society built in ways that perpetuate longstanding gaps, intentionally or not?

For Northam the answer was clear: Call it systemic racism, call it by another name, but when you trace the origins of those divides, he found, they almost always lead to political and personal decisions involving race. Mid-twentieth-century housing policies denied many Black citizens home ownership, even as government-backed mortgages allowed White citizens to acquire housing that today remains a bedrock of White financial security. Late twentieth-century criminal justice policies incarcerated a huge segment of young Black males while wrist-slapping many young White males for similar drug crimes. Current housing policies that limit affordable housing stock in the best school districts have the effect, if not the intention, of perpetuating educational divides by class and race.[2]

Whatever the label, all are potent examples of societal structures that have helped keep people of color at the low end of the American social order. There are obvious exceptions. Many African Americans and other racial minorities have solidly entered the middle class. Others have reached the highest echelons of American society. Their progress dwarfs that for minority groups a half century ago. Yet circumstance freezes millions of others in a cycle of perpetual scarcity. Income dictates housing. Housing dictates educational opportunity. Educational opportunity dictates income. Whether individual citizens are racist or not, racial distinctions and consequences are bred into many of the ways society functions.

The challenge of disrupting attitudes and processes embedded over centuries would not be the work of a year, or three years, or even decades. It would take more than one governor or one legislature, especially when the way forward would surely not be a straight path. Still learning himself, Northam could not undo four centuries of history, but he could help spearhead progress. And he could empower citizens and staff to envision a more inclusive future and to lay out roadmaps for getting there.

Part of his legacy, as his term edged toward conclusion in January 2022, would be blueprints left behind by the Commission to Examine Racial Inequity in Virginia Law, the Virginia Commission on African American History Education in the Commonwealth, and the "ONE Virginia Strategic Plan for Inclusive Excellence," which aimed to disrupt structural inequities in the state workforce. Scores of men and women of every race and ethnicity contributed to those plans, but the leadership and experiences of three particular Black women appointed by Northam speak to the contributions of many.

CYNTHIA HUDSON, TAPPED BY NORTHAM to head the racial inequity commission, had built a sterling résumé in her sixty-plus years. She was born in Nottoway County in south-central Virginia, next door to Prince Edward County. The date was 1959, the same year Prince Edward County shuttered its schools for five years rather than integrate. Hudson grew up not knowing that history. Her fourth- and seventh-grade history classes, which each focused for an entire year on the story of Virginia, managed not to sully the narrative with the tragedy at her doorstep.

Thanks to her parents, Hudson did become the beneficiary of *Brown v. Board of Education*, however.

Her father's mother had died when he was young. The children were scattered. "My father had to live with relatives who didn't care as much about sending him to school as they did about him working the farm," she said, relating the family history. His education stopped in fifth grade, but his desire for learning did not. "He would watch kids getting on the school bus or see kids with schoolbooks in town. It hurt him the rest of his life that he wasn't able to complete his education, and he always said, 'If I ever have children, they will never suffer educationally as I did.'"

Hudson's mother finished high school but saw her dreams of college founder because of finances. So when, post-*Brown*, Nottoway offered a handful of select Black students positions in the county's White schools, Hudson's parents saw to it that she was among them. She remained one of the few Black students in her elementary school until 1968 when the Supreme Court finally had its fill of foot-dragging on integration. The next year, she recalled, "was like the Rapture." Most of the White students vanished to private academies.

Even so, those early years, combined with her studies at Virginia Common-wealth University and William & Mary Law School, had led Hudson to put a high premium on racial integration. "That experience informed my sincere be-lief that we won't break down the barriers of misunderstanding or intolerance or hate until we interact with each other in a very meaningful way—and the first meaningful way to do that is in an educational setting."

By 2019 Hudson had joined a prestigious Richmond law firm, following stints as Virginia's chief deputy attorney general and as Hampton city attorney. Composed and approachable, with rounded cheeks and a wide smile, Hudson sat at a polished conference table in a downtown office tower, describing the commission's work.

She recalled hearing, in the aftershock of Northam's blackface scandal, that he was about to create a commission on racial inequity in the law. Excited by the idea, she considered submitting her name for legal counsel. When a call came offering her the chairmanship instead, the usually measured lawyer was elated. "It spoke to my heart. It was almost as if, 'Gosh, I was born to do this,'" she said.

Over the years Hudson had sometimes wondered how she would have responded to the civil rights movement had she been older in the 1960s. "Would I have been in the street? Would I have been willing to go to jail? Would I have been one of those folks on the Edmund Pettus Bridge?" In the work she was about to do, she found an answer. "It's the manner in which I march," she said, recalling the "Bloody Sunday" encounter in 1965 in Selma, Alabama, that led to passage of the Voting Rights Act. "It's my Edmund Pettus Bridge."

Joining Hudson on the racial inequity commission were a distinguished panel of leaders in the law, many of them people of color. A group of University of Virginia law students, under the guidance of Andrew Block, one of the White commission members and the director of the state and local government law clinic at the university, provided essential research. For those who doubt that government policies have contributed to racial disparities, their reports should be mandatory reading.

Consider just two of the many categories unraveled by the researchers: housing and education.

"Racial disparities in housing are widely acknowledged to be the direct result of government action, including state and local zoning and lending choices," observes the second of three commission reports. Beginning in the 1930s and extending deep into the twentieth century, the federal Home Owners' Loan Corporation graded neighborhoods by lending risk. Black neighborhoods—even the better ones—were routinely designated subpar. That so-called redlining quashed sales to Black would-be homeowners, depriving them of a mainstream way to build capital that was available to White citizens. Even today, three-quarters of Virginia's White families own homes versus less than half of Black families.[3] Moreover, the loan-denial disparities have not gone away. Even when calibrating for income, families of color were nearly twice as likely to be denied a government-backed loan in Virginia in 2015 as White families, according to data from the state housing department.[4]

Housing disparities do not stem from government actions alone. Far from it. Private covenants barring home sales to Black people, Jews, and other marginalized groups were once ubiquitous across the United States. Even after the Supreme Court banned the practice in 1948, many individual White homeowners simply refused to sell to Black buyers, perpetuating the housing segregation that continues in many communities.

Such limitations on home ownership increase demand for rental stock, which has drastically declined in Virginia for low-income individuals in the last decade. The National Low Income Housing Coalition in 2018 estimated a 150,000 rental-unit gap for Virginians earning less than 80 percent of regional median income.[5]

The commission's reports are chock-full of such evidence not only of housing disparities but also of state and local government policies either contributing to or failing to fix them. The reports also prescribe remedies—many of which, if history is a guide, will stir resistance from homeowners protective of property values and suburban ambiance. Two critical housing recommendations:

- Loosen the state's grip on "inclusionary zoning laws." Such laws either require or create incentives for developers to include affordable dwelling units in their plans. Yet under Virginia's so-called Dillon Rule, which requires state approval for many local actions (another dip into historic White control), most Virginia localities can only encourage such programs, not demand them.

- Limit "exclusionary zoning laws," which reduce affordable housing by setting lot size, density, and other restrictive building requirements. Such restrictions have a direct link to educational segregation by limiting the opportunity for low-income families to move into often high-achieving school districts.

In such prescriptions the racial inequity report reveals ways in which a seemingly benign status quo perpetuates racial inequality. Donald Trump spotlighted that reality on the last day of the 2021 Virginia gubernatorial race when he warned that Democrats would "literally abolish the suburbs as you know them today" by allowing for more affordable multifamily housing. Trump's "beautiful and successful suburbs" have no room for the less-affluent children who would people those apartments.

As for education, Virginia's long history of segregating schoolchildren by race, then marshaling the full force of government to skirt the *Brown v. Board of Education* decision well into the 1960s, needs no retelling. The update does. "Since 2003, the number of racially-isolated, underserved public schools has nearly doubled" in the state, the commission reported.[6] The New York-and-Washington-based Century Foundation, among other groups, has documented the considerable value of integrating lower-income children into middle-class educational settings: fewer dropouts, more college attendance, and higher overall test scores.

Yet Virginia—like most of the nation—is moving in the opposite direction. To confront that problem, the commission proposed a startling structural solution: allow regional solutions by repealing the state statute that requires school districts to follow county and city lines. Since the 1970s federal courts have moved away from allowing race-based solutions to inequality in schools. Yet structures long in place—the method of drawing school-district boundaries prime among them—contribute to a universe in which poor children, often Black and Latino, are clustered in low-performing inner-city classrooms while White and Asian families dominate in more affluent suburban settings.

Shuffling the outlines of those school districts would be one way to disrupt clusters of educational disadvantage. And yet, judging from the outrage typically greeting bold educational prescriptions related to race, good luck with that. If parents can go ballistic over the teaching of Toni Morrison's *Beloved* or Angie Thomas's *The Hate U Give*, as they have, one can only imagine the outrage in public hearings over reconfigured school districts that would bring a whole new level of racial integration to public schools.

The less volatile option, and the one both Virginia and most other states have long embraced, is trying to lift struggling schools with influxes of cash. The limits of that approach are broadly evident in the fact that expenditures rarely match need. While funding techniques vary by state, Virginia is illustrative. The commission cites a 2018 study from the Urban Institute in arguing that, from an equity standpoint, Virginia's "educational funding scheme ranks in the bottom half of states nationwide, creating vastly different low- and high-income school experiences."[7]

Virginia uses a complex formula to divide school funding responsibility between the state and localities. Various studies show that the portion borne by the state in Virginia is strikingly low. A report from the progressive Commonwealth Institute, published in 2018, found that Virginia's highest-poverty school districts received 7 percent fewer dollars overall from local, state, and federal sources than their peers in the wealthiest districts. The report identified that gap as "one of the largest of such disparities nationwide."[8]

A problem with assigning a large portion of school funding to localities lies in the most likely method for raising local funds: property taxes. That, too, links to structural racism, because wealthier, Whiter districts typically have much higher property values than poorer, Blacker ones. Northam, the Virginia Legislative Black Caucus, and their allies worked to increase state funding to poorer districts through an outlay known as an at-risk add-on. That helped to balance the scales somewhat. However, an overhaul of the state funding formula, one of multiple recommendations from the racial inequity commission, would be a more permanent fix.

Even among progressives, retooling funding formulas proves to be a big ask. Much of the state's wealth, as well as Democratic political clout, is concentrated in Northern Virginia. Lawmakers hoping to improve the lot of poor children downstate must weigh that goal against the needs and demands of their own constituents. Self-interest often prevails, reinforcing the racial status quo.

Despite such challenges, Hudson refused to despair. The commission Northam created, she believes, points a way forward. "If you're trying to achieve big things, big ideas have to be embraced and explored," she said. "Nothing this fundamental is easy. What is easy is continuing to do what you've always done."

CASSANDRA NEWBY-ALEXANDER AND JANICE UNDERWOOD also faced challenges in seeing their work come to fruition. The degree of difficulty was on full display as Republican gubernatorial nominee Glenn Youngkin scoured Virginia for votes through the summer and fall. The wealthy businessman and political newcomer drew enthusiastic cheers as he opened many rallies with a pledge to ban the teaching of critical race theory on his first day in office. Less volubly he promised to "teach all history, the good and the bad." That was not the line that prompted applause.

The meaning of critical race theory varied with the listener. Some critics thought the term meant teaching White school children to feel guilty about their race. Others saw in it a belief that America's founding principle was the oppression of Black, Brown, and Indigenous people. Still others thought the term boiled down to seeing life through a racial lens and castigating any who disagree. Whatever it meant, scores of Virginians had decided that they did not like it.

Such resistance and misinterpretation collided with the work of Newby-Alexander and Underwood. Newby-Alexander's focus on teaching US and Virginia history in more honest ways and Underwood's on instilling awareness of impediments to minority success in the state workforce both fit, in a general way, under the rubric of what Youngkin was pledging to ban. Both came back to the central idea of critical race theory: that structures in place across generations have perpetuated racial inequalities and need to be aggressively dismantled.

On the campaign trail, exasperated Democrats countered that the theory, a graduate school concept, was not being taught in public schools. That was true. Even so, Republicans were correct that public school curricula and government practices surrounding race were under revision and that White ancestors and culture did not come off entirely well. For those intimately aware of Virginia's and the nation's long history of elevating White perspectives and authority to the exclusion of minority views and experience, the changes were not overstepping. They were a necessary correction.

As a cochair of Northam's African American History Education Commission, Newby-Alexander had overseen a review of state standards governing history education in the commonwealth. Step 1 had been enacting scores of technical edits to the standards that prescribe "essential knowledge" for Virginia history students. The board of education had approved changes recommended by her history-education commission in October 2020. Step 2 would be a more comprehensive standards redesign, part of a regular review due for completion in November 2022.

The technical edits suggest the degree to which African American history had been incomplete or missing altogether. Four examples among scores of additions for high school history courses:

"African Americans faced injustice, increased violence, and discrimination immediately after the end of slavery."

"[During Reconstruction] African Americans pushed for education for their children. This directly resulted in Freedom's First Generation of who became doctors, lawyers, and teachers. . . . Despite the obstacles they faced, many African Americans achieved excellence."

"African Americans were disproportionately impacted by the Great Depression and they were discriminated against when New Deal agencies were created, both in hiring, pay, and access."

"Churches and homes were bombed by white opponents of the Civil Rights Movement."

These are not "woke" concepts. They are factual statements, describing essential parts of the African American experience at significant junctures in American history. Yet they and many other such omissions were not part of what was considered essential for high school history students to learn prior to the commission's work.

For Newby-Alexander the core of that work lay not in such technical edits, critical as they were, but in the prospect of a broader rethinking of the history standards, one that better incorporated what she liked to call the silences in American history. Much like Cynthia Hudson, she could see her life's work as a preparation for helping conceive such a structural framework.

Born into an upper-middle-class Black family in Norfolk, with a physician father and an educator-turned-housewife mother, Newby-Alexander describes herself as an early bookworm whose first history lessons were at her parents' side. "I was given a foundation of pride, of understanding that no one defines who you are. You define who you are by yourself," she said.

Tall and robust, with a hearty laugh and confident manner, she vowed as an undergraduate at the University of Virginia in the 1970s not to be intimidated by the White male students who sometimes muttered racial epithets while blocking her path or pushing her against a wall in the hallways. "I would steel myself so that they were hitting an immovable force," she said. "I saw the hate and the nastiness, how these people were brought up."

In response, she said, "you have to find a way to be bold and fearless."

By 2019, when Northam appointed her to the history commission, Newby-Alexander had established her academic credentials as a scholar of the early racial history of Virginia, including the Underground Railroad in Hampton Roads. She also had come to believe that the Virginia history standards needed more than an insertion here or there about Black lives. Whole concepts were missing. There was little mention of free Black people prior to the Civil War, for instance, even though they were a substantial segment of the state's Black population. The history of lynching, which claimed the lives of at least eighty-six

Virginians between 1880 and 1930 and served as a potent means of Black intimidation, was not uniformly taught.[9] Aside from a few prominent figures, "Blacks were either victims or they were objects," she said.

Left untold was a broader narrative of African American agency, stories of what Black Virginians were doing throughout American history to actively improve their standing, contribute to society, and make sense of their lives.

With Newby-Alexander's encouragement the commission urged a standards redesign addressing ten concepts that better integrate African American history with US history: freedom, imperialism and nationalism, colonialism, racism and systemic racism, capitalism and economic motivation, citizenship, servitude and enslavement, advocacy and agency, cultural expressionism, and invasion and colonization. The goal would be for teachers to instruct thematically, in a way that made marginalized groups more than an addendum to a history of White domination and advancement.

Talking about the ugly parts of the American story "does not make people who are talking about it hate America," Newby-Alexander insisted. "Talking about these issues helps America to become what it says it is. . . . You can't say, 'Oh, we've come a long way,' but then you deny that you took land from native peoples, that you murdered and massacred them, that you had a system of oppression and dehumanization that is still present in our society."

Considering founding fathers such as George Washington and Thomas Jefferson in complex, sometimes unflattering ways does not erase their merit; it makes them human. "If you're teaching history, you're teaching the complications and the contradictions," she said.

In her view too many White Americans think the nation's racial problems are being overblown. "If you are not the one directly impacted by this [racial injustice], you don't believe it exists," she countered. Experiences such as a recent hospital stay for her husband tell her otherwise. While visiting, she encountered several former students on the nursing staff. Even in 2021, she learned, some White patients do not want to be touched or treated by a Black nurse.

"ONE VIRGINIA," THE DOCUMENT that Janice Underwood was bequeathing Virginia government, laid out a toolkit for state agencies to use in creating a more inclusive workplace. The first-of-its-kind statewide, strategic plan had been shaped by Underwood in conjunction with state human resources officials. The manual offered a primer in the burgeoning field of diversity, equity, and inclusion (DEI).

Dissected, DEI consists of recruiting and promoting a diverse workforce; allocating resources to weed out discrimination within the office culture; and creating a welcoming environment for all. The introduction to "ONE Virginia" synthesized the work as "a model of inclusive excellence, kindness, and respect."

Implementing the plan was unlikely to be as benign as that description. Exposing embedded patterns of behavior risked arguments and bruised feelings. As DEI had expanded in both public and private workplaces nationwide, so had resistance. Some conservative commentators claimed that "equity" was a code word for socialism, an insistence on equal outcomes.[10] Underwood and others discounted that assertion. DEI aims to erase disparities, not by lowering standards or dictating uniform results but by toppling entrenched barriers to advancement and opportunity, they said.

Tangentially, through the summer and fall of 2021, culture wars around schools exploded in wealthy and increasingly diverse Loudoun County, outside Washington, DC. Much of the initial furor had to do with transgender bathroom privileges, but it soon dipped into what was being taught about cultural competency, a bedfellow of DEI. The setting made national headlines, trumpeted by Fox News, when training materials for teachers turned out to include a slide attributing various attitudes to "White Individualism" and others to "Color Group Collectivism." The White column included "fostering independence and individual achievement" with "an emphasis on taking care of yourself and your needs," while the Color Group column was assigned "fostering interdependence and group success" with an emphasis on "helping others, considering their needs (or how your needs affect others)." White Individualism "promotes self-expression, individual thinking, personal choice" and association with private property, according to the material. The Color Group "promotes adherence to norms, respect for Authority" and was associated with shared property, the authors said.

The slide, a tiny part of a large packet, did not appear in classrooms and was shown only to a few Loudoun County Public Schools administrators as a part of a training on various schools of thought involved in equity work, a school spokesman said.[11] Still, the ensuing outrage over stereotyping was part of the landscape as Underwood bucked headwinds to promote increased opportunity in the state government workforce.

Two new laws strengthened her hand. One cemented her position by statute, not just the Northam executive order that created it. The other required every state agency to submit an annual DEI plan to the governor. The first such reports had been due on July 1, 2021, and Underwood and her tiny staff were in the midst of reviewing them.

Excited as she was at the prospect, Underwood was equally aware that her budget for reviewing the plans was wholly inadequate and that she had almost no authority to enforce compliance. Her chief accountability tool remained persuasion. "[Agencies] make these goals, and if you don't hit them, it's the only field where there's no accountability," she said. "I have zero sticks at this point."

She recognized also the precariousness of her position as she argued for ground-up systemic change. Throughout state government top leadership remained "very, very lacking in diversity," she said, even within the Northam administration's tiny inner circle. Yet "racism is so incredibly endemic to the American experience that even when you call out the manifestation of it, it looks so normal that you will be blamed for attacking America."

Even White allies such as the governor could fail to see ways in which they impeded progress, she argued. Her request for a $3 million emergency appropriation to hire help for evaluating the dozens of agency reports piling her desk had gone unattended to. She and one deputy were pouring through the mass. Similarly Northam's inner-office staff had shuttled to a study her recommendation that $20 million from the federal American Rescue Plan Act be used to create a language portal for immigrant communities struggling to access health, employment, and other state services. To her mind the need—amplified by the COVID-19 pandemic—was too obvious to tolerate that delay.

When her office was created, she asked, had there been a study? No. The blackface episode had created a crisis, and money had been found. Now, because appropriations routinely demanded a study, the request for language access was on hold. "You don't see the level at which you're perpetuating these racist ideologies because it's normal. We've always needed a study, so therefore, we're not asking for anything out of the ordinary. This is how government has worked for generations."

The danger, she pressed on, is when White allies "get so caught up in your 'we are champions' that you don't see the inequity right under your nose. And there's inequity and bad decisions and racism in the governor's office on the third floor right now."

Given that such patterns existed even among allies, she fretted over what might happen to the DEI work once Northam's administration was gone. "What will this office look like twenty years from now? That's what I think about, worry about," she said.

Underwood was not alone in concern as she watched races for governor, lieutenant governor, attorney general, and the one-hundred-seat House of Delegates play out through the fall. Who would be sitting in those positions come January? What would be their commitment to the equity work that she, Hudson, Newby-Alexander, and their colleagues had begun? Would the trio's reports inform state policy going forward? Or would the accumulated wisdom be relegated to some dusty shelf?

Whatever the outcome, one thought offered solace. Northam had given each a crucial charge. They had risen to the task. Each was leaving behind a body of evidence and a plan.

CHAPTER 24

Republicans Take Charge

Virginians charted a new direction on November 2, 2021, voting in record numbers for three Republicans to replace Democrats Ralph Northam, Justin Fairfax, and Mark Herring in the state's top offices. In the governor's race, Glenn Youngkin, a former executive for the Carlyle Group, a multinational private-equity firm, scored a narrow, come-from-behind victory over Terry McAuliffe. The former Democratic governor had entered the race as a solid favorite. Winsome Sears, a Jamaican-born businesswoman and Marine Corps veteran, captured the number-two spot. And Jason Miyares, a tough-on-crime former prosecutor whose family had fled Cuba, became the state's first Latino attorney general.

Completing the Republican sweep, voters returned the House of Delegates to GOP control, giving the party a narrow 52–48 majority. The Senate, none of whose members had faced reelection, remained in Democratic hands, but a single defection would create a 20–20 split with Sears as the tiebreaking vote.

The returns stripped away the blue-majority veneer that Virginia had acquired during the Obama and Trump presidencies. Instead the Old Dominion reverted to the list of states capable of tilting in one political direction or another depending on the candidates and the year.

Driving to Northern Virginia for McAuliffe's election-night rally, the Northams, Mark Bergman, and press secretary Alena Yarmosky were sobered but not surprised when the first exit-poll reports reached them. The main thrusts of Youngkin's campaign—the economy and education—had spiraled upward to the top of voter concerns, according to the polling. COVID, Donald Trump, and abortion rights, three of McAuliffe's mainstays, did not appear to be motivating voters to the same extent.

"About a week out, it had become clear that it was not going well" for McAuliffe, Bergman recalled. The first significant narrowing of the race had come in late summer when President Biden's popularity tumbled in the wake of the chaotic evacuation of Afghanistan, marking the end of the nation's twenty-year war there. As Biden's poll numbers plummeted, Youngkin's improved.

Throughout October the Republican candidate's momentum grew. Voter sentiment in pivotal suburban swing districts appeared to be coalescing around parental frustrations over schools. Anxiety stemming from long months of at-home learning and debates over mask wearing and back-to-school timetables merged with unease over transgender and race issues in schools, strengthening Youngkin's case for change.

Arriving at the Hilton McLean Tysons Corner on election night, Northam and his entourage watched from a private suite as the tally turned grim for Democrats. In midevening the Northams joined the McAuliffe family before a throng of well-wishers. Opening his remarks with a gracious nod to the outgoing governor, McAuliffe gamely insisted that uncounted votes could yet tip the outcome. Working the crowd moments later, he appeared as ebullient as if he was already en route back to the governor's mansion.

That facade crumbled as the Associated Press declared Youngkin the winner shortly after 12:30 AM Wednesday. By then the Northams were back in Richmond, where the governor and Bergman chatted into the night. The next morning, shortly after McAuliffe officially conceded his loss, Northam telephoned congratulations to Youngkin and invited the governor-elect and his wife for their maiden tour of the home that Ralph and Pam would soon be vacating. Modeling a mature transfer of power, the couples met for lunch the next day.

IN THE WEEKS THAT FOLLOWED, Northam's inner circle had one overriding concern: making sure that the election results were not interpreted as a rebuke of his stewardship. Both they and members of the Virginia Legislative Black Caucus worried also over how much of the legacy they had constructed might be overturned. Youngkin had not directly attacked Northam on the campaign trail, but it was hard to read a Republican sweep as anything less than a rebuff of eight years of Democratic rule.

Many also detected a classic pattern in the results: White backlash to Black progress. The post–Civil War Reconstruction era had been followed by the racial apartheid of Jim Crow. The advancements of the civil rights era gave way to the devastating prison sentences of the war on drugs. A racial provocateur, Donald Trump, had succeeded the nation's first Black president. Virginia Republicans made major gains on the heels of the 1990–94 term of the nation's first elected Black governor, Doug Wilder. And in 2021, after a term in which Black Democrats had held unparalleled sway over the public agenda, that pattern had recurred. Were Virginians witnessing a repeat of the 1880s pattern, in which subsequent governors and legislatures erased the Black political advances made from 1881 to 1883? And were the Virginia election results a harbinger of a national retrenchment from the post–George Floyd racial awakening?

With a margin of fewer than sixty-four thousand votes separating the gubernatorial candidates out of 3.3 million cast, the outcome by one interpretation seemed tantalizingly close.[1] However, the fact that Joe Biden had defeated Donald Trump by ten percentage points in the previous year's presidential race, and that no Republican had won a statewide contest in Virginia since a 2009 GOP sweep, heightened Democrats' gloom and fueled national speculation about a Democratic collapse in the 2022 federal midterm elections.

In fact, based on normal turnout expectations, McAuliffe had performed well in many Democratic strongholds. What few had anticipated was a flood of rural Republican voters who, combined with independents in several major suburban counties and cities, propelled Youngkin's victory. According to a *New York Times* analysis, only four small Virginia counties had given Republican John McCain 70 percent or more of the vote in the 2008 presidential race. By 2021 Youngkin won 70 percent in forty-five counties and passed 80 percent in fifteen of them.[2]

Democrats were a vanishing breed in much of the Virginia countryside.

Democratic decline in rural Virginia overlapped with strong support there for former president Trump. McAuliffe had counted on an equally robust rebuke of the divisive, autocratic leader by urban and suburban voters. The Democrat's scorched-earth, anti-Trump media assault had fizzled, however, against a Republican candidate deftly straddling the line between embracing Trump and distancing from him. Youngkin welcomed Trump's endorsement and said he would vote for the former president if he became the party nominee in 2024. He did not invite Trump to campaign for him, however, and he rarely invoked Trump's name.

During the nomination process, Youngkin sidestepped the issue of whether Biden had been properly elected. Post-nomination, he dropped the qualifiers on Biden's legitimacy, even as he pledged to tighten voting-access laws. In perhaps the clearest signal that Youngkin had not drunk conspiracist Kool-Aid, he unapologetically disavowed a Richmond-area, Trumpian campaign event in which attendees recited the Pledge of Allegiance to a flag said to have flown at the rally preceding the January 6 Capitol insurrection.

Asked about the episode, Youngkin called pledging to that particular flag "weird and wrong." "As I have said many times before," he added, "the violence that occurred on January 6 was sickening and wrong." The comment boosted his fleece-vest-wearing, hoops-shooting image of normalcy.

In theory such outspokenness might have tamped down Youngkin's support among Trump loyalists. But as Mark Rozell, dean of the Schar School of Policy and Government at George Mason University, pointed out in a postelection recap sponsored by the Virginia Public Access Project, Youngkin did not have to moor himself to Trump. A barrage of McAuliffe ads did the work for him.

TEASING OUT THE ROLE OF RACE in the election outcome was, as always, an imprecise science.

Unquestionably multiple factors—not just race—produced Youngkin's victory. Concerns about the economy, inflation, high gas prices, and the pandemic created a sour mood. Bickering between Democratic progressives and moderates in Washington over the Biden agenda chipped away at claims of governing competency. McAuliffe's defeat in the primary of three Black candidates left a hint of lingering bitterness among some progressive voters. And much postelection quarterbacking expressed dismay at McAuliffe's failure to trumpet a positive agenda or to herald the accomplishments of not just his term but the Northam years as well.

Astonishingly, in a state with an unemployment rate below 4 percent, designation by CNBC in 2019 and 2021 as the top state for business,[3] a budget surplus of $2.6 billion, the highest rainy-day reserves ever, and private capital investment in Virginia over the previous four years quadruple that of any prior administration, Youngkin had campaigned on the notion that the state's economy needed rescuing.

Race also factored in the complex mix of election influences, however. The impact began with a Democratic primary in which the eventual nominee, a White man, defeated three Black competitors. While McAuliffe had strong Black support in the primary, including prominent state senate leaders, the White-privilege optic was unavoidable.

"You have a White male come in and say, 'I'm the guy. I'm the only one that can win,'" observed Delegate Jeff Bourne. "A lot of Black folks interpreted that as another example of the privilege that comes with being White." Their takeaway? "This is your world and we're just bit players."

Northam had contributed to that feeling by endorsing McAuliffe a month ahead of the Democratic primary. He coupled the action with backing for an up-and-coming Black delegate, Jay Jones, against incumbent attorney general Mark Herring and of Delegate Hala Ayala for lieutenant governor. Ayala, who had grown up in a financially struggling family in Alexandria, was the daughter of a Salvadoran immigrant father and a mother with Irish and Lebanese roots.

Behind the scenes Northam had met with each of the three Black gubernatorial hopefuls. He recalled counseling them to coalesce. "Unless it becomes one of you versus Terry, the numbers don't add up," he told them. "That went over like a lead balloon." With McAuliffe's opponents struggling in the polls, Northam also tried to persuade Jennifer McClellan, the one of the three to whom he was closest, to drop back and run for lieutenant governor. He believed election to the second spot would create a glide path for her to the governorship in 2026. His overture, made through counselor Rita Davis, fell on deaf ears. Angered, McClellan was far too invested in the governor's race to quit.

With his advances rebuffed and convinced that McAuliffe had by far the best prospects for continuing Democratic hold on the state, Northam endorsed him on April 8. The backing added to the sense of inevitability. It also deeply disappointed McClellan, who learned of the endorsement in a 5:45 AM text message from Northam on the morning the story broke in the *Washington Post*. "I'll try to call you later," McClellan remembered his texting. "And he didn't." Months later, voicing a complaint similar to that leveled by Northam against various political allies after the blackface scandal broke, she added, "We've talked around it, but we've never really talked about it." In her view her legislative work on the Clean Economy Act, voting rights, and numerous other measures had been critical to the success of Northam's legislative agenda. "All of that will be part of his legacy," she said. "Given what I did for him, I felt in a lot of ways used."

In the election postmortems, memories of Northam's role in endorsing McAuliffe raised "what if" questions among supporters of the Black candidates. Critics also wondered why Northam had not garnered a specific commitment from McAuliffe to campaign on the legislative gains and broader racial equity agenda Northam had championed. "Terry likes to talk about what Terry's been able to do," Northam said, shrugging when asked prior to the election why so little of the campaign was focusing on the achievements of his administration.

On the Republican side, one indicator of racial backlash lay in the rejection by rural voters of referenda aimed at removing Confederate statues in their localities. While cities like Richmond and Charlottesville were busy disposing of their Confederate images, nine rural counties—including three in the 2021 election and six the previous year—voted overwhelmingly to keep their statues in place. The margins of support ranged from a low of 55 percent in Charles City County to a high of 87 percent in Tazewell County. That outpouring reflected in microcosm the cultural chasm between rural and urban voters so evident in the election results. It also suggested that an Old South view of race relations still held throughout much of the state.[4]

Within the Youngkin campaign, the most overt racial appeals lay in the frequent and loud promises to ban the teaching of critical race theory. Black assessments of the impact of that emotional trigger, drawn from a national Republican playbook, ranged from substantial to huge.

"When there are racial dog whistles in every single thing that they talked about, and then you have an increased turnout, it has to be reckoned with," said Marcia Price, who believed the attack on critical race theory was the thread stitching together Youngkin's victory. Bourne gave the offensive tactic slightly less weight, even as he lamented the ploy. "It certainly was a piece," he said. "Using that was something probably that plagues politics nationally, playing to people's least common denominator to energize or inspire, motivate."

Will Ritter, Youngkin's media strategist, pushed back on the idea that the approach constituted a racist dog whistle, a subtle political message whose true intent is audible only to a select audience. None of Youngkin's more than three dozen television ads mentioned the term, he pointed out during the Virginia Public Access Project postelection forum. Ritter also rejected Democratic claims that the theory had not impacted public education in Virginia. "Sure, there was not a critical race theory textbook being handed out, but it was there and everybody knew that there was something there," he said, noting correctly that instruction about the term had appeared on some Virginia government websites.

More generally, Ritter continued, Youngkin's disavowal of critical race theory offered a way to synthesize concerns "about bullying, lack of control over the curriculum and people feeling that they did not have control over what their kids were being exposed to in the curriculum in their public schools."[5]

If so, that meant the candidate was wrapping up all those frustrations and deliberately laying them at the doorstep of a widely misunderstood term, one overlaid with racial suspicion and innuendo. At best such charged rhetoric did not advance the cause of racial understanding. At worst it deliberately exploited and deepened racial antagonism and fears for political gain.

The most explosive moment galvanizing parental frustrations came in the final McAuliffe-Youngkin debate. The moderator asked McAuliffe about a controversial veto in 2016, made during his first term as governor. The vetoed bill would have let parents excuse their children from required reading if it contained sexually explicit material. The legislation also would have saddled teachers with the cumbersome task of discerning what constituted sexually explicit content and notifying parents in advance of any such planned reading. It would have made Virginia the first state nationwide to require such action.[6]

During the debate McAuliffe offered a vigorous defense. "I'm not going to let parents come into schools and take books out and make their own decisions," he replied with familiar gusto. Then he issued twelve fateful words: "I don't think parents should be telling schools what they should teach."

McAuliffe's 2016 veto had held merit. Individual parents could create chaos if allowed to trump teacher and school board decisions indiscriminately. But the implication in 2021 that frustrated parents needed to just be quiet ignited smoldering ire. Almost overnight Youngkin rallies were packed with "Parents Matter" signs.

Simultaneously the campaign rolled out a television ad featuring the mother whose complaints had triggered the 2016 legislation. The book she had sought to keep her teen from reading was Toni Morrison's Pulitzer Prize–winning novel, *Beloved*. Drawn from an actual incident, the powerful story tells of a formerly enslaved woman who would rather murder her daughter than have the child returned to bondage. Morrison's authorship and the book's graphic narrative about the horrors of slavery injected yet another racial twist into the campaign.

THE VIRGINIA ELECTION LEFT DEMOCRATS generally, and Black political leaders in particular, conflicted about how to respond to future allegations about critical race theory. The divide reflected historic patterns within Black circles, pitting militancy against a more collaborative response.

In a postelection memo developed by ALG Research, a Washington-based firm that polled for the Joe Biden–Kamala Harris presidential ticket in 2020, researchers laid out the challenge in preventing political independents from drifting to Republicans over issues lumped under the label. Based on conversations with voters who had crossed party lines to vote for both Biden and Youngkin, they reported: "CRT in schools is not an issue in and of itself, but it taps into these voters' frustrations." A feeling that "they have to walk on eggshells even on seemingly innocuous topics" extends to discussions around race in schools. Regarding schools, the voters "were less concerned with critical race theory as an idea or curriculum but expressed frustration with the black-and-white approach they see taken toward such complicated subjects."

The memo reported several telling comments from focus-group participants

- "In an attempt for inclusion, there's a lack of respect for opinions that don't match yours identically. It's so divisive and if you don't think exactly what I think then we can't even be friends."

- "I feel like what I was taught in school was mainly Virginia history, and it was all white people and leaders. So I understand why they're doing that, but I feel like there's a certain way to go about those things."
- "It doesn't need to be aggressive, in your face. It needs to be smoother and with a variety of approaches, and not accusatory."

The researchers warned against the dominant Democratic response, dismissing critical race theory as a graduate-school discipline not taught in public schools. Many swing voters understood that distinction, they said. "They absolutely want their kids to hear the good and the bad of American history, at the same time they are worried that racial and cultural issues are taking over the state's curricula."

Democrats should expect continued backlash on the topic, especially as it overlaps with parental frustrations stemming from the pandemic, the memo warned. When parents feel unable even to control whether schools are open, critical race theory may be an easy scapegoat.

Jennifer McClellan saw value in heeding that advice. "There's a lot of fatigue, and people are a little sensitive. We need to be more conscious of meeting them where they are," she said, pondering over the right message. "We need to focus a little more on our common humanity, frame it a little less as us against them. We have to create a safe space for everybody to be in the discussion."

Some other Black lawmakers saw irony in taking a quieter approach. "The notion that we need to be softer and easier and more sensitive to the holders of the privilege is expressing that privilege in and of itself, right?" said Jeff Bourne.

"That's why we can't get ahead," added Marcia Price. "Because as soon as White folks are made uncomfortable, we have to shut it down."

The open question of whether White parents truly want their children to be taught accurate Black and Indigenous history hangs over such conversations. Delores McQuinn bridled at the memory of a television news segment during the 2021 election in which a White woman rejected critical race theory by saying, "I don't want my children to feel bad about themselves." The woman saw the term as shorthand for blaming contemporary White people for long-gone sins.

"She didn't say she wanted her children to understand the truth," McQuinn continued. "Obviously she didn't understand that generations of Black people have felt bad about themselves, about who we are, what we look like. It's been changing, but it's what we've had to live with all our lives." A few years earlier, McQuinn had been stunned when her four-year-old granddaughter announced. "I want to be White with falling down hair, because I want to be a princess."

In a house filled with artistic representations of strong Black people, that child had latched on to the dominant media representation of beauty. "Nobody's trying to pain or shame anyone, but it is high time that the truth is told," McQuinn said. "It's part of the growth if we expect to grow as a nation."

THE DEGREE TO WHICH THE ELECTION results grew from a repudiation of the agenda of Northam and the Legislative Black Caucus would be answered over time, initially in the actions of the newly elected team. Since McAuliffe had done so little to highlight that record, the Northam team hoped that the returns were not a statement on what had been achieved. The hope was short-lived.

Youngkin's lack of a public record made predicting his actions as governor little more than a barstool guessing game. His campaign had included hints of moderation, as in his refusal to answer a questionnaire from the National Rifle Association and his pledge not to pursue a Texas-style abortion bill, one setting severe limits on the procedure and leaving enforcement to civil lawsuits.

The governor-elect had also promised dramatic upheaval, however. "Together, we will change the trajectory of this Commonwealth. Friends, we are going to start that transformation on day one," the governor-elect thundered as he met with supporters the morning after his victory. He proved to be as good as his word. Youngkin's first executive order after his swearing in on January 15 banned the teaching of "inherently divisive concepts," including critical race theory. Without naming the work of Cassandra Newby-Alexander and her colleagues, he pointedly ordered a review of all changes to the state educational curriculum made within the last forty-eight months, and he forbade a series of actions, including suggesting that "any individual bears responsibility for actions committed in the past" by members of the same race, ethnicity, sex, or faith. Never mind that no prescribed teachings suggested any such thing. The new governor sparked further Democratic outrage by setting up a tip line to report teachers who dipped into "inherently divisive concepts," a largely undefined term.

Within months, newly appointed Superintendent of Public Instruction Jillian Balow, a Wyoming transplant, was on track to rescind all vestiges of racial equity–based initiatives at her department. In the Youngkin administration's interpretation, the term *"equity"* had been redefined as a totalitarian expectation that all children would perform equally. Lost in translation was the dictionary meaning of the word: just, impartial, and fair. Despite Youngkin's pledge to teach all the history, the good and the bad, there was no commensurate effort to deepen or expand instruction about the roles of Black citizens and other minority groups in American and Virginia history. Even so collaborative a project as including the stories of enslaved workers in the governor's mansion tour for schoolchildren had dropped off the radar, seemingly a victim of the prohibition against "inherently divisive" teaching.

Youngkin quickly put his stamp on Janice Underwood's domain also. Naming a former executive with the conservative Heritage Foundation as her successor, he imposed a new title: the Office of Diversity, Opportunity, and Inclusion. Opportunity was in; equity was out. In an executive order, he expanded the office's portfolio to include promoting "diverse free speech" and "viewpoint diversity in higher education," serving as "an ambassador for unborn children," and being "responsive to the rights of parents in educational and curricular decision making," among other items. Forced by law to staff such an office, Youngkin clearly intended it to remake it on his own terms. Within months, many of Underwood's initiatives had been eliminated or curtailed.

Meanwhile, continued Democratic control of the Senate and the possibility of House elections in November 2022, due to court-ordered redistricting, both militated against dramatic policy changes in the next year, Democrats believed—or hoped. "What we've done is what we've learned from the people by listening. It's what they wanted," Northam said. Republicans "know where the polling is, and they know that lines are being redrawn."

If so, such knowledge did not stop numerous GOP lawmakers from introducing bills that would roll back recent Democratic initiatives. On the eve of the 2022 legislative session, outspoken voices in the new GOP House majority wanted to eliminate the newly enacted one-a-month limit on gun purchases, the power of civilian boards to review law enforcement actions, constraints on student discipline, higher thresholds for determining when a theft becomes grand larceny, and many other measures enacted during Northam's term.[7]

By the session's end Democrats had warded off many proposed changes, including banning abortions after twenty weeks of pregnancy, rolling back increases in the minimum wage, restoring a photo ID requirement for voting, and prohibiting by statute the teaching of "inherently divisive concepts." Youngkin and his allies had prevailed on other matters, however, including requiring parental notification when teaching sexually explicit material in schools, abandoning a mask mandate, opposing a new level of civilian oversight at the Department of Corrections, and defeating a constitutional amendment that would have ended Virginia's status as the rare state not automatically restoring voting rights to most felons once their societal debt is paid.

On racial matters one reality gave Republicans a measure of confidence. Ironically, considering the Democratic drumbeat on diversity, Republicans had just elected the most racially and ethnically diverse governing team in Virginia history. The 2021 selection of a White man, a Black woman, and a Latino man to run Virginia was rivaled in diversity only by the 1989 Democratic ticket, in which a Black man, a White man, and a White woman gained the state's top posts.

Those who had lost faith in the promise of the American dream would have to reconcile their theories and strategies to the 2021 Republican model of success. Those wedded to an up-by-the-bootstraps narrative, in which any American child with sufficient effort could rise above birth conditions of race and class, faced a deeper challenge. They must either confront or ignore data exposing that vision, for many, as a mirage.

CHAPTER 25

An Ending and a Beginning

The idea came to Ralph Northam in August as his term was winding down. He had just read a book by Ty Seidule, professor emeritus of history at West Point, and the message resonated. After a youth and early manhood of hero worship for Robert E. Lee, Seidule had come to see the former Confederate general in a much different light. "No other enemy officer in American history was responsible for the deaths of more U.S. Army soldiers than Robert E. Lee," Seidule wrote.[1]

That was true.

The clarity and the force of Seidule's words inspired Northam. They also reminded him of his own personal evolution and of the resistance he had faced in ordering a ground-up investigation of racism and sexism at the Virginia Military Institute. The order had created intense backlash. Substantial numbers of alumni and some cadets still held him in contempt.

Northam decided to go back to Lexington before he left office to speak the truth about his actions, as he saw it, to the young men and women in the corps. He wanted them to better understand his metamorphosis on race and why he had acted as he did. Many of them were probably as oblivious to racism as he had been as a young man, he thought, and his words might widen their vision.

The message also might speak to many far beyond the confines of the military school.

In late summer the governor began crafting the speech he wanted to give. Some mornings, arriving at the office before his staff, he would sit at his desk writing out the words in longhand. This was one address, he felt, that should come from his heart and his own pen and not from speechwriters. He intended to delay delivery until after the gubernatorial election. No one should regard this as a political stunt.

Freshly returned from a European trade trip, Northam spent part of the November 13–14 weekend polishing the final product. Monday evening, with reporters barred from the hall and cadets ordered to leave their cellphones in their rooms lest comments be posted to social media before he had finished, Northam stood before the seventeen-hundred-student cadet corps and began.

"If I could go back and talk to seventeen-year-old Rat Northam,[2] I would tell him, Ralph—you have a lot to learn about the world," Northam said, delving into the crux of his message. "And one of the most important lessons I've learned is that the world is filled with people who are different from me. People who think differently from me. Who experience things differently from me."

As a student a VMI, he did not ask a lot of questions, Northam said. "I just did what I was told—trying to avoid ten more pushups. . . . It didn't occur to me to ask, who is that a statue of? When was it erected? Why is that person being honored? Who decided that we would all salute him?

"When I saw the Confederate flag, it didn't occur to me to ask, what does flying the Confederate flag, or playing 'Dixie,' symbolize? Why are we glorifying the Lost Cause? And might these symbols be offensive to some of my fellow cadets? Those questions simply were not on my mind when I sat in your chair.

"But forty-four years have passed since I sat there, and over that time, I've come to understand what a large and diverse world we live in—and how much the world looks to our country for honest leadership. And as your governor, I have emphasized the importance of embracing diversity, being inclusive, being welcoming, and treating people fairly and with dignity."

He paused to let the words sink in. "Over the years, I've helped train many new young doctors. And I've always taught them this lesson: the eyes can't see what the brain doesn't know." What that means, he elaborated, is that if you've never been told or learned about a particular medical diagnosis, your brain won't recognize it "even if all the symptoms are staring you right in the face."

That, in many ways, is where the nation stands on racism, he continued. "If you haven't experienced sexism or racism yourself—perhaps because you look like me—and you haven't paid much attention to what it looks like, you're going to have a very hard time recognizing it. Until you learn what it looks like. Until you learn how to see it.

"That is where I was when I was Rat Northam and for a long time afterward. I thought I knew everything I needed to know. But I was wrong." Correcting those blind spots had required hard work—a conscious, deliberate effort.

As he continued, his words focused on VMI, but he could just as easily have substituted "Virginia" or even "America" for the school's name. "There's a proverb that says, 'A wise man changes his mind. A fool never will,'" he said. "Here at VMI, we have built up a lot of traditions over the generations. Many of those traditions have great value in molding young people. But others do not. We must understand our past, both the good and the bad, if we are going to move forward together as one."

In other words it would take understanding both the noble and ignoble parts of American history and confronting the legacies born of the bad, not just celebrating the good, for VMI, Virginia, and the United States to advance.

Winding up, he addressed the changes he had helped orchestrate at the school, and he urged the students to model themselves on the noble service of graduates such as Gen. George C. Marshall, who oversaw the rebuilding of post–World War II Europe. "Keep your heads up. Do good things for others. Learn from your mistakes. And take care of each other and your families," he concluded. That had been his credo through three turbulent years.

LEARN FROM YOUR MISTAKES

What had Ralph and Pam Northam learned in the months since the blackface photograph upended their privileged lives, and how had it changed them?

Several weeks before they returned to South Hampton Roads for the governor to resume his medical practice and for Pam to explore still-unfolding possibilities, the couple tackled those and other questions in a joint interview. Living through the scandal and its aftermath had been a shared experience. They had grown separately and as a unit.

Seated side by side on a gray leather sofa underneath a serene painting of marshland and coastal waters, with the gleaming-white Virginia capitol visible through office windows, the Northams reflected on a journey unlike anything they had envisioned in the comparatively innocent days just after his election as governor.

"The worry ages you. It keeps you up at night," said Pam, addressing her own evolution. At the same time, the experience had reinforced her belief in writer Glennon Doyle's mantra, "We can do hard things." Sometimes "you need to do them when it's the most difficult. It's easy to do the right things when it's all sunshine and the birds are tweeting. And it's really hard when it's dark and difficult days, but that's when it's most important to stand up for what you believe," she said.

"Hard things," for her, at one point had been simply putting on a public face. Outside the capitol the day of the interview, scaffolding was going up for the bleachers that would hold dignitaries and onlookers at the Youngkin inaugural. Four years earlier, "the first time the scaffolding went up, I felt like it was going up for a hanging," she recalled, smiling. "I was so worried about changing my life and career and everything else."

After more than eleven thousand miles of travel around Virginia, much of it aimed at understanding and promoting early childhood education, Pam no longer chafed at public appearances. "The public scrutiny is very difficult for a person who's very much an introvert," she said. "But you put on your armor, so to speak, and get out and get the job done." She balanced discomfort against the opportunity to impact the lives of children.

"In the end, do you really care what people think about how you dress and what you wear? They can say whatever they want about you. It doesn't change who you are."

Ralph's description of how he had changed echoed his VMI speech. "I'd say I'm much more knowledgeable about the world around me," he said. "My brain knows a lot more right now than in the past." Returning to medical practice, he hoped to put that learning to use. As a physician "I never had anybody tell me that they weren't comfortable with me," he said. But he had heard with his own ears from numerous people of color who feel they are not understood or valued by White professionals.

He had thought deeply about how he might incorporate that understanding into his practice. "I don't think I ever really looked at it like this," he said. "But there are maybe very sophisticated or more educated White families that come in and a ten-minute visit or fifteen-minute visit won't do. You have to pull out the literature and the textbooks." In contrast some of his Medicaid patients were actually better at describing what was wrong with their child, he said. But he wonders if he short-changed them on answering questions and giving detailed explanations.

"Perhaps I didn't spend as much time with folks like that as I should have. Maybe I didn't make them understand that I was there to give them the best care I could." In the future "I want to make sure that I take care. I think I'll put more into it, into the teaching. I will do it now with everybody with more vigor."

Asked if they could synthesize what they'd learned about race in America and how White people could deepen their understanding of it, the Northams suggested a dozen or so steps. They cautioned that their recommendations grew out of their personal experience and would not fit everyone.

A starting point, the governor warned, is knowing that "there's a lot [of White people] who don't want to be helped, and we have to understand that. Some people I thought were pretty well-rounded have been really frightened by critical race theory. 'Don't be teaching my children that, because they're not racist and I'm not racist.' What I've tried to explain to some of my friends who are so worried about critical race theory: don't be scared about teaching the truth.

We're not asking to force-feed anybody. We just want to understand our history —and an accurate history.

"It's kind of like religion," he said, reverting to his original point about not everyone being open to confronting concepts such as White privilege. If someone is uninterested or their mind is closed, initiating conversation is likely pointless. "But if they ask you about it, you can explain it to them," he said. He foresaw that his future might involve some form of teaching about race, growing out of his personal experience. "If they're willing to listen," he added. "I won't ever force it on anybody."

For those who are open to knowing more, the road begins with listening, both Northams believe. "I realize now, at age sixty-two, you learn every day. The answer is to understand that we don't know everything and to listen to people's stories and experiences," the governor said. That was how he learned— hearing firsthand how a Black aide had felt hearing a White aide walk by whistling "Dixie" or, from Senator McClellan, how a person of color felt about minstrel shows. "Most of us have empathy. We don't get up in the morning to be offensive," he said, so coming to understand different perspectives is key.

Few, if any, White people can immerse themselves in hearing Black voices to the extent the Northams did during their listening tour. However, for those willing to do the work, community conversations, podcasts, and books can substitute to a degree, they said. Critical as personal conversations proved, the governor's learning was also deeply informed by the documentary *13th*, by Seidule's *Robert E. Lee and Me*, and by numerous other texts. Such sources are widely available. "Some people may need a little more convincing than others," said Pam, "but, for the most part, as we learn from the stories of people like Gayle, we can do better."

She was referring to Gayle Jessup White, a community engagement officer at Monticello, Jefferson's home. Jessup White is the author of *Reclamation*, a book describing her search for the truth behind family lore claiming an ancestral link to Thomas Jefferson and Sally Hemings. The twists and turns of such struggles reveal much about the Black experience of navigating a White-dominated world.[3]

Learning may lead to a next step. "One of the things that can be difficult, and I say this personally, not giving advice to anybody else, but it can difficult to admit that you're wrong and to admit that you don't know everything you think you do," the governor said. A level of humility is required.

In the Northams' experience, having open conversations about race requires the courage to make a mistake. Finding a safe space for dialogue may ease discomfort. For many that may involve a faith arena, they said. For others unconnected to a faith tradition, community organizations such as the YMCA or YWCA may offer opportunities to tackle racially charged topics. Having on hand a trained facilitator in the role Jonathan Zur or Janice Underwood played for them can help elevate understanding over anger or defensiveness, they noted.

The possibility of saying something offensive, a fear that often shuts down White people in racial conversations, needs confronting. "It's painful to learn that way," said Pam, recalling her experience with the mansion kitchen. Turning her focus to understanding the perspective that lay behind the criticism helped her navigate it. Redoubling her efforts to seek out the descendants of the enslaved people who had worked at the mansion and deferring to their guidance allowed her to feel that she had turned bad to good.

Trusting in forgiveness and goodwill can often, if not always, ease the path, the pair said. Simply asking, "Can you help me?" conveys an openheartedness and a willingness to learn. In their experience many people will forgive errors born more from ignorance than malice. "It's all part of making mistakes, learning, and doing better the next day," Northam added.

Factual information can also be invaluable in building understanding, they said, citing Northam's inaugural address as an example. "A child born two miles that way can expect to live to about age sixty-three," he had said, pointing north from the capitol. Then, pointing west, "But a child born five miles in that direction can expect to live twenty years longer. You don't have to be a doctor to know that something's wrong." That, they believe, is the sort of easily understood messaging that needs no elaboration. "For me as an educator, it's always about bringing facts to the table and letting people draw their own conclusions," Pam said.

When dealing with hard truths or hostile audiences, the governor said, he tries to start with a point of connection, something everyone can agree on. "It may just be a slim thread," he said. At VMI, for instance, he began with a joke about how he had arrived at the school with a girlfriend and a full head of hair. Within weeks both had disappeared. The hair had been buzz-cut and the girlfriend had gone the way of a "Dear Ralph" letter. From that common thread of connection, he moved on to laying out the more challenging truths that he wanted to convey.

One important reality, said both the governor and First Lady, is that healing racial wounds is often more about deeds than words. "It's not lip service. It's what you do that says more to people," Pam said. "That's what we've tried hard to do, to speak with our deeds about what we care about and prioritize in equity."

For both their work in early childhood education is central to hopes for a better American future. If education is what can bring someone out of poverty, then it is critical that all children be given an opportunity to learn from a young age. "You pick a baby up and look into the eyes, and you don't see the hatred and bigotry," said the governor. "That's learned from somewhere, and most of the time from home. But if we're able to provide access to early childhood education, let people know that we're all in this together, that will help defuse some of the hatred and bigotry that maybe is learned later in life."

At least he would like to think so. His tenure as governor had left him knowing that not everyone shares the sentiment. "There are just a number of individuals out there who don't want to lose their parking spot. It's just the way it is," he said. "We have to be realistic and accept that. We're not going to be batting one thousand."

In his final weeks as governor, Northam was still swinging for the bleachers. He wanted to do all in his power to ensure that his legacy extended beyond a blackface photograph. A treasury flush with cash allowed him to roll out proposals for both tax cuts and spending increases in the 2022–24 budget proposal that he would bequeath to Youngkin. The governor-elect and the assembly would determine the final spending plan, but as proposed by Northam, it included pay hikes for teachers, state troopers, and other government workers; eliminated the state portion of the sales tax on food; invested in the Chesapeake Bay and its tributaries at record levels; dramatically increased state spending for historic Black colleges; brought Virginia closer to meeting its goal of universal broadband; and much else.

Northam had no illusion that careful stewardship would blot out the blackface stain. In a highly partisan era and a time of deep racial mistrust, the story could expect a long life. "At the end of the day, it would be nice to put that behind us. But, no, it's not behind us," he said. "It'll probably be with me until they put me in an urn, the ground, whatever." He sighed. "And that's okay. It's part of my life story."

He revisited the persistent questions one more time. "When you say, 'Are you positive?' I have no recollection of dressing up and being in that photograph," he said. The fact that he clearly remembers donning blackface to imitate Michael Jackson and also blackening his face for night maneuvers in the military convinces him that he would remember a medical school blackface moment if it had occurred. He also has no memory of submitting the photograph. "That's about all I can say," he concluded. "I would have liked someone to say, 'Northam, that wasn't you. It was me.' That didn't happen. And right now, it's like I've done what I could do to make good from it. I've moved on from that.

"The story is what's happened since, at least in the way I look at it."

As Northam packed his bags and prepared to leave public office, commentators and constituents reflected on the results of a remarkable tenure. Rarely had so many dramatic events been packed into a Virginia governor's single four-year term. Multiple lessons—personal, political, and societal—had emerged from the fallout surrounding the blackface photograph. From this author's perspective, these are among them.

PERSONAL REDEMPTION

If the blackface photograph was to be a permanent part of the Northam narrative, then his refusal to quit and his determination to respond by doing the work of racial repair deserve equal or greater billing. The story began as that of a proud and accomplished man who faced deep humiliation. His decision to respond not by slinking away but by learning from his mistakes and by making amends is a model worth emulating. "We're all human, and we all make mistakes. I've never been a quitter. I think because I didn't quit, we've been able to do some good things for Virginia," he said.

Conservative partisans and some far-left progressives continued to question Northam's motives and actions. For one group he had gone too far; for the other not far enough. However, many Virginians who observed Northam closely saw an admirable model of humility and personal growth. "People are going to say, 'It's just a politician trying to redeem himself,'" said Cassandra Newby-Alexander. "It may have started out that way, but somewhere along the line, it became real to him." Watching Northam speak at various events, comparing the old Ralph to the new, she saw a changed man, one whose eyes had been opened to a reality he had not known. Knowledge empowers, and the knowledge Northam had acquired had made him bold, as when he took down the Lee statue or pardoned the Martinsville Seven or demanded an accounting at VMI. "The experience helped him start to become fearless. He's acquired a depth he didn't have," she said.

AN INTOLERANT POLITICAL CULTURE

Some abusive and dishonest actions clearly should disqualify politicians from office. A thirty-five-year-old racist photograph that does not comport with a life filled with commitment to principled causes, though deeply disappointing, is not one of them. It falls into a grayer area. Many African Americans were willing in February 2019 to judge Northam by his whole life, not by a worst moment; more loudly, many others, feeling betrayed and incensed by evidence of escalating racism in Trump-era America, demanded blood. Yet an ugly image

deserved to be balanced against such acts as Northam's critical role in bringing medical coverage to four hundred thousand needy Virginians and his years
of compassionate service to the children of Hampton Roads. Unquestionably
Northam spurred his own near demise by his confusing response to the photograph. His clumsy back-and-forth between acceptance and denial came close
to destroying him politically. No matter how many advisers contributed to his
actions, responsibility for that misstep rests with him.

Politically, on the night of February 1, Northam should not have let himself
be pressured into a premature statement. The demands of a twenty-four-hour
news cycle did not have to be instantly satisfied. Sometimes the best course for a
politician, as for any other person, is to say nothing until certain of what is correct and needs to be said.

Still, in a fed-up, rush-to-judgment era, the Northam story shows how the
backlash to centuries of wrongdoing involving race, sex, and gender risks breed-
ing overreach and intolerance of its own. When it comes to race, the lesson of
Ralph Northam is that "everyone deserves a restorative path back when you
make a mistake," Underwood said. Far more was accomplished by his staying in
office than if he had left.

HOW TO BE AN ANTI-RACIST (THE FIFTY-NINE-YEAR-OLD
SOUTHERN WHITE MAN'S VERSION)

Guided by African American lawmakers and others, Northam took a deep dive
into exploring his own privilege and inadequate understanding of both Black
history and the reality of racial injustice in America. The steps he took can be a
guide to others. For a White person, dismissing concepts such as systemic racism
and White privilege is easy from a sheltered world that includes little in-depth
interaction with Black lives. It becomes harder when and if a White person is
willing to listen, truly listen, to the realities of another person's experience.
Even after listening, there may be legitimate differences in prescriptions for healing, but those remedies will be grounded in deeper truth. Such understanding
can lessen vitriol and reduce the easy manipulation of terms such as critical race
theory.

BLACK AGENCY IN CREATING CHANGE

The role of the Virginia Legislative Black Caucus and other Black voices in
Northam's and Virginia's transformation cannot be overstated. At first furious
with the governor, feeling deceived, many Black leaders shunned him. Gradually
they came to recognize both his sincere willingness to embrace their counsel

and the unique opportunity that presented them to shape the state's policy agenda. For Black lawmakers the two-year period after Democrats took control of the legislature in 2020 offered a flowering unparalleled in Virginia since the aftermath of the Civil War. Prior to that "we were certainly a voice for uplifting the Black community and a voice for pointing out inequity, but we had very few victories," said Senator McClellan. Suddenly the victories flowed.

Even if retrenchment awaited, Black lawmakers had seized the opportunity when it arose. "I feel like the Black caucus was a phoenix. We rose through the fire in this moment of strength," said Marcia Price with pride. Northam's predicament and the deference paid by White Democrats to the Black caucus created a rare opening. The response "required a sense of discipline and preparedness that I'm really glad we were able to meet," she said.

TENSIONS AMONG ALLIES

Close-knit as the alliance became, not every interaction went smoothly. The connections were tested by COVID-19, both when declining tax revenues in 2020 forced budget cuts in progressive programs and when administration strategies failed to deliver vaccines to Black and Brown communities as rapidly as to White ones. In a moment of national panic, once again, centuries of White advantage and Black mistrust prevailed.

Some Black leaders also found themselves assessing the importance—and the danger—in working with White allies. The value lies in not having to carry the burden of anti-racism alone and in the potential for White allies to enter spaces largely off-limits to Black people. The danger, summed up by Delegate Price, comes "when you have White progressives that, instead of amplifying the voices of those that have the lived experience of the injustice, will grab the mic to speak for us." She did not see Northam as being in that group.

A second danger comes if White allies backpedal or forget their commitment when pressure subsides. On that account Price was waiting to see where Northam would land. "I'm just hopeful that time will show that he was serious about this and that in his private life he will continue to excavate the opportunities to do this work," she said.

PROBLEMATIC TOOLS

The complaint of Democratic political strategist and pundit James Carville that Democrats were being swamped among independents by an overly righteous sense of "stupid wokeness" gained credence after party losses in the Virginia and New Jersey elections in November 2021.[4] The danger with that analysis, on point as it might be politically, lay in the prospect that it granted permission to ignore fundamental, ongoing injustices in education, housing, policing, and economics.

The imperative to keep a laser focus on essential goals does not preclude owning up to unnecessarily hostile, confusing, or outdated messages, however. Responding to the Loudoun County training that assigned various characteristics to White and Color groups, for instance, Newby-Alexander was dismissive. "All of that is foolishness," she said. "There are not groups of people who are kinder, gentler, more thoughtful than other groups of people. Privilege will beget a certain amount of selfishness and abusiveness toward other people. But that's a matter of privilege; it's not race-based. It's societal." Underwood echoed the concern: "There are a lot of professional development and cultural competency trainings that don't meet the mark."

The critical point voiced by both women is that such shortcomings demand revision, not rejection. As racial and ethnic diversity grows, both children and adults will need better tools for understanding and accepting the ways in which society is changing. To reject such efforts because some individual decisions need rethinking or some teaching materials need retooling would be tragic.

NAVIGATING THE CONTRADICTIONS

While some on the far left prefer to dispose entirely of Thomas Jefferson, James Madison, and other founders who enslaved human beings, more sober thinkers will evaluate people by the times in which they lived and by the whole of their lives. Lee, a general whose primary claim to historical significance was leading an insurrection against the United States in defense of slavery, is one calculation. Jefferson and Madison, individuals who drafted frameworks for the Declaration of Independence and the US Constitution, even as they enslaved human beings, are another.

To suggest, as some do, that telling a full history teaches children to hate America misconstrues the imperative of looking honestly at the past. Surely it is possible to acknowledge the founders' sins while also praising their achievements. Even as turmoil swept the nation after George Floyd's death, across the globe simultaneous police and government crackdowns against pro-democracy demonstrators in Hong Kong showcased the differences in an autocratic, militarized state and the far superior, if imperfect, government conceived by Jefferson, Madison, and their peers.

Katherine Rowe, president of the College of William & Mary, spoke to that complexity in April 2021 as she described the school's process for evaluating how various statues and building names would be considered going forward. "With respect to our nation's Founding Fathers," Rowe said, "we cannot sweep them away and ignore the revolutionary ideas of liberty and democracy they launched; those ideas have empowered oppressed peoples around the world. Nor can we rest easy with simple stories of their achievements, without honestly grappling with how those ideas rose in a society defined by enslavement."

Unfortunately, the quest to strike that balance is "inherently divisive," but it is what is required of a mature society at this point in our history. We can do hard things.

STAY THE COURSE

As activists make the case for concepts like systemic racism and White supremacy, they have no better allies than the facts. Whole segments of the histories of Black and Indigenous peoples in the United States have been whitewashed in school curricula. Much middle-class White wealth was built on twentieth-century housing policies that excluded Black people. The crack cocaine epidemic of the 1980s and '90s resulted in the criminalization of many Black people and the decimation of Black families, while the opioid epidemic of the 2000s affected many more White people and has been viewed largely as a health crisis. School district lines nationwide are drawn in such a way that poor children of color are largely clustered together, a bundling that contributes to inferior educational outcomes in many of those schools. Exclusionary housing policies often perpetuate educational problems.

Those are all facts, as are the data affirming racial disparities in so many aspects of American life.

"You've got to stay the course, because inequity has had a 402-year head start," said Janice Underwood. "People have very unrealistic expectations of how do we resolve this." Some think that the nation's race problem was resolved in the 1960s. What they ignore, she said, are "the deep, structural inequities that are inherent in all those funding formulas and systemic inequities across housing and financial systems and educational systems. We have been socialized to think we don't have a racism problem because it's much easier to think that and move on with the status quo."

Northam's mission as a White ally had been to expose that lie. "I don't think you can say we've gone too far or overplayed our hand in wanting to learn the truth," he said. The role he had played since 2019 was to use his powerful office to elevate messages that had been muted or silenced. "I've got a pulpit to speak from, and I'm speaking for voices that have never been heard," he said. He left office with no regrets about having tried to meet that challenge.

NO MATTER WHAT HAPPENED in the aftermath of the Northam administration, those who had worked closely with him celebrated the racial progress that had been made. In many ways their actions had merely scratched the surface of structural racism. Even so, "we did more to address racial inequity in Virginia between 2019 and 2021 than at any other time in my lifetime," Jennifer Mc-Clellan said. Soon many of the changes of those years—even the dismantling of Confederate statues—would look normal and would be broadly accepted, Cassandra Newby-Alexander predicted. "We're a society that fears change," she said. "But then after it's happened, we realize how important the change really was and how beneficial the change has been."

Members of the Virginia Legislative Black Caucus detected changes not only in Northam but in other White colleagues. As a spotlight had been turned on the governor's shortcomings and as the reckoning spurred by George Floyd's death had unfolded, other White people had quietly assessed their own misunderstandings or failings around race. Some had brought new determination to share in the responsibility for correcting those ills, not simply leaving the task to Black lawmakers. "Ralph Northam is not the only person that grew during that time," said Jeff Bourne. "His going through it makes others understand."

The important challenge going forward was to see that those White allies not waver in what promised to be a more hostile political environment. Working with a new Republican administration, the Black caucus hoped to find points of common ground. They had few illusions about the probable difficulty of that task. White people sympathetic to the cause, whatever their party, needed to step up. "Be an ally always," urged Marcia Price. "The need exists whether you're caught with your pants down or not. There are actual people that live in these communities, that need funding, that need not to be criminalized for being poor and for being Black."

The legacy of Ralph Northam lay not just in legislative achievements. He had demonstrated also how a White man, even a highly accomplished one with Black friends and a record of support for civil rights, can be race-ignorant about what it means to live as a person of color in America. Do not indulge yourself by imagining that Northam is unique in that blindness. Equally important, he showed a path for making amends. Jarred into a new perspective, he committed to serious learning. Then he adjusted his policy goals and joined with Black advocates to chart better directions.

How different might the narrative have been had a blackface photograph not surfaced on Ralph Northam's yearbook page in 2019? Very different. Perhaps many White people need a blackface scandal to tear down their defenses and force them to look at America—and at themselves—through cleared eyes.

FINALLY, WAS IT HIM IN THE PHOTOGRAPH?

Based on Northam's high regard for truth-telling and the failure of anyone to come forward with evidence placing him in the picture, I believe not. Others may disagree. The mystery remains unsolved. Does it matter? Barring proof of deliberate falsehood, not really. What matters most is what happened in the second half of the story.

The blackface photograph that surfaced in the 1984 Eastern Virginia Medical School yearbook on February 1, 2019, will remain one of the most consequential images in Virginia history, just not in a way anyone first imagined.

It changed a White man, who then joined forces with Black lawmakers and many others to create a racial regeneration in the state that gave birth to some of the noblest aspirations and worst evils of American history. Their work was a beginning, not an end.

ACKNOWLEDGMENTS

Any book is a blend of subject and author. An author's worldview inevitably influences the way she interprets her subject. Inevitably, also, immersion in a subject will expand an author's view of the world.

The opportunity to speak in depth with multiple members of the Virginia Legislative Black Caucus and other Black activists at a particular crossroads in history left me, a White woman, changed. How?

Here are three ways. First, the stories. I was struck by the fact that almost every Black leader I interviewed had a very tangible story about how they or their family had been significantly harmed by racism. A job had been denied. A community had been terrorized. A parent had been ostracized. A police stop had triggered fear. These were not theoretical movie versions of how it is to live as a Black person in America. They were real stories, and almost everyone I interviewed, no matter how accomplished they had become, had one.

Second, I saw more clearly than previously how the same incident can be interpreted in totally different ways based on life experiences, including those tied to the color of one's skin. Over the years, friends of color have sometimes mentioned an episode to me that paralleled some experience of my own. They had taken the event as a reflection of racism; I'd taken it as someone having a bad day or acting poorly.

Reporting this book, I had the opportunity to flesh out a couple of such episodes. Listening to the White version and the Black version of the same event, I could see how life experience colored or dictated the interpretation. Both views, in fact, were founded in lived truth. The revelation reminded me how many times, through a long reporting career, the voices of authority I encountered had been White. Consequently, the stories I told often were grounded in their perspective. How much, I now wonder, was left untold?

Third, I had never before thought so consciously about the degree to which skin tone influences first impressions. If you doubt that this is the case, ask yourself if you have ever—*ever*—felt a hint of fear when the face coming toward you on a darkened sidewalk did not match your own, or a smidgeon of doubt when a business owner or a professional was of a different race, or a bit of concern if your child's newly assigned teacher's skin tone differed from your own.

If you are White, and you have felt any of those tugs, multiply your outlook by the likely similar feelings of tens of millions of Americans, and you might glimpse the underpinnings of structural racism. If you are Black, or any other race or ethnicity, you may have similarly stereotyped a White person. The human damage is comparable, but simply because you are in the minority, the impact on how society functions will be less.

This book had its start on June 4, 2020, when Ralph Northam announced that he intended to take down the Robert E. Lee statue in Richmond. The contrast between that day and February 1, 2019, when a photograph of Northam in blackface came to light, struck me as a potentially powerful story, one worth telling. My first interview with Governor Northam, on June 24, 2020, was followed by thirteen others over the next eighteen months.

Somewhere along the way, it became clear that this was much more than Northam's story. It also was an account of the Black lawmakers, activists, historians, and other professionals who tutored, prodded, threatened, and supported him through the journey. My gratitude to them, as to the former governor, for their candor and trust is profound. They recognized the value of my attempt, however imperfect, to record for history the inner workings of an astonishing period in the evolution of a state and nation.

Where a quotation is not sourced, either in the text or footnotes, the reader may assume that it emerged from the author's recorded interviews with dozens of public officials, community activists, and personal acquaintances of the former governor. I regret that more Republican leaders were not among those interviewed. Most GOP leaders whom I approached saw little political benefit for themselves in public comment. As one leading Republican who had called for Northam's resignation put it, "After the Governor's yearbook photo was publicized in 2019, I had no communication with the Governor himself aside from bumping into him at one or two events. Because of our extremely limited contact, I'm afraid I don't have anything to offer you in the way of insight or analysis."

Where appropriate, I have tried to give credence to a Republican perspective. Determination to combat racism should not be viewed as a Democrat-Republican binary.

Considerable effort went into unearthing the roots of the Eastern Virginia Medical School yearbook blackface photograph. Ultimately, I was unable to shed more light on the origins of the picture than the investigators assigned the task separately by the medical school and the governor were. However, some previously unpublished details of their investigations appear in the text, as do the first published comments from the 1984 yearbook editor, whom investigators had been unable to reach.

Several people played important roles in bringing this book to publication. First among them is Suzette Denslow, who provided the introduction to Northam and his staff. Thank you, Suzette. I would also like to thank agent David Black for his early confidence in the project; readers Lucretia McCulley, Dan Ream, Bill and Carol Obrochta, and Glenn Frankel for the many improvements they brought to the manuscript; friends Bonnie Winston, Stephen Retherford, Claudia Jemmott, Elizabeth Roark, and Earl Swift for their help; and UofSC Press acquisitions editor Ehren Foley for his instantaneous understanding of and enthusiasm for the story.

So many people ground me with friendship that I must resort to thanking them in groups. Hurray for the best book and potluck groups; the Women Rowing North, who were there for the book's inception and followed all its twists and turns; the Grace-Patterson women; and the Richmond Friends Meeting community. Thanks also to my diverse and wonderful family. You are the source from which I grow. If every book under my name should be dedicated to a single person, it would be my friend and life partner Bob Lipper.

NOTES

LIST OF ABBREVIATIONS USED IN NOTES

Associated Press (AP)
Daily Press (DP)
Encyclopedia Virginia (EV)
New York Times (NYT)
Richmond Dispatch (RD)
Richmond Free Press (RFP)
Richmond Times-Dispatch (RTD)
Roanoke Times (RT)
Virginia Magazine of History and Biography (VMHB)
Virginia Mercury (VM)
Virginian-Pilot (VP)
Washington Post (WP)

PART I

1. Brent Tarter, *The Grandees of Government: The Origins and Persistence of Undemocratic Politics in Virginia* (Charlottesville: University of Virginia Press, 2013), 13.

2. James Horn, *1619: Jamestown and the Forging of American Democracy* (New York: Basic Books, 2018), 116; Joseph C. Miller, "Transatlantic Slave Trade, The," *EV*, https://www.encyclopediavirginia.org/Transatlantic_Slave_Trade_The#start_entry.

CHAPTER 1

1. Ronna McDaniel (@GOPChairwoman), Twitter, January 30, 2019, 2:02 PM, https://twitter.com/gopchairwoman/status/1090686730934644736; Marco Rubio (@marcorubio), Twitter, January 30, 2019, 2:04 PM, https://twitter.com/marcorubio/status/109068733 6827011074; Donald Trump quoted in Vince Coglianese and Saagar Enjeti, "Trump Rips Virginia Democrat's Abortion Comments," *Daily Caller*, January 30, 2019.

2. Trip Gabriel and Michael M. Grynbaum, "With Northam Picture, Obscure Publication Plays Big Role in Virginia Politics," *NYT*, February 4, 2019.

3. McGuireWoods, "'Report to Eastern Virginia Medical School," summary of statements by Clark Mercer, May 21, 2019, 5.

4. "'He Should Step Down': Racist Photo Sparks Near-Universal Calls for Northam to Resign," *WP*, February 2, 2019. This article provides a detailed list of prominent figures calling for Northam's resignation on either February 1 or February 2, 2019.

5. Ibid.

6. VLBC (@VaBlackCaucus), Twitter, Feb 1, 2019, 10:56 PM, https://twitter.com/vablackcaucus/status/1091545949716004864.

CHAPTER 3

1. Jonathan Martin and Alan Blinder, "Second Virginia Democrat Says He Wore Blackface, Throwing Party into Turmoil," *NYT*, February 6, 2019.

2. Margaret Edds, *An Expendable Man: The Near-Execution of Earl Washington Jr.* (New York: NYU Press, 2003); Rob Warden and Steven Drizin, eds., *True Stories of False Confessions* (Evanston, IL: Northwestern University Press, 2009); Michael Radelet, Hugo Bedau, and Constance Putnam, *In Spite of Innocence: The Ordeal of 400 Americans Wrongly Convicted of Crimes Punishable by Death* (Boston: Northeastern University Press, 1992).

3. Geoffrey Skelley, "Calls for Northam's Resignation Reflect White Democrats' Changing Attitude on Racism," FiveThirtyEight, February 4, 2019.

PART II

1. Patrick Breen, *The Land Shall be Deluged in Blood: A New History of the Nat Turner Revolt* (Oxford: Oxford University Press, 2015), 10.

2. Peter Wallenstein, *Cradle of America: Four Centuries of Virginia History* (Lawrence: University Press of Kansas, 2007), 144–47; Gregory Schneider, "The Birthplace of American Slavery Debated Abolishing It after Nat Turner's Bloody Revolt," *WP*, June 1, 2019.

3. Breen, *Land Shall be Deluged in Blood*, 2.

4. James M. Campbell, *Slavery on Trial: Race, Class, and Criminal Justice in Antebellum Richmond, Virginia* (Gainesville: University of Florida Press, 2007), 150.

CHAPTER 4

1. Darren Sands, "Black Officials in Virginia Have a List of Demands for the Governor and Attorney General if They Won't Resign," *BuzzFeed News*, February 11, 2019.

2. Greg Schneider, "Va. Gov. Ralph Northam Says He Wants to Focus Rest of His Term on Racial Equity," *WP*, February 9, 2019.

3. Julissa Natzely Arce Raya (@julissaarce), Twitter, Feb 1, 2019, 10:56 PM, https://twitter.com/julissaarce/status/1094643414786662401.

4. Kurt Eichenwald (@kurteichenwald), Twitter, Feb 10, 2019, 3:16 PM, https://twitter.com/kurteichenwald/status/1094691561189924864?ref_src=twsrc%5Etfw.

CHAPTER 5

1. 1960 US Census: Population, Vol. 1., Characteristics of the Population, Part 48 (Virginia), General Social & Economic Characteristics, Table 88.

2. 1850 and 1869 US Census Slave Schedules, www.ancestryinstitution.com. For manumission records, see Richard H. Smith, "Manumission Deeds of Accomack County, Virginia."

3. John A. Brownlee, https://www.geni.com/people/John-Brownlee/6000000000507003640.

4. John Ewing Brownlee, https://www.wikitree.com/wiki/Brownlee-112, and "The Premium Which Capt. J. E. Brownlee Bore Off—His Victories and Triumphs in Later Years," *Abbeville (SC) Press and Banner*, April 27, 1910, https://www.newspapers.com/clip/412 55425/john-ewin-brownlee-story/.

5. T. Stephen Whitman, *Challenging Slavery in the Chesapeake: Black and White Resistance to Human Bondage, 1775–1865* (Baltimore: Maryland Historical Society, 2007), 5; T. H. Breen and Stephen Innes, *"Myne Owne Ground": Race and Freedom on Virginia's Eastern Shore, 1640–1676* (New York: Oxford University Press, 2005), 104.

6. Kirk Mariner, *Slave and Free on Virginia's Eastern Shore: From the Revolution to the Civil War* (Onancock, VA: Miona, 2014), 18–19.

7. Matthew Krogh, "The Eastern Shore of Virginia in the Civil War," MA thesis, Virginia Tech, 2006, 10–11.

8. Adopted by a rump legislature, the 1864 Virginia constitution was recognized only in those parts of the state under US military control, including the Eastern Shore.

9. Brooks Miles Barnes, "The Onancock Race Riot of 1907," *Virginia Magazine of History and Biography* 92 (July 1984): 336.

10. Mariner, *Slave and Free on Virginia's Eastern Shore*, 229.

11. McGuireWoods, "Report to Eastern Virginia Medical School," 2.

CHAPTER 6

1. Beverly Daniel Tatum, *Why Are All the Black Kids Sitting Together in the Cafeteria?* (New York: Basic Books, 1999), 7.

2. Robin DiAngelo, *White Fragility: Why It's So Hard for White People to Talk about Racism* (Boston: Beacon, 2018), 3, 20.

3. Peter Wade, "In Interview, Virginia Gov. Northam Shows He Still Doesn't Understand Race in America," *Rolling Stone*, February 9, 2019.

4. Writer's Program of the WPA, *The Negro in Virginia* (New York: Hastings House, 1940), quotation from introduction by Roscoe Lewis, supervisor of Negro workers.

5. "Slavery, 1825–1860," exhibit of the Virginia Museum of History and Culture; Charles Dew, *The Making of a Racist: A Southerner Reflects on Family, History, and the Slave Trade* (Charlottesville: University of Virginia Press, 2016), 99–100.

6. Brent Tarter, "The Abolition of Slavery in Virginia," *EV*, https://encyclopedia virginia.org/entries/the-abolition-of-slavery-in-virginia/ (accessed March 8, 2022); Jaime Amanda Martinez, "Slavery during the Civil War," *EV*, https://encyclopediavirginia.org /entries/slavery-during-the-civil-war/ (accessed March 8, 2022).

7. Wallenstein, *Cradle of America*, 228–29.

8. A. E. Dick Howard, "1902: The Era of Disenfranchisement," *RTD*, December 20, 2020; J. Douglas Smith, *Managing White Supremacy: Race, Politics, and Citizenship in Jim Crow Virginia* (Chapel Hill: University of North Carolina Press, 2002), 26.

9. Margaret Edds, *We Face the Dawn: Oliver Hill, Spottswood Robinson, and the Legal Team that Dismantled Jim Crow* (Charlottesville: University of Virginia Press, 2018), 115.

10. Equal Justice Initiative, "Lynching in America: Confronting the Legacy of Racial Terror," 2013. The report argues that the decline of lynching in the South was linked to an increase in capital punishment, often after speedy trials. https://eji.org/wp-content /uploads/2020/09/lynching-in-america-3d-ed-091620.pdf.

11. Eric Rise, *The Martinsville Seven: Race, Rape, and Capital Punishment* (Charlottesville: University Press of Virginia, 1995). Statistics on executions for rape are discussed on p. 102.

12. For two of the many stories, see Gregory Schneider and Laura Vozzella, "Virginia First Lady under Fire for Handing Cotton to African American Students on Mansion Tour," WP, February 28, 2019; and Laura Vozzella, "Virginia's 'Cotton Situation' Is a Matter of Dispute," WP, March 1, 2019.

13. Jonathan Zur, "Jonathan Zur on Virginia's Moment of Reckoning," DP, February 12, 2019.

14. Richard Reeves and Christopher Pulliam, "No Room at the Top: The Stark Divide in Black and White Economic Mobility," Brookings, February 14, 2019.

CHAPTER 7

1. Michael Rosen and Helen Oxenbury, *We're Going on a Bear Hunt* (New York: Little Simon, 1997).

2. "Opinion: Ralph Northam: I Won't Sign Another Mandatory Minimum Sentence Bill into Law. Here's Why," WP, May 1, 2019.

3. Laura Vozzella and Antonio Olivo, "Legislature Sustains Northam's Vetoes and Backs Major Highway Plan, Despite Scandal," WP, April 3, 2019.

4. Wason Center Surveys, "Virginia Voters Are Tuned into Upcoming State Legislative Elections," April 9, 2019.

5. Nathaniel Cline, "Black Leaders, Republicans Protest Governor's Northern Virginia Visit; Northam Retreats," *Loudoun (VA) Times-Mirror*, April 15, 2019.

6. Jonathan Martin, "Terry McAuliffe Will Not Run for President," NYT, April 17, 2019.

CHAPTER 8

1. Ned Oliver, "Good Teeth, Big Legs and a Bow Tie: Inconclusive Report Details Chaos in Northam's Office," VM, May 22, 2019.

2. Alston & Bird, memo re: "Investigation of Photograph Appearing on Governor Ralph Northam's Student Page in the 1984 Eastern Virginia Medical School Yearbook," April 1, 2019; McGuireWoods, "Report to Eastern Virginia Medical School."

3. Brett Murphy, "Blackface, KKK Hoods and Mock Lynchings: Review of 900 Yearbooks Finds Blatant Racism," *USA Today*, February 20, 2019 (updated April 23, 2020).

CHAPTER 9

1. "Following Virginia Beach Massacre, Gov. Ralph Northam Calls Special Session on Guns," AP, June 4, 2019.

2. NBC12 Newsroom and Eric Perry, "'Part of My Heart Is Missing': 9-Year-Old Girl Shot, Killed at Richmond Park," NBC News, May 26, 2019 (updated May 28, 2019).

3. Gregory Schneider, Laura Vozzella, and Antonio Olivo, "Gun Debate Ends Abruptly in Virginia as GOP-Controlled Legislature Adjourns after 90 Minutes," WP, July 9, 2019; Alan Suderman and Sarah Rankin, "GOP-Led Virginia Legislature Abruptly Adjourns Gun Session," AP, July 9, 2019.

PART III

1. Smith, *Managing White Supremacy*, 91; Warren Fiske, "The Black & White World of Walter Plecker," *VP*, August 18, 2004.

2. Smith, *Managing White Supremacy*, 107, 117.

3. *Buck v. Bell*, 274 U.S. 200, May 2, 1927.

4. Paul Lombardo, *Three Generations, No Imbeciles: Eugenics, the Supreme Court, and* Buck v. Bell (Baltimore: Johns Hopkins University Press, 2008), xii, 139–40, 262.

5. *Loving v. Virginia*, 338 U.S. 1, June 12, 1967.

CHAPTER 10

1. Lisa Vernon Sparks, "Northam Calls for Jefferson Davis Arch on Fort Monroe to Come Down," *DP*, April 18, 2019.

2. Mel Leonor, "Janice Underwood, ODU Official, Is the State's First Director of Diversity," *RTD*, September 9, 2019.

3. Gregory Schneider, "'A Rare Position': Va. Gov. Ralph Northam Could Wind Up with Great Power, Months after Almost Resigning," *WP*, June 10, 2019.

4. Ervin Jordan Jr., *Black Confederates and Afro-Yankees in Civil War Virginia* (Charlottesville: University of Virginia Press, 1995), 83–84; Ira Berlin, *The Long Emancipation: The Demise of Slavery in the United States* (Cambridge, MA: Harvard University Press, 2015), 159–60.

5. Jack Stripling, "U. of Richmond's Leader Pushes City to Face Its Slave History," *Chronicle of Higher Education*, June 12, 2011.

CHAPTER 11

1. Erik Eckholm and Kim Severson, "Virginia Senate Passes Ultrasound Bill as Other States Take Notice," *NYT*, February 28, 2012.

2. Jonathan Martin, "Primary for Virginia Governor Tests Power of an Anti-Trump Campaign," *NYT*, February 26, 2017.

3. A term coined by Kimberlé Crenshaw in a 1989 academic paper, *intersectionality* refers to the ways race, class, gender, and other individual characteristics intersect in a person's interactions with the world. In the theory of intersectionality, a Black man and a Black woman, for instance, will experience the world differently, even though they are of the same race. Similarly, a White woman and a Black woman will be impacted by varying identities, even though they share sex and gender. Along with critical race theory, *intersectionality* has become a controversial term, less for its original meaning than for the way it is interpreted by various political groups. For a fuller explanation of both, see Jelani Cobb, "The Limits of Liberalism," *New Yorker*, September 20, 2021, 20–26; and Jane Coaston, "The Intersectionality Wars," *Vox*, May 28, 2019.

4. Andrew Cain, "Northam Calls for Taking Down Confederate Statues in Virginia and Moving Them to Museums," *RTD*, August 16, 2017.

5. "A List of Virginia's 200-Plus Confederate Monuments and Public Symbols," *RTD*, August 17, 2017. The article cites a Southern Poverty Law Center report, "Whose Heritage? Public Symbols of the Confederacy." The 2019 update of that report listed 110

Confederate monuments and 244 Confederate symbols, including buildings, streets, and schools in Virginia. The data, which the report acknowledges is not complete, can be found at https://docs.google.com/spreadsheets/d/17ps4aqRyaIfpu7KdGsy2HRZaaQiXU fLrpUbaR9yS51E/edit#gid=22299898.

6. Laura Vozzella and Gregory Schneider, "Virginia General Assembly Approves Medicaid Expansion to 400,000 Low-Income Residents," *WP*, May 30, 2018.

CHAPTER 12

1. Gregory Schneider, "Virginia Republicans Thought Calling Ralph Northam 'Gov. Blackface' Would Help Them. That's Changed," *WP*, September 6, 2019.

2. Noah Robertson, "After Blackface Scandal, Va. Governor Has Hung On—and Is Making Amends," *Christian Science Monitor*, October 3, 2019.

3. A Roanoke College poll conducted August 11–19 gave Northam a 37 percent approval rating. The Virginia Survey of the University of Mary Washington, conducted September 3–15, put Northam's job approval at 47 percent, as did a *Washington Post*-Schar School poll conducted September 25–30. A poll conducted September 4–30 by the Wason Center at Christopher Newport College put Northam's approval at 51 percent.

4. Gregory Schneider, Laura Vozzella, and Scott Clement, "Poll Finds Va. Voters Focused on Gun Policy Ahead of Pivotal Election," *WP*, October 4, 2019.

5. Fredreka Schouten, "How a Bloomberg-Funded Gun-Control Group Helped Turn Virginia Blue Tuesday," CNN, November 6, 2019; Mike Valerio, "Bloomberg Bankrolled 1 in 5 Northern Virginia House Candidates, Targeting Pivotal Races with Donations," *WUSA-9*, February 19, 2020, https://www.wusa9.com/article/news/politics /bloomberg-donations-to-democratic-candidates-virginia-elections/65-c051cac9-a78b-40 14-8439-795ad6037636.

6. Francis Butler Simkins, Spotswood H. Jones, and Sidman P. Poole, *Virginia: History, Government, Geography*, rev. ed. (New York: Scribner, 1964), 368–69; Adam Wesley Dean, "Who Controls the Past Controls the Future: The Virginia Textbook Controversy," *VMHB* 117 (2009): 318–55; Bennett Minton, "The Lies Our Textbooks Told My Generation of Virginians about Slavery," *WP*, July 31, 2020.

7. Simkins, Jones, and Poole, *Virginia*, 388.

8. Amy Friedenberger, "Gov. Northam Lays Out Budget Priorities for 2-Year State Budget," *RT*, December 17, 2019.

9. Jerry Lazarus, "Gov. Northam Releases Progressive 2020–22 Budget Plan," *RFP*, December 20, 2019.

CHAPTER 13

1. Tarter, *Grandees of Government*, 246–51.

2. For a listing, see "African American Legislators in Virginia (1967–1899)," *EV*, July 15, 2021, https://encyclopediavirginia.org/entries/african-american-legislators-in-virginia -1867-1899/.

3. Graham Moomaw, "In Five Weeks, Virginia Democrats Reshape Decades of State Policy," *VM*, February 12, 2020.

4. Timothy Williams, Adam Goldman, and Neil MacFarquhar, "Virginia Capital on Edge as F.B.I. Arrests Suspected Neo-Nazis before Gun Rally," *NYT*, January 16, 2020.

5. Michael Kunzelman, "Neo-Nazis Discussed Killing Va.'s Filler-Corn," AP, October 2, 2021.

6. Alan Suderman and Sarah Rankin, "Pro-gun Rally by Thousands in Virginia Ends Peacefully," AP, January 20, 2020; Gregory Schneider and Laura Vozzella et al., "Virginia Pro-gun Rally: Despite Anger, Threats of Insurrection, Massive Rally Is Carried Out Peacefully outside State Capitol," WP, January 20, 2020.

7. Laura Vozzella, "Ban on Assault Weapon Sales Dies in Va. Senate Committee," WP, February 17, 2020.

CHAPTER 14

1. Ty Seidule, *Robert E. Lee and Me: A Southerner's Reckoning with the Myth of the Lost Cause* (New York: St. Martin's, 2020), 223. A retired Army brigadier general and professor emeritus of history at West Point, Seidule argues that the Constitution clearly names Lee's action as treason. "When one tries to answer the question of why Lee left, the simplest reason works best," he continues. "Lee left for the same reason the southern states seceded. The southern states went to war to protect and expand chattel slavery because they felt threatened by Lincoln's election" (226).

CHAPTER 15

1. Lauren Hirsch, "Trump Says, 'Anybody Who Wants a Test Gets a Test' . . . ," CNBC, March 6, 2020, https://www.cnbc.com/2020/03/06/trump-anybody-who-wants-a-test-gets -a-test-amid-shortage-for-coronavirus.html; Daniel Wolfe and Daniel Dale, "A Timeline of Trump's Claims That Covid-19 Will Vanish," CNN, October 31, 2020, https://www .cnn.com/interactive/2020/10/politics/covid-disappearing-trump-comment-tracker/; Daniel Funke, "In Context: What Donald Trump Said about Disinfectant, Sun and Coronavirus," POLITIFACT: The Poynter Institute, April 24, 2020, https://www.politifact.com /article/2020/apr/24/context-what-donald-trump-said-about-disinfectant-/.

2. Of the six men charged with federal crimes, two pleaded guilty. Two were acquitted in April 2022, and the jury deadlocked on counts against two others, producing a mistrial. At the time, federal prosecutors vowed to retry those two. Defense attorneys argued that FBI agents had entrapped their clients.

3. Giulia McDonnell Nieto del Rio and Neil MacFarquhar, "Virginia Governor Was also a Possible Target of Anti-government Plot, F.B.I. Says," *NYT*, October 18, 2020.

4. The *Richmond Times-Dispatch* first reported the testing discrepancy in articles such as Mel Leonor, "Criticism Mounts as Virginia Includes 15,000 Antibody Results in COVID-19 Testing Data," *RTD*, May 14, 2020. See also Alexis Madrigal and Robinson Meyer, "How Virginia Juked Its COVID-19 Data," *Atlantic*, May 13, 2020, https://www .theatlantic.com/health/archive/2020/05/covid-19-tests-combine-virginia/611620/.

5. Laura Vozzella, "Gov. Northam Slammed for Mingling in Virginia Beach Crowds without a Mask," *WP*, May 24, 2020.

PART IV

1. Transcript of Barbara Rose Johns's personal journal, property of the Robert Russa Moton Museum, Farmville, Virginia.

CHAPTER 16

1. CNN, "President Trump's Call with US Governors Over Protests," June 1, 2020, https://www.cnn.com/2020/06/01/politics/donald-trump-race-police/index.html.

2. "The Statue Is Here," *RD*, May 6, 1890.

3. "Patriotic Pullers: Men, Women, and Children Draw the Lee Statue to the Pedestal," *RD*, May 8, 1890, 1.

4. Headlines taken from *RD*, May 30, 1890.

5. "The Moving of the Lee Statue," *Richmond Planet*, May 10, 1890.

CHAPTER 17

1. Sarah Rankin, "Black Contractor Braves Threats in Removing Richmond Statues," AP, October 25, 2020.

2. Ibid.

3. Ibid.

4. Interviewed by the author at his home at 1833 Monument Avenue on November 14, 2020, Mr. Massey died on March 10, 2021, after a brief illness.

5. Peter Galuszka, "Massey's Tragic Legacy," *Style Weekly Magazine*, September 11, 2012.

CHAPTER 18

1. Whitney Blair Wyckoff, "Jackson State: A Tragedy Widely Forgotten," National Public Radio, May 3, 2010, https://www.npr.org/templates/story/story.php?storyId=126426361; Rachel James-Terry and L. A. Warren, "'All Hell Broke Loose': Memories Still Vivid of Jackson State Shooting 50 Years Ago," *Jackson (MS) Clarion Ledger*, May 15, 2020.

2. Department of State Police, *Crime in Virginia*, 65, https://www.vsp.virginia.gov/pdf/Crime_in_Virginia/Crime_In_Virginia_2019.pdf; Virginia Department of Corrections, "State Responsible Offender Demographic Profile," FY 2019, https://vadoc.virginia.gov/media/1472/vadoc-research-state-responsible-demographic-report-2019.pdf.

3. Jerry Lazarus, "New Review of Marcus-David Peters Case Finds Shooting Justified," *RFP*, November 12, 2020.

4. "Peters' Sister: 'Marcus Alert' Law Is Not Enough," *RTD*, December 16, 2020.

CHAPTER 19

1. Ian Shapira, "At VMI, Black Cadets Endure Lynching Threats, Klan Memories and Confederacy Veneration," *WP*, October 17, 2020.

2. Claire Mitzel, "VMI Black Alumni Speak Out about Racism, Demand Changes amid Swell of Racial Justice Protests," *RT*, June 13, 2020.

3. Ibid.

4. See HB 1537, 2020 General Assembly session, Virginia's Legislative Information System.

5. VMI, "Way Forward for Greater Understanding Fair and Equality," July 29, 2020, https://www.scribd.com/document/470892835/Way-Forward-for-Greater-Understanding-Fair-and-Equality-VMI#from_embed (accessed November 30, 2020).

6. Addressed to John W. Boland and the VMI Board of Visitors, the October 19, 2020, letter was signed by Northam, Lieutenant Governor Justin Fairfax, Attorney General Mark Herring, House Speaker Eileen Filler-Corn, Senate president pro tempore Louise Lucas, Legislative Black Caucus chair Lamont Bagby, Senate Finance chair Janet Howell, House Appropriations chair Luke Torian, Senate Majority Leader Richard Saslaw, House Majority Leader Charniele Herring, and Senate Democratic Caucus chair Mamie Locke.

7. John William Boland to Gov. Ralph Northam, October 20, 2020, Governor's papers.

8. J. H. Binford Peay III to John William Boland, October 26, 2020, Governor's papers.

9. L. Scott Lingamfelter, "The Glittering Pyrite of Political Correctness," *RTD*, November 25, 2020.

10. Steven McAuliffe to Gov. Ralph Northam, Oct 19, 2020, Governor's papers.

CHAPTER 20

1. Rebecca Tan, Samantha Schmidt, et al., "Before Trump Vows to End 'Lawlessness,' Federal Officers Confront Protesters outside White House," *WP*, June 2, 2020.

2. Tom Jackman and Carol Leonnig, "Report: Park Police Didn't Clear Lafayette Square for Trump Visit," *WP*, June 10, 2020.

3. "Editorial: Northam Has Been Dizzingly Transformational," *RT*, January 13, 2021.

PART V

1. Kirt von Daacke, "The Memorial to Enslaved Workers Virtual Tour," University of Virginia, Alumni, Parents, and Friends, July 23, 2020, https://alumni.virginia.edu/learn/program/the-memorial-to-enslaved-laborers-virtual-tour/.

CHAPTER 21

1. Richard A. Rutyna, "Virginia: An Historical Sketch," paper presented to the Virginia State Crime Commission advisory committee on capital punishment, September 17, 1973, 33.

2. "State by State: Virginia," Death Penalty Information Center, https://deathpenalty info.org/state-and-federal-info/state-by-state/virginia (accessed October 10, 2021).

3. Ngozi Ndulue, "Enduring Injustice: The Persistence of Racial Discrimination in the U.S. Death Penalty," Death Penalty Information Center, September 15, 2020, 16, https://deathpenaltyinfo.org/facts-and-research/dpic-reports/in-depth/enduring-injustice -the-persistence-of-racial-discrimination-in-the-u-s-death-penalty.

4. Ibid., 29–30.

5. Corrina Barrett Lain, "Three Observations about the Worst of the Worst, Virginia-Style," *Washington & Lee Law Review On-line* 469 (2021): 77, https://lawreview.wlulaw .wlu.edu/three-observations-about-the-worst-of-the-worst-virginia-style/.

6. James S. Liebman, Jeffrey Fagan, and Valerie West, "A Broken System: Error Rates in Capital Cases, 1973–1995," Columbia Law School Public Law and Legal Theory Working Paper Group, June 12, 2000, 47. When state and federal actions were combined, the study found, only 18 percent of Virginia's death sentences were overturned between 1973 and 1995, compared with 68 percent nationally.

7. Gregory Schneider, "Virginia Is About to Abolish the Death Penalty. It Was a Long, Surprising Road to Get There," *WP*, March 23, 2021.

8. Joint Legislative Audit and Review Commission, "Key Considerations for Marijuana Legalization, 2020 (draft report)," November 16, 2020, 10.

9. Dean Mirshahi, "Black Virginians Four Times as Likely to Be Cited for Marijuana Possession," WRIC-TV, March 3, 2021, https://www.wric.com/news/virginia-news/black-virginians-more-likely-to-be-cited-for-marijuana-possession-even-after-decriminalization/; Ned Oliver, "Push to End Marijuana Prohibition This Year Instead of 2024 Hinges on Northam," *VM*, March 11, 2021.

10. Mel Leonor, "Legal Marijuana Sales in Virginia Could Start in Less than 2 Years under Northam's New Proposal," *RTD*, January 13, 2021.

11. Nixon Peabody LLP, "Report to the Governor of the Commonwealth of Virginia, et al., Concerning Policies, Process, and Procedures Employed by the Office of the State Inspector General during its Investigation of the Virginia Parole Board's Handling of the Vincent Martin Matter," June 14, 2021.

12. Timothy Bella, "Suit: Police Threatened, Sprayed, Struck Army Officer," *RTD*, April 11, 2021.

13. Rise, *Martinsville Seven*, 43–44.

14. Holly Kozelsky, "An Old Wrong Was Righted. Gov. Ralph Northam Pardons Martinsville Seven," *Martinsville (VA) Bulletin*, August 31, 2021.

CHAPTER 22

1. Opinion, *Helen Marie Taylor, et al., v. Ralph S. Northam, et al.*, Record #210113, September 2, 2021, and Order, *William C. Gregory against Ralph S. Northam*, Record #201307, September 2, 2021.

2. Douglas Southall Freeman, *R. E. Lee: A Biography*, 4 vols. (New York: Scribner, 1935), 4: 494.

3. Ibid., 4: 505.

4. James C. Cobb, "How Did Robert E. Lee Become an American Icon?" *Humanities*, 32 (July/August 2011), 28.

5. Connelly laid out his views in *The Marble Man: Robert E. Lee and His Image in American Society* (Baton Rouge: Louisiana State University Press, 1977).

6. Freeman, *R. E. Lee*, 4: 498.

7. Lee, as quoted in Elizabeth Brown Pryor, *Reading the Man: A Portrait of Robert E. Lee through His Private Letters* (New York: Viking, 2007), 151.

8. J. C. Cobb, "How Did Robert E. Lee Become an American Icon?"

9. Pryor, *Reading the Man*, 260–61.

10. Ibid., 261, 270–72.

11. Allen C. Guelzo, *Robert E. Lee: A Life* (New York: Knopf, 2021), 3, 432–33.

12. Seidule, *Robert E. Lee and Me*, 244–45.

CHAPTER 23

1. VCU Center on Society and Health, "Mapping Life Expectancy," November 12, 2015; Statisticatlas.com, "Household Income by Neighborhood in Richmond,"

https://statisticalatlas.com/neighborhood/Virginia/Richmond/Windsor-Farms/Overview, https://statisticalatlas.com/neighborhood/Virginia/Richmond/Gilpin/Household-Income (accessed November 8, 2021).

2. Many sources document these disparities. Among them are Richard Rothstein, *The Color of Law: A Forgotten History of How Our Government Segregated America* (New York: Liveright, 2017); Michelle Alexander, *The New Jim Crow: Mass Incarceration in the Age of Colorblindness* (New York: New Press, 2010); Genevieve Siegel-Hawley, *When the Fences Come Down: Twenty-First-Century Lessons from Metropolitan School Desegregation* (Chapel Hill: University of North Carolina Press, 2016).

3. Commission to Examine Racial Inequity in Virginia Law, "Identifying and Addressing the Vestiges of Inequity and Inequality in Virginia's Laws," November 15, 2020, 15.

4. Ibid., 18.

5. Ibid.

6. Ibid., 28.

7. Ibid.; Cary Lou and Kristen Blagg, "School District Funding in Virginia," Urban Institute, December 2018, 4.

8. Andrew Warren and Chris Duncombe, "In Funding High-Poverty Schools, Virginia Gets a Failing Grade," Commonwealth Institute: Half Sheet, August 28, 2018.

9. Brendan Wolfe, "Lynching in Virginia," *EV*, https://encyclopediavirginia.org/entries/lynching-in-virginia/ (accessed March 8, 2022).

10. For example, Charles Lipson, "'Equity' Is a Mandate to Discriminate," *Wall Street Journal*, March 4, 2021.

11. Michael Ruiz, "Virginia District Spent $34K on Critical Race Theory Coaching for Administrators, Documents Show," Fox News, July 2, 2021.

CHAPTER 24

1. According to the Virginia State Board of Elections, Youngkin won 50.58 percent of the vote; McAuliffe, 48.64 percent; and Princess Blanding, 0.70 percent under a Liberation Party banner.

2. Astead Herndon and Shane Goldmacher, "In Rural Areas, Prospects Sink for Democrats," *NYT*, November 7, 2021.

3. The Northam administration had been notified that CNBC intended to name Virginia the top state for business in 2020. However, the COVID-19 pandemic disrupted plans for the announcement.

4. Glenn Youngkin addressed the Lee Monument by saying that "we have a court ruling, so the statue's going to come down." He coupled that statement with the hope that "we recognize how wrong the graffiti and the violence was." He then pivoted to support for law enforcement. See *Richmond's Morning News with John Reid*," WRVA, September 7, 2021, https://www.audacy.com/newsradiowrva/podcasts/richmonds-morning-news-20797/glenn-youngkin-september-7-2021-722923901.

5. "After Virginia Votes 2021," Virginia Public Access Project, https://www.vpap.org/about-us/events/after-virginia-votes-2021/.

6. Jenna Portnoy, "McAuliffe Vetoes Bill Permitting Parents to Block Sexually Explicit Books in School," *WP*, April 4, 2016.

7. Mel Leonor and Andrew Cain, "In Va., Assembly Session Kicks off a New GOP Era," *RTD*, January 12, 2022; Mel Leonor and Michael Martz, "Va. Legislature Convenes, Prepares to Share Power," *RTD*, January 13, 2022.

CHAPTER 25

1. Seidule, *Robert E. Lee and Me*, 216.

2. "Rat" is the nickname for VMI students during the first six months of their freshman year. They are subjected to a series of harsh, boot-camp-type requirements during that period.

3. Gayle Jessup White, *Reclamation: Sally Hemings, Thomas Jefferson, and a Descendant's Search for Her Family's Lasting Legacy* (New York: Amistad, 2021), 214.

4. "Why the Dem Strategy in Virginia Failed, and How Youngkin Flipped the State," *PBS News Hour*, November 3, 2021, https://www.pbs.org/newshour/show/why-the-dem -strategy-in-virginia-failed-and-how-youngkin-flipped-the-state.

INDEX